IN THE
COMPANY
OF
RILKE

Also by Stephanie Dowrick

Fiction
Running Backwards over Sand
Tasting Salt

Nonfiction
Intimacy and Solitude
The Intimacy and Solitude Workbook
Forgiveness & Other Acts of Love
The Universal Heart
Free Thinking
The Almost-Perfect Marriage
Choosing Happiness
Creative Journal Writing
Seeking the Sacred

IN THE
COMPANY
OF
RILKE

*Why a 20th-century visionary poet
speaks so eloquently to
21st-century readers*

STEPHANIE
DOWRICK

JEREMY P. TARCHER/PENGUIN
a member of Penguin Group (USA) Inc.
New York

JEREMY P. TARCHER/PENGUIN
Published by the Penguin Group
Penguin Group (USA) Inc., 375 Hudson Street, New York, New York 10014, USA • Penguin Group
(Canada), 90 Eglinton Avenue East, Suite 700, Toronto, Ontario M4P 2Y3, Canada (a division of
Pearson Penguin Canada Inc.) • Penguin Books Ltd, 80 Strand, London WC2R 0RL, England •
Penguin Ireland, 25 St Stephen's Green, Dublin 2, Ireland (a division of Penguin Books Ltd) •
Penguin Group (Australia), 250 Camberwell Road, Camberwell, Victoria 3124, Australia (a division
of Pearson Australia Group Pty Ltd) • Penguin Books India Pvt Ltd, 11 Community Centre,
Panchsheel Park, New Delhi–110 017, India • Penguin Group (NZ), 67 Apollo Drive, Rosedale,
North Shore 0632, New Zealand (a division of Pearson New Zealand Ltd) • Penguin Books
(South Africa) (Pty) Ltd, 24 Sturdee Avenue, Rosebank, Johannesburg 2196, South Africa

Penguin Books Ltd, Registered Offices: 80 Strand, London WC2R 0RL, England

Previously published in Australia by Allen & Unwin 2009
First American edition Jeremy P. Tarcher/Penguin 2011
Copyright © 2011 by Wise Angels Pty Ltd.

Most Tarcher/Penguin books are available at special quantity discounts for bulk purchase for sales
promotions, premiums, fund-raising, and educational needs. Special books or book excerpts also
can be created to fit specific needs. For details, write Penguin Group (USA) Inc. Special Markets,
375 Hudson Street, New York, NY 10014.

Page 343 constitutes an extension of this copyright page.

Library of Congress Cataloging-in-Publication Data

Dowrick, Stephanie.
  In the company of Rilke: why a 20th-century visionary poet speaks so eloquently to 21st-century
readers / Stephanie Dowrick.—1st American ed.
      p.   cm.
  Previously published by Allen & Unwin, 2009.
  Includes bibliographical references and index.
  ISBN 978-1-58542-867-0
  1. Rilke, Rainer Maria, 1875–1926—Criticism and interpretation. 2. Rilke, Rainer Maria,
1875–1926—Religion. 3. Spirituality in literature. I. Title.
  PT2635.I65Z6686   2011   2011018963
  831'.912—dc23

Printed in the United States of America
10 9 8 7 6 5 4 3 2 1

Book design by Emily O'Neill

For Jane Moore,
and in memory of my mother,
Estelle Mary Dowrick

CONTENTS

[Reading Rilke,] I felt a sense of release as if I had been let out of a cage I had not known I was in.

Joanna Macy

Rilke, the tenderest and most spiritual man I knew—a man who more than anyone else possessed all the wonderful anguish and secrets of the spirit.

Paul Valéry

To be a poet in a destitute time means: to attend, singing, to the trace of the fugitive gods. This is why the poet in the time of the world's night utters the holy.

Martin Heidegger

PREFACE

Rainer Maria Rilke is one of the most praised and praising of modern poets. What is more astonishing is that he is a poet who is widely read. Why people read poetry—what they are seeking from this intense, condensed form of literary, perhaps soulful, communication—can't be disentangled from the question as to why you or I might read Rilke. Writer and monk Thomas Merton gives us a clue: "He *is* a poet. Is that a small thing?"[1]

Merton was asking his question rhetorically, but spending time in the company of Rainer Maria Rilke makes it easy to respond: *This is no small thing.* Rilke is one of few poets on the world stage who genuinely "transcends the sphere of the literary,"[2] whose voice is welcomed far from libraries and lecture theaters. In fact, at a time of massive indifference to the quietly subversive art of poetry, Rilke's life and work are of increasing interest.

Three reasons stand out. Most obvious is that Rilke is a highly innovative and exhilarating, even "great," poet. (Yet there are other great poets whose poems lie unread.) He is authentically "European" and "saw himself as a mediator between various cultures and nations."[3] That internationalism suits these times. But what Rilke also does, sometimes sublimely, is to avow and express a spirituality or spiritual yearning that is not dependent upon belief in any conventional sense, nor on any kind of "middleman." Dogma and priests, in fact, got in the way for him. So did secondhand ideas about God.

This last is, I believe, most crucial of all. Like the Psalmist who cried out, in Psalm 42, "My soul thirsts for God," there is tremendous longing in Rilke—for direct experience but not for certainty. In Rilke, the mystery can remain mysterious, and he affirms something of that same need for the contemporary reader. Here is a poet who speaks directly to God while doubting God; who meets the reader through a sensibility that is simultaneously transcendent *and* uncertain. That paradox could not be timelier. And my sense is strong that it is Rilke's unfettered spirituality and inwardness, as well as the piercing beauty of much of what he writes, that drives a steady unfolding of new editions, translations and new and faithful readers.

Born in Prague in 1875 and dying in 1926 in a French-speaking canton in Switzerland, Rilke is also close enough in time to us to have had recognizably modern—even postmodern—concerns about what we call our outer and inner worlds and the incoming and outgoing tides that unite them. Through his eleven thousand extant letters Rilke left a vast and vivid "memoir" that makes no secret of his numerous affairs and stark internal ambiguities. This makes thinking about him and engaging with his ideas and poems a more intense and more personally affecting experience than reading poets of similar spiritual significance (like John of the Cross, Rumi or Kabir, Hildegard of Bingen or Mechthild of Magdeburg, for example) whose daily reality can barely be imagined and whose works express a degree of spiritual conviction that many might find equally out of reach.

So at a time when public indifference to poetry generally could not be greater, and the idea of someone "living for poetry," as Rilke undeniably did, is simply laughable, new translations of Rilke's work continue to appear—and not just of his early *Stunden-Buch* (*Book of Hours*), which offers some of his most accessible poetry to readers. His magnificent but demanding *Duineser Elegien* (*Duino Elegies*) and *Die Sonette an Orpheus* (*Sonnets to Orpheus*) also inspire, resisting a contemporary culture that seems to threaten to desacralize or dehumanize us. Reading Rilke, reading in his company, we literally witness the elusive vanishing "Things" within ourselves, the Things that *"endure, just as the tongue does [and] still is able to praise."*

> Here *is the time for the* sayable, here *is its homeland.*
> *Speak and bear witness. More than ever*
> *the Things that we might experience are vanishing, for*
> *what crowds them out and replaces them is an imageless act.*
> *An act under a shell, which easily cracks open as soon as*
> *the business inside outgrows it and seeks new limits.*
> *Between the hammers our heart*
> *endures, just as the tongue does*
> *between the teeth and, despite that,*
> *still is able to praise.*[4]

By any measure, Rilke's writing achievement is exceptional. It includes a huge variety of poetry, some arguably as fully realized as poetry has ever been; plays; a modernist novel,

The Notebooks of Malte Laurids Brigge, not much read these days; semi-philosophical writings; and that mountain of surviving letters "drawn out of his loneliness like silk threads unwound from a cocoon."[5] He was a highly introverted, sensitive man, whose life has been laid bare, theorized, pilloried, sanctified, misunderstood—*and* interpreted with the greatest sophistication and understanding. But I think it is fair to say that reading Rilke offers something else, too, of unexpected value. It opens our eyes to the power of human creativity more generally and of poetry specifically. This may challenge some of our ideas about reading and especially about the value of reading exceptional poetry. Rilke lets us participate in his ambivalent, compelling inner world. Just as crucially, reading Rilke lets us discover and rediscover our own depth, yearnings and "innerness."

It was while thinking about reading—as much as about reading Rilke—that I turned to a vital reference and essay. To mark the twentieth anniversary of Rilke's death, the German philosopher Martin Heidegger chose to respond to a question posed earlier by the poet Hölderlin in his elegy "Bread and Wine": "What are poets for in these destitute times?"

With the Second World War just ended, and Germany shamed by the Holocaust as well as the obscene violences of war, the question was stark. It would never have been a question about poets' *usefulness*. "The part of art which is art, and not device, unshackles us from usefulness almost entirely," writes the poet Jane Hirshfield.[6] It is a profound question about meaning, and especially the depth of meaning that is "indispensable" in human life if we are to maintain the dignity and consciousness that ought to be, but are not always, the transformative hallmarks of our species.

Heidegger's English-language translator, Albert Hofstadter, is adamant in his response to the question: "Without the poetic element in our own being, and without our poets and their great poetry, we would be brutes, or what is worse and what we are most like today: vicious automata of self-will."[7]

Rilke himself believed in art as a "cosmic, creative, transforming force"[8] and in the power of art to "change the normal world"[9] and therefore our experiences of it. When we abandon inwardness and a search for meaning, we lose a depth of perception that makes the world more real to us. Going inward, the "outer" more easily reveals its dimensionality and tenderness and our fragility. "We empty ourselves, we surrender, we unfold," Rilke wrote.[10] And then:

> No, what my heart will be is a tower,
> and I will be right out on its rim:
> nothing else will be there, only pain
> and what can't be said, only the world.
>
> Only one thing left in the enormous space
> that will go dark and then light again,
> only one final face full of longing,
> exiled into what is always full of thirst,
>
> only one farthest-out face made of stone,
> at peace with its own inner weight,
> which the distances, who go on ruining it,
> force on to deeper holiness.[11]

We are freed to discover that at the tower's rim a whole self is risked, a self that floods with adrenaline and comes fully to life. This kind of awakening, and a lovely glimpse of what a rare poet or poem might be *for*, is given by the

American critic Harold Bloom when he recalls that his sense of self "came to its belated birth" when he was about nine or ten. This was achieved, he explains, by "reading visionary poetry [in his case, Crane and Blake], a reading that implicitly was an act of knowing something previously unknown in me." The "something" to which Bloom is referring is a sense of "possible sublimity."

This is Rilke's territory precisely. Bloom goes on: "To fall in love with great poetry when you are young is to be awakened to the self's potential. . . . The self's potential as power involves the self's immortality, not as duration but as the awakening to a knowledge of something in the self that cannot die, because it was never born. . . . At more than half a century away from the deep force of reading and loving poetry, I no longer remember precisely what I then felt, and yet can recall how it felt. It was an elevation, a mounting high on no intoxications except incantatory language."[12]

My own interest in Rilke began in a way that is similar to Bloom's experiences. I doubt that I read visionary poetry as a child, other than the Psalms that I didn't then understand or "hear" as poetry. My sense is that I was in my teens before I read and learned by heart the "incantatory language" of Gerard Manley Hopkins, T. S. Eliot and Emily Dickinson. I remember, as Bloom does, *how that felt*. Fortunately, I have never recovered. I did, however, have a religious upbringing that was unusual in that it did not begin until I was nine, the very age Bloom was when he discovered Crane and Blake.

In those days, and those were the days of traditional Roman Catholicism, the intensity of spiritual, even mystical experience was a given in the life of the church. Mystery was at the center of daily living: everyday human experience radiated outward from it. The one-true-faith ideology was fierce and many of the rules for daily living were extreme. Nevertheless, there was (literally) no questioning the possibility of an ordinary person aspiring to an authentic spiritual awakening, something that drives much of Rilke's poetry.

Those experiences were made more vivid, I believe, because my mother had died a year before we entered this new world. My father, older sister and I were "converts." The contrasts between old and new were stark. Our new Roman Catholic lives were to be in every way different from our previous, casual-Protestant, barely believing, non-Catholic lives. I noticed the reversals: God first.

It was my first startling experience of transcendent *seeing* that is, like *ripening*, a constant Rilke theme. The intensity of spirituality, the rhythms of ritual, music, contemplation and prayer, the repeated references to the vulnerable fate of one's soul, repelled and compelled me. I never ceased to feel utter loss about the circumstances that preceded and followed my "conversion." But this time was also when I discovered that language could be used to talk about and pray to God, to seek God and to feel sought, and to know that life centers upon a profound mystery of which we are an integral, inevitable part. The genesis of my eventual fascination with Rilke belongs in that time.

～

Rilke's pious, superstitious Roman Catholic childhood a hundred fifty years earlier was not the same as mine. Some of the traces it left on his personality and in his work were nevertheless familiar to me. And nothing was more familiar to me than the yearning so dazzlingly characteristic of some of Rilke's poetry. What's more, and is more surprising, in Rilke's vision this is not an experience outside "daily" life; it is securely within it. However inconsistent Rilke may be in some ways, he is not inconsistent in this. *It is life in its fullness that is sought*: darkness as well as light, the unseen with the seen, uncertainty frequently triumphing over certainty; questions mattering much more than answers. Here, in Rilke's world, engagement is demanded and risk assumed. The Ungraspable is not for grasping.

> *Don't believe it, that I'm wooing.*
> *Angel. And even if I were! You are not coming. For my*
> *call is always dense with farewelling. Against such*
> *strength of current, you can't come forward. My call*
> *is like an arm outstretched. And its hand, held open*
> *as if for touching, remains before you,*
> *open, like defense and warning.*
> *Ungraspable One, far out . . .*[13]

PART ONE
READING

Let us not be satisfied with recounting a fable of the heart; let us create its myth. Is not love, with art, our only license to overreach the human condition, to be greater, more generous, more sorrowful if need be than is the common lot? Let us be so heroically. . . .

Rainer Maria Rilke, 18 November 1920

"GOD IS STILL SPEAKING"

As I walk most days from my house to the local shops or park and back again, doing the ordinary chores that anchor and shape daily life, I pass a large wooden notice board outside a sturdy suburban church. God is still speaking, it tells me. What it doesn't and cannot tell me is how God speaks, or who is listening.

We live in a society where God was long ago banished from most mainstream intellectual discussion. Freudian psychology is now no more fashionable than Marxist theory. Nevertheless, Freud's assumptions that religious belief is driven by neurosis, especially Oedipal anxieties, wishful thinking or "primal horde" instincts, continue to have significant influence. Many people are literally embarrassed to "confess" to their religious or spiritual impulses and feelings. Their yearnings and desires for the "holy" remain easily trivialized.

With its facility to bridge the boundaries between the conscious and the unconscious mind in both the writer and the reader, literature might have retained its power to explore and engage spiritual questions long after other disciplines have turned away. After all, literature has on its side the immense forces of imagination, emotion, instinct and story. It can call on and speak of inquiry and awe. It is more embodied, more sensual and personal than theory can ever be. It can precede the Zeitgeist and not just trail after it. And literature has always been concerned with questions of meaning. *What is the "nature" of human nature? Why do we live as we do? What makes life worth living? How does belief, or its absence, shape us? Beyond matter, what, if anything, are we?*

Perhaps literature has that facility still. That's sometimes true at the essential meeting point between writer and reader: words on the page. It is less true in the worlds of scholarship and literary criticism, however, where something different has long dictated what (and who) matters. In 1935, the poet and critic T. S. Eliot was fiercely decrying that ". . . the whole of modern literature is corrupted by what I call Secularism, that it is simply unaware of, simply cannot understand the meaning of, the primacy of the supernatural over the natural life: of something which I assume to be our primary concern."[1]

In our own time there is not much enthusiastic scholarly engaging with the supernatural as a "primary concern." The interest in Rilke, for example, from the general public clearly centers on at least some sense of him as an inspirational or visionary poet, yet this is the first full-length study of his work from that perspective since Federico Olivero's 1941 publication. The effects of this lack of serious interest—or confidence—are neatly summarized by David Burrell. A Roman Catholic priest as well as an academic, he is reflecting on the aftereffects of teaching in universities for more than forty years and speaks of colleagues intent on preserving their "[Max] Weberian 'neutrality,'" and says, "I often tweak colleagues . . . reminding them that as a Catholic priest (and so a 'professionally religious' person), I usually find religion quite boring, whereas I find God infinitely interesting."[2]

In this climate, questions of spiritual meaning remain marginalized, robbed of drive and even language by lack of context, as much as interest. It is a rare privilege to speak openly of one's longing for, need for, experience of or confusion about the transcendent. With brave exceptions, austere forms of rationalism have come to prevail, sometimes ruthlessly.

Yet while many intellectuals have largely been looking away, or discussing "God" as theory or as a quaint or redundant creation of the human mind, and rarely as a legitimate, passionate and authentic experience, our world has come to be dominated and threatened by competing religious ideologies. The majority of the world's people continue to see religion as the principle around which their lives are organized, and significant numbers remain ready to kill or to be killed in the name of religion ("inspiration" of a most perverse kind). Beyond anything that could have been predicted in the dying years of the twentieth century, in twenty-first-century life God continues to engage and preoccupy us.

Something else is also happening. More difficult to analyze, and certainly less determined by common sets of beliefs or behaviors, this "something" is a felt or lived desire for the sacred. And as deeply rooted as it is in our human nature, I am confident this is a desire that has never gone away.

It is not a renewal of religious dogma but of religious *feeling*. It has resonances of late-nineteenth- and early-twentieth-century transcendentalism but would now more often and more simply be called *spirituality* or perhaps *mysticism.* Resistant to explanations or external authority and dogma, sometimes tentative yet palpable in its effects, this is increasingly the focus of books, discussions, personal and shared reflection, and committed spiritual practice. It can coexist with formal religious belief or practice, yet is not dependent on them. In fact, as independent as it often is, it is curiously democratizing while decidedly not being "spirituality lite." In fact, in its broad inclusiveness and emphasis on self-knowledge and responsibility, it brings into clear relief what human beings share beyond the conventionally divisive labels, creating a turning point as important as any earlier reformation in how we think about spirituality and religion, and our spiritual and religious selves more generally.

Revelation and insight play their part here. For millions of people, God or the divine does "speak." For others, the sacred or holy does "call." Yet familiar questions linger: Who is listening? *How* are they listening? And what could they possibly hear?

⁓

"We are these transformers of the earth; our entire existence, the flights and plunges of our love, everything qualifies us for this task (besides which there exists, essentially, no other)," wrote the poet Rainer Maria Rilke in a letter to his Polish translator and friend, Witold von Hulewicz. It is one of more than eleven thousand surviving letters he wrote before his death, at the age of fifty-one, in December 1926.[3]

Was Rilke speaking to us—or about us? Are we *transformers of the earth*? Or are we simply our beloved earth's failed guardians?

There can't be anything remotely like an absolute or

even partially consoling answer to those questions. Nor to the question that lies secreted inside them, like the smallest Russian doll inside the largest: *Are we transformers of ourselves?*

Perhaps it is the sheer impossibility of subduing those questions with any kind of a definitive answer that makes them exhilarating to contemplate, and especially exhilarating to contemplate alongside Rilke. Who better to remind us through example, not theory, that there are countless ways to discover the depth of life, the *hiddenness* of life, coexistent with the rational, self-evident and material, or that there are countless ways to challenge the familiar explanations of institutional religions, without reflexively abandoning or attacking what is at their heart?

Language is a mixed blessing here, almost literally. Theologian Sallie McFague writes what we know: that "religious language is a problem for us." I would go further. For many people "religion" is a problem and, worse, *causes* problems. McFague usefully elaborates the problem when she writes, "For most of us, it is not a question of being sure of God while being unsure of our language about God [as in classical times]. Rather, we are unsure both at the experiential and the expressive levels . . . We do not live in a sacramental universe in which the things of this world . . . are understood as connected to and permeated by divine power and love. Our experience, our daily experience, is for the most part nonreligious . . . If we experience God at all it tends to be at a private level and in a sporadic way."[4]

In the years since McFague was writing, God (or, rather, some limited and tragic ideas about God) has moved far from the "private." In fact, it seems God has "gone public" (again) to a far greater extent than McFague or anyone else could possibly have imagined. And perhaps partly in reaction to those public images of a partisan "God," counting faults and ruthlessly sorting goats from sheep, as well as everything that "God" ostensibly encourages and determines, it becomes more necessary still to affirm the mysterious and tentative. God may be the Absolute, but there are no absolutes on the way to God.

Here are some singularly apt lines from French philosopher Simone Weil. "There is a God. There is no God. Where is the problem? I am quite sure that there is a God in the sense that I am sure my love is no illusion. I am quite sure there is no God in the sense that I am sure there is nothing which resembles what I can conceive when I say that word."[5]

Within all these possibilities, doubt remains a constant. Not doubt that the questions are worth asking. Not doubt that asking the questions is timely and necessary. But doubt that a single answer would ever do.

~

Meanwhile, a few lines of words lie on a page, creating the reading experience we call a poem. Space falls quite naturally around them and is also part of what they are. In the place that words and space create, questions can be seen as an expression of a yearning that seeks to connect us to what might arguably be called "the best in us" and perhaps even the best that is beyond us.

That may be what many serious readers quite ravenously seek. And it is the territory where the complex, self-centered, occasionally repugnant and undeniably visionary poet Rainer Maria Rilke most skillfully takes them. Readers go willingly. Not just because Rilke is a poet of brilliance but because he promises that:

Overflowing heavens of squandered stars
flame brilliantly above your troubles. Instead
of into your pillows, weep up toward them.
There, at the already weeping, at the ending visage,
slowly thinning out, ravishing
worldspace begins . . . Breathe.
Breathe the darkness of the earth and again
look up! Again. Lightly and facelessly
depths lean toward you from above. The serene
countenance dissolved in night makes room for yours.[6]

It is precisely this "breath," this renewal of vision, that I suspect many readers seek, along with visions upon visions of *Overflowing heavens of squandered stars* that may possibly *flame brilliantly above [our] troubles*, not even knowing that was what they sought, nor how eager they were for the permission Rilke gives them to *breathe the darkness of the earth* as it takes them not down but up. This is not poetry as consolation. It speaks the language of awe and speaks it directly. The "poet" does not stand between.

Lightly and facelessly
depths lean toward you from above. The serene
countenance dissolved in night makes room for yours.

Finding room in the night for our own "countenance," we experience one of countless examples of the geographical/theological play of words so characteristic of visionary writing—and of Rilke. Is deep not also wide, it asks; and is wide not also high? And is "face" not also and at once faceless?

The ultimate spiritual experience is union with the divine and the dissolution of any contradictions inherent in dualism. *The One that you are looking for is also looking for you.* Increasing intimacy is a prelude to union. Rilke is shockingly and wonderfully unafraid also to say, in one of his typically declamatory, possessively intimate opening lines: *Herr, es ist Zeit.* Lord, it is time!

What's thrilling here is that *it is time*—it becomes "time"—in whatever time we find ourselves. This brings to mind Schopenhauer's famous question: "Can anything happen to you for which you are not ready?"

Perhaps you will immediately think of the unwelcome, the tragic, the desolating or terrible for which you were never ready but could only—somehow, however unwillingly—be *readied*. Yet in this poem, and without preliminaries, placelessness yields to place, timelessness to time. Not every reader is listening to God, we can assume. Rilke is insisting, however, that God should and can listen to us. *Lord, it is time.*

> *Lord, it is time. The summer was so full.*
> *Lay your shade upon the sundial,*
> *and loose your wind across the fields.*
>
> *Command the last fruit to ripen.*
> *Give them two more southerly days.*
> *Bring them to fullness, and gather*
> *the last sweetness for the heavy wine.*
>
> *Those without a house won't build one now.*
> *Those who are alone will remain so for a long time;*
> *they'll lie awake, read, write long letters,*
> *and wander the streets restlessly, back and forth,*
> *as the leaves begin to fall.*[7]

Intensity and intimacy are the characteristics of poetry generally and of Rilke's poetry quite specifically. The excitement of extreme tensions is often present, between the visible and the hidden, for example, or what's clear and what's opaque; between the ecstatic and the despairing; between what is highly engaged and what is oddly distancing; what is spoken and what is yet to be spoken. Most crucially, these tensions exist not to be resolved or appeased, but to be experienced. This demands a certain kind of surrender.

Readers who cling too closely to the familiar cannot willingly be thrown into the air with no idea of where they will land. "A belief in the magical power of art to transform life lies at the heart of Rilke's poetry," is how the British critic B. D. Barnacle describes it. More contentiously, Barnacle suggests that the "transformations in Rilke are poetic not actual." He likens this to "dream work" and aligns it to Freud's notions of the working out of desire and the potent role the unconscious plays in that. (As I write this I am wondering when you last woke, astonished by the strangeness of your own dream, yet intrigued also?)

Desire powers "Rilke's kind of poetry," Barnacle writes, "which aims for the evocation of states of being which are largely beyond the grasp of language."[8]

Is that so? Much of the desiring that Rilke speaks to and sometimes exquisitely evokes is indeed "largely beyond the grasp of language." Yet isn't it also true that Rilke's medium *is* language, as well as the space around language and, prominently, the feelings that drive language and seek expression through it? Reading this book, reading about reading Rilke as well as reading Rilke, are complex acts that language allows.

If you and I were, at this moment, in a room together, we might not need words to express our thoughts and feelings; gestures, "looks," silence might be more eloquent. But for the countless interchanges that cannot depend on proximity or intimacy, it is language that provides both. Rilke was language's instrument (a most exceptional "instrument");

language was Rilke's instrument. He "played" it magnificently and allowed himself also to be "played." Besides, Rilke's use of his chosen form pushes the boundaries superbly of what language, precisely, can do.

I also want to argue a little more with Barnacle because it seems to me that the transformations that arise from reading Rilke are grounded in real life, in *this* world (albeit a rather unfamiliar view of "this world"), rather than in some unknown "next" or "other" place, or only in "poetic" realms.

> *Earth, isn't this what you want, to arise*
> *invisibly within us?—Isn't it your dream*
> *to become invisible eventually?—Earth! Invisible!*
> *What is it, if not conversion, that you are here to accomplish?*

> *Earth, beloved: I want this. O, believe that you*
> *no longer depend upon springtime to take me for yours—one,*
> *oh, only one is already too much for my blood.*
> *Namelessly am I joined to you across the distances.*
> *You were always in the right, and your holy notion*
> *is death in all its familiarity.*

> *Look: I'm alive. But how? Neither childhood nor future*
> *grow less . . . Immeasurable existence*
> *bursts forth in my heart.*[9]

A strange and rich picture builds of Rilke drawing ordinary life and things into his consciousness from one direction, and inspiration from beyond himself—though still within the world—from another "direction," and churning and turning it all into who he became and what he wrote and what we, variously, read and perhaps also become. (The use of "direction" here must be taken with a ton of salt.) Of the *Sonnets* and *Elegies*, for example, Rilke wrote in 1922,

"Both works were actually given me as if they were not mine (because somehow, by their nature, they are *more* than '*by* me'). . . ."[10]

Yet if that is alchemy of a most awesome kind, and if "work" as well as inspiration is also always present, it must be said it was always quite a selective view of "daily life" that Rilke was turning into poetry. In a letter to Countess Margot Sizzo-Noris-Crouy, written in 1922, just a few years before his death, Rilke complains that it is only writers who are pushed away from their craft and into "life."

"No one," he writes, "would think of thrusting a ropemaker, cabinetmaker or shoemaker away from his craft 'into life' . . . Only, with regard to him who writes, the craft seems to be slowly, so naturally accomplished (everyone can write), that some [. . . are . . .] of the opinion that the person occupied with writing would immediately fall into empty play if left alone too much with his craft!"[11]

Patricia Pollock Brodsky has written extensively on Rilke. She believes that "the subject of [Rilke's] poetry was poetry itself."[12] Traces of Barnacle re-emerge here, with his idea that the "transformations in Rilke are poetic not actual." And again I want to protest that this separates poetry from life in a way that I find false, just as false as imagining that the "spiritual" is found somewhere other than in daily living.

After all, what is "poetry itself"? Where are its horizons? What draws a reader to "read" the world and their own self through this particular medium, even if only occasionally? Because it is often on "occasions"—sacred or ritualized moments, or moments made holy by celebration or grief—that poetry is reached for, its peculiar intensity and compression instinctively demanded. But this is not a separation from life; rather, it is an illumination of it.

It is perhaps the greatest of all the many transfigurations

offered by Rilke that the worlds of spiritual and temporal breathe in and out of one another and that, in the "place" that is the poem, the evolving subjectivities of poet and reader are simultaneously concealed and revealed. In that placeless place, their histories create a brief communion.

The writer's history shapes what sits on the page; the reader's own history and conditioning are also inevitably present, shaping the encounter and limiting or delimiting comprehension and appreciation. Philosopher and poet John O'Donohue builds this sense of communing relationship when he describes the human being as "an in-between presence, belonging neither fully to the earth from which she has come, nor to the heavens toward which her mind and spirit aim. In a sense, the human being is the loneliest creature in creation. Paradoxically, the human being also has the greatest possibility for intimacy."[13]

The intimacy that takes place on the page between writer and reader with the poem as the medium can only be partially described. "Understanding" is not an adequate currency: not challenging enough, not risky enough. Poetry, like the human being, is also an "in-between presence": in between what is understood and still sought; in between what is conscious and what is not; in between what is perceived and what is given. Rilke himself proposed that even his "most recalcitrant obscurities," as they are described by his translator Edward Snow, "may require not elucidation (*Aufklärung*) so much as 'submitting-to' (*Unterwerfung*)."[14]

I had been thinking of much the same process as surrendered reading. *Surrendered* is a word I have come to relish through years of spiritual practice, learning—slowly—to enter potentially transformative experiences with less reservation, and to allow them to enter me. Surrendered reading could be seen particularly as a way of ritualizing the meeting point between the writer and the reader that requires a willing letting-in as much as a letting-go. Reading then becomes a brave and profound experience of being, not simply of "doing." More crucially, like all intense experiences, "submitting-to" or surrendered reading illuminates process rather than goal. It leaves some "ends" open.

That sense of "unfinished business" can be powerful, even and sometimes especially when reading a highly finished (polished) work. After all, it may be at least momentarily finished for the writer but for the reader the complex processes of engagement may have just begun. "Where will this take me?" "What am I, right now, witnessing within myself?" "Am I 'lost' in this—or found?"

Such questions don't have to be conscious to be effective. They must leave space open, however, for wonder, pleasure and new discoveries. "Art is childhood, after all," wrote Rilke in 1898, when his own physical childhood was still fresh. "Art means to be oblivious to the fact that the world already *exists* and to create one. Not to destroy what one encounters but simply not to find anything complete . . . God was too old at the beginning, I think. Otherwise he would not have stopped on the evening of the sixth day. And not on the thousandth day. Still not today. This is all I hold against him. That he could expend himself. That he thought that his book was finished with the creation of the human and that he has not put away his quill to wait and see how many editions will be printed. That he was no artist is so very sad. That *yet* he was no artist. One wants to cry over this and lose all courage for everything."[15]

God as *failed* artist? There is humor in this tragedy, nicely disrupting any notions that Rilke was unceasingly earnest. While no one would claim that humor was prominent in Rilke's repertoire, it was certainly there, particularly in some letters and in some of the brief inscriptions to his own books that he generously signed for countless admirers.[16] Rilke scholar Mark S. Burrows goes further and identifies a "distinct sense of comedy, in the classic sense, that permeates Rilke's early and middle-life writing."[17]

More generally, reading Rilke's work may best be achieved in a state of mind the English poet John Keats wonderfully called, in a letter to his brothers written in December 1817, "negative capability." Keats was referring to poetry's relationship to what is not known, and described this as the ability "of being in un-certainties, Mysteries, doubts, without any irritable reaching after fact or reason." Such reading is braver than it might first appear. It defies the conventions of Keats's time and ours. It calls for a rare degree of intellectual openness, even innocence of a kind, which gives curiosity and anticipation the spaciousness they need. It also calls for a willingness to be "moved," even "disrupted," by the intimate processes of reading, and not just informed or affirmed. Conventional criticism stands apart from the text itself, yet stays close to the reassurance of currently approved theories and sources.

Any version of "irritable reaching after fact or reason" excludes the reader from all but the most familiar of contexts. It makes satisfying reading of visionary poetry impossible. Such poetry, like prayer, depends on the nondiscursive languages of inspiration and intuition contributing to what the twentieth-century priest and writer Dom Bede Griffiths called "a higher mode of thought."[18] This seems to echo Plotinus: "You can only apprehend the Infinite by a faculty superior to reason, by entering into a state in which you are your finite self no longer—in which divine essence is communicated to you . . . Like can only apprehend like; when you thus cease to be finite, you become one with the Infinite."[19]

Such writing, such poetry, is not limited by or to the linear, so-called rational universe and nor are its creators. Poetry is, after all, the writing form where inner reflection and internal impressions quite naturally take precedence over outer event. It is the natural home of ambiguity. It is also the writing form that goes and takes us beyond analysis and criticism, although only if we are willing to go.

And perhaps at least part of where the "going" takes us is to "the imaginal world," vividly described by Jungian analyst Robert Romanyshyn as "an intermediate world, a hinge or pivot between the intellectual and the sensible worlds, a world which is neither that of fact nor reason, a world [and here he quotes Henry Corbin on the great Sufi mystic Ibn Arabi] 'where the spiritual takes body and the body becomes spiritual,' a world whose organ of knowledge is the heart."[20]

You need courage to go there. The heart is dangerous territory to enter and difficult to leave. Heading in that direction it is, again, not change in some external sense that is risked but transformation. ("You can't go back," Rilke knows.) This is the place of the wound and of healing; of abandonment and of reconciliation. Yet, to insist on this same point, what is a poem *for* if it is not potentially transformative?

> . . . *Be earth now, and evensong.*
> *Be the ground lying under that sky.*
> *Be modest now, like a thing*
> *ripened until it is real,*
> *so that he who began it all*
> *can feel you when he reaches for you.*[21]

The reader is, or should be, shaken.

The chances to be shaken by Rilke are tremendous. The call to *Be earth now, and evensong / [to] Be the ground lying under that sky* challenges and disturbs, yet also connects and soothes. The sonnet below also gives some sense of these extremes. Written in 1922, the translation I have chosen has, like the fragment above from *The Book of Hours*, been freely rendered into English by Anita Barrows and Joanna Macy. Purists will point to some loss of authenticity. Yet what these translators have achieved is spaciousness, perhaps a "negative capability" in which the reader's own consciousness or truth can move.

Breath, you invisible poem!
Pure, continuous exchange
with all that is, flow and counterflow
where rhythmically I come to be.

Each time a wave that occurs just once
in a sea I discover I am.
You, innermost of oceans,
you, infinitude of space.

How many far places were once
within me. Some winds
are like my own child.

When I breathe them now, do they know me again?
Air, you silken surround,
completion and seed of my words.[22]

That breath could be seen as a poem, and perhaps poetry as necessary as breath, brings us to a realization of our own selves as the medium here. Through us breath is breathed; thanks to breath, we are breathed. The very intimacy of breath speaks of absolute connection between all life forms. *How many far places were once/within me.* And now some "claiming"—*Some winds/are like my own child*—and some letting go. The "I" that is each of us is birthing breaths, winds; is discovered in "a sea," yet in *the infinitude of space* familiarity remains fragile: *do they know me again?*

"Perhaps creating something is nothing but an act of profound remembrance," Rilke had written in 1902.[23] Reading Rilke, we *listen* in order to remember. We read through ears as much as eyes. As we listen, we tune and are tuned to the sacred. *What lingers/is what consecrates us,* we hear through the following "Sonnet to Orpheus," packing into brisk, shortened lines—unusual for Rilke—warning against the speed it demonstrates, implicitly insisting on the holy power of what lingers.

> *We press forward.*
> *But this march of time—*
> *consider it a glimpse*
> *of what endures.*
>
> *All that hurries will*
> *soon enough be over,*
> *because what lingers*
> *is what consecrates us.*
>
> *O, young ones, don't waste*
> *your courage on speed*
> *or squander it in flight.*
>
> *Everything is at rest:*
> *darkness and light,*
> *blossom and book.*[24]

Like his *Duino Elegies*, *Sonnets to Orpheus* was written at a time when Rilke was actively mourning the disappearance of "the lived and living things."[25] In fact, what was disappearing was not the "things" but the depth of our connection to them—our capacity to notice. The *Sonnets* themselves speak to our ancient past and atavistic longings and, like Rilke's poetry more generally, speak or sing repeatedly to neglected realms of our experience, perhaps to the timeless souls we were and are. One critic wrote of their "sound magic" and how, through them, "The perceptive reader . . . is transported into a state of rhythmic equipoise."[26] Describing the self-created (imagined) horse on which his Orpheus "arrived," Rilke himself wrote, "Across so many years he bounded, with his complete happiness, into my wide-open feeling."[27]

The "many years" Rilke refers to was a painful but far from empty time of waiting for a particular level of intensity and inspiration that brought him the writing he valued most. But for us it may be the "wide-open feeling" that is captivating.

When a previously unfamiliar poem evokes a feeling of "belonging" or coming home, it is exceptionally affecting. Our bridges are relatively few between the outer world and our inner world. Increasingly, we need those bridges and those mythical horses—and the gods they carry. They may feel life-engendering if not lifesaving. Is this one more way to conjure up what the heart seeks?

In the face of increasing abstraction, and mechanization of almost every aspect of life, Rilke feared that his might be the last generation to know those "lived and living things." This is challenging to us also. Without falling into sentimentality about a preindustrial past (an idyll for very few), it is nevertheless tempting to think of a world emptied of "divine radiance" and filled up with worship of the technological and mechanical as a relatively recent phenomenon. Yet in 1918, when Rilke was only in his early forties and the horrors of the First World War were raw, the pioneering sociologist Max Weber (then in his fifties) was already speaking of "modernity's rationalized approach to reality" and grieving that "there are no mysterious or incalculable forces that come into play." In short, "The world is disenchanted."[28]

Or is it? I would suggest that it is not the world that is stripped of enchantment; it is we "conscious" beings who—out of our unconsciousness or what the Buddhists so correctly call our ignorance—are stripped and stripping. Thomas Carlson extrapolates from this: "We see a model of the modern human subject as one who, through its rational and technological self-assertion, *empties the world of mystical presence.*"[29]

Rilke's work can be read as a profound response to those incalculable losses, to a familiar version of "flat-earth" thinking that literally reduces the dimensions of living and meaning, "flattening" what we might experience within life and how we might respond to it. Yet why are we reading Rilke if not to protest this, and to assert stubbornly with him that, as in Sonnet II, X, *for us existence still can enchant; in a hundred/places it's still Origin. A play of pure forces, / which no one touches who doesn't kneel in wonder?* The *hand's more masterful lingerings* are essentially subtle, inviting us to reflect but not always directly. This is not a view of existence gained secondhand; rather, it is a broadening of vision that takes some settling of the mind before the mind is ready to receive what is offered.

All that we've gained the machine threatens, as long
as it dares to exist as Idea, not obedient tool.

21

To inure us to the hand's more masterful lingerings,
for rigid buildings it cuts starker stone . . .

. . . But for us existence still can enchant; in a hundred
places it's still Origin. A play of pure forces,
which no one touches who doesn't kneel in wonder.

Words still softly give way before the unsayable . . .
And music, forever new, out of the most tremulous stones
builds in unusable space her house fit for gods.[30]

In 1917, a year before Weber had given his lecture and while war was still desolating Europe and beyond, Rilke was mourning that "'Victories,' however striking, do not lead us one step forward, and inwardly no one is prepared for a real change, everything is false and superficial; the old, fatal tendencies are still doing their evil work all the time and everywhere . . . only through one of the greatest and innermost renovations it has ever gone through will the world be able to save and maintain itself."[31]

Two years later, the "Great" War just over, Rilke was suggesting that the task of the intellectual in the post-war world would be to "prepare in men's hearts the way for those gentle, mysterious, trembling transformations, from which alone the understandings and harmonies of a serener future will proceed."[32]

His conviction that *life holds mystery for us yet* is central to a sacred reading of his work, or, more precisely, to a sacred rereading of *life* through his work, for that vision is surely needed now. The power of the "machine" and the temptations to regard one another "mechanically" has not lessened. Functionalism denies us our holiness. This is a great violence. It is also a betrayal and we are all tainted by it. This makes it all the more powerful when Rilke insists *for* us as well as *to* us that a life relentlessly fixed on the visible (or, often, a secondhand, flattened version of the visible) is a life cut off from its roots, dangerous in its lack of truth and dimensionality.

Poetry cannot save the world. What it can do is arouse the essential mystery within the world. Observing Rilke from a slightly different angle, while writing primarily about houses and their metaphorical as well as actual contents, the French philosopher Gaston Bachelard sees that in Rilke's work, "house and space are not merely two juxtaposed elements of space. In the reign of the imagination, they awaken daydreams in each other. . . ."[33]

I cannot think of a more moving or apt description when this same thought is applied to reading, and to reading poetry most of all. Writing must have its genesis in stillness and reverie: deep daydreaming. Otherwise it is simply the recording or reordering of other people's opinions, or the surface regurgitation of facts. When writing "works," it arouses daydreaming also in readers. Writing and reading must be born from the same place and meet there. Writing, reading: like Bachelard's house and space, they "awaken daydreams in each other."

"The sacred remains latent in poetry, which was born in ancient ritual and cult," writes the critic Camille Paglia. She continues: "Poetry's persistent theme of the sublime—the awesome vastness of the universe—is a religious perspective, even in atheists like Shelley. . . . Poets have glimpses of other realities, higher or lower, which can't be fully grasped cognitively. The poem is a methodical working out of fugitive impressions. It finds or rather projects symbols into the inner and outer worlds."[34]

"I do not want to tear art from life," Rilke wrote. "I know that somehow and somewhere both belong together."[35]

TRANSLATION AND
RECEPTION

To nourish the sacred rather than the certain is no small thing. It is not surprising then that it is often other poets who write about Rilke best; poets who can coax a brave openness and unimpeded response out of Rilke's readers; poets who write with least judgment (not the same as "least critical") and are most open in their *experiencing* of what they are reading. It is also not suprising that it is often "ordinary readers"—reading for love and not career—who will find it quite natural, even self-evident, to read Rilke in much that same way.

Of the many poets who have written about Rilke or translated him into English and contemporary idiom, American poet and writer Robert Bly is something of a beacon carrier. All kinds of Rilke readers in English have, I suspect, fallen in love with Rilke lines or been turned upside down by them when they have discovered them through Bly's lavishly openhanded translations. As with the more recent translations from Anita Barrows and renowned Buddhist teacher and scholar Joanna Macy, in the versions according to Bly, massive liberties are taken. Often as much of the translator sits on the page as Rilke does. Often the "intuitions" are less Rilke-reflective than self-reflective. And if we are reading Rilke only in English, then the question must be asked: Are we, in fact, reading Rilke or a *representation* of him?

There are other significant Rilke translators. Stephen Mitchell's wide-ranging *Selected Rilke* has been the primary source of Rilke discovery for many, who may also have enjoyed his more contemporary translation of the most accessible of Rilke's prose writing, *Letters to a Young Poet*. Edward Snow has given rich life in English to Rilke's words. These include journals and letters (with Michael Winkler) as well as several key volumes of poems. Snow, in fact, deserves special mention. He has translated more of Rilke's work into English than any other Rilke scholar. He has lived "inside" Rilke's work for decades and is an outstanding scholar/ translator in a crowded field, yet the calm restraint of his scholarship is admirable. In the world of Snow, the finger that points to the moon is never greater than the moon.

There are many others, including William Gass and Ulrich Baer, whose prose translations are invariably elegant and persuasive. And there is Mark S. Burrows, whose new translations add so much to this book less because he is able to think and breathe in German than because he himself is a "true poet" who lives by and through the sacred *tempi* that Rilke "heard" so exceptionally.

In my earliest days of reading Rilke, it was Bly, however, never less than a poet himself, who not invariably but often enough delivered Rilke's tone and concepts, perhaps his hidden meaning, with a particularly sinewy force. Bly seemed unafraid of Rilke and especially unafraid of Rilke's god-hunger; that's what made the difference.

I came to Rilke via Bly. It wasn't a perfect route. In fact, partly because of Bly's reservations about Rilke's *Elegies* ("almost too cultured"[1]), which are generally regarded as the peak of his writing, it was rather an idiosyncratic route. Yet even as my appreciation of the efforts made by other translators has accelerated, it feels a little like a lineage.

What is clear is that through the medium of each translator a somewhat different poet appears. I have noticed that when people tell me they are reading or have read Rilke I barely wait for them to stop speaking before I'm asking, "Which translation?"

A more central question also hovers: Should the freer, more popular translations be called representations rather than translations? Would that further liberate translators and readers? And perhaps this term should be applied not to the freer versions only but also to some of those that are formally "correct" but stripped of inner wit and rhythm and sometimes of vision and of life. Should we call those *translations*?

After all, what's going on here is rather like a grown-up version of the children's "Telephone" game, where I whisper something into your ear and you hear what you *believe* I said and whisper it into the ear of the person next to you, and so it goes around until something "appears" at the other end that may—but often does not—resemble or even represent that first moment I pressed my mouth to your ear.

It's the variety of translations in this book that best shows the intense subjectivity of our inner listening and, therefore, our reading. (What is reading if not "listening"?) If I am in a room with twenty or a hundred people, for example, and give each person a Rilke poem to think about, I know that soon we would have twenty or a hundred "readings" that are effectively translations not from one language to another, but from one sensibility to another.

Constantine Contogenis is a contemporary critic and translator. He suggests that ". . . the language *into which* one translates also deserves loyalty." But he sees this "loyalty" as complex. He writes, "A literary translation is like a wartime collaboration between two enemies of roughly equal power and moral standing. A translator ought to have divided loyalties and risk appearing a traitor to both languages . . . Deliberately not using a technique from the original—say, a pun available in both languages—is a minor betrayal of the original. But finding another technique in the second language—perhaps a rhyme—that better achieves the original effect enacts a fuller loyalty to the original."[2]

This question of what is gained and lost when words move from one language to another, from the mind of the poet to and through the mind of the translator, was also something that intrigued Rilke. According to Donald Prater, one of his biographers, Rilke's own "versions of [the poetry of French poet Paul] Valéry were Rilkean re-creations rather than faithful transpositions of the original into German . . ."

Prater continues, ". . . his images are often subtly different, and the thought sometimes elusively changed, resulting in a German poem with a beauty of its own but going beyond translation in the strict sense—'as if a piece written for the harpsichord were played on an organ.'"[3]

J. B. Leishman is an early Rilke translator. He quotes a note that accompanied Rilke's inscription in a copy of the *Elegies* that he signed for his Polish translator and friend, Witold von Hulewicz, in 1924. In the note, Rilke calls Hulewicz an "intermediary."[4] A nice sense emerges of a baton being passed, each person gripping it somewhat differently.

IN THE COMPANY OF RILKE

It anyway seems fair to suggest that much of what we read of Rilke in translation goes "beyond translation" while implicitly raising questions about what translation is. Prater asserts that this freedom, when exercised from French into German by Rilke, ". . . may be why he found as great a pleasure in this work as in production of his own, while at the same time feeling he had achieved a *tour de force* of equivalence and continuing to consider Valéry—whose more cerebral poetry was in fact very different from his—as 'the one nearest to me among the poets of my generation.'"[5]

The issue is not about language only, after all, and I found it fascinating to discover that C. F. MacIntyre, in his relatively early (1940) translated *Selected Poems*, is already making it clear how much partisan subjectivity there is in interpretations and criticisms of the man himself as well as in translations of his work. MacIntyre writes: "After I had got on with my personal Rilke for some ten years, I was surprised to discover I'd been living with a sort of Proteus who seems to have been all things to all critics, and to have trifled with me—even with the Nordic Diotima, Ellen Key, with the astute but vague Paul Valéry, and with the florid, oily Federico Olivero of the University of Turin [author of the 1931 study, *Rainer Maria Rilke: A Study in Poetry and Mysticism*]. Every man had his own Rilke."[6]

It seems likely—and desirable—that each serious reader will also have their own Rilke (no one "true" faith) and that this subjective "Rilke" will and must change over time. Critic Patricia Pollock Brodsky writes, "I've been interacting with Rilke for nearly forty years, yet I still find new things with every reading."[7]

How lovely that Brodsky would choose the word *interacting*, so much more vigorous and engaged than *studying* or *reading*, or *commenting upon*. Like any reader I, too, am aware that I am "drawing Rilke"—my own Rilke—and also drawing him in through the prism of my needs and experiences, taste, conditioning, desires and expectations. Rilke enhances the process quite wonderfully. Many of his poems invite self-reflection. They make sense of "seeing" and of the yearning to "see": a profoundly Rilkean idea and ideal. My sense is strong that a reader's devotion arises quite naturally when that particular yearning is articulated or met.

⁓

The British philosopher George Steiner (born in France) offers some general remarks about reading and translation that may also help us to understand better why we read and what we are seeking beyond words when we read deeply. He quotes Dante's idea of "motion of spirit," itself invaluable, and then writes: "Facing the text, we presume that it has meaning, however elusive or hermetic. . . . We proceed as if there was 'sense to be made' and transferred. This assumption is, in fact, audacious . . . Any such operative belief or 'leap of reason' in respect of the meaningfulness of words and signs, has psychological, philosophical and ultimately theological intuitions or entailments at its roots. . . ."[8]

We may or may not recognize them as such, but it is toward these "theological intuitions" that the Rilke reader is repeatedly returned, sometimes landing, more often circling. But Steiner raises something else, too, citing the possibility of a translator "killing" a text, or, perhaps more surprisingly, surpassing it.

"The translator invades the original. He decomposes it into lexical, grammatical parts. This dissection comports obvious dangers. So many translations kill, literally. Imperatively, unavoidably, the translator severs the ligaments which, in any serious text, make 'form' and 'content' reciprocally generative and rigorously fused. Not only in the obvious case of poetry, such dissolution is, more often than not, fatal. Paradoxically, there can be fatalities and betrayals 'from above.' If the vast majority of translations fall short of the source-texts, there are those which surpass them, whose autonomous strength obscures and marginalizes the humbler 'self' of the original. I call this betrayal 'transfiguration.'"

The example Steiner uses is of Rilke not as *translated* but as translator. "The high music of Rilke's *Umdichtung* all but obscures the domestic warmth and privacy of the sonnets of Louise Labé [Rilke translated some sonnets from this sixteenth-century poet in 1911]." Steiner concludes: "Ortega y Gasset speaks of the 'sadness of translation' . . . But there is also a *tristitia* that comes, as in eros of too violent and transforming a possession."[9]

The extent to which the different translators have served Rilke's work well—unafraid of its "theological intuitions," preserving its life, not "invading" or "killing" it—inevitably varies. (The same could be said of the efforts of critics and biographers.) Yet as long as it remains difficult for us to read poetry in its original language rather than in our own we will remain dependent on translators, on their sensitivity as well as their sensibility. This is particularly delicate when it comes to Rilke.

Reviewing William Gass's *Reading Rilke*, critic Marjorie Perloff comments on the "high degree of untranslatability that characterizes [Rilke's] poems" and mourns the current unwillingness of serious readers to learn a language in order to read a significant writer in the original. She writes of James Joyce learning Norwegian to read Ibsen. (And Rilke learned Danish to read Jens Peter Jacobsen, along with Russian, French and Italian, traces of English and passable

Czech.) Perloff also relates an anecdote that itself comments on the challenges of contemporary reading and translating.

"At a recent poetry festival, a highly respected American poet, when asked about her influences, spoke movingly about her special attachment to Rilke. Afterward, I asked her if she could read Rilke in German. She said no. I then asked her what translation she was using. She couldn't quite remember. "Have you wanted to take time off to learn a little German so that you might have a sense of Rilke's sound and rhythm?" I asked. She merely shrugged, as if to say that such study would be too much of a chore for a successful mid-career poet like herself."[10]

This anecdote raises many questions about what and why we are reading—and also how. Do we want to read Rilke in the "voice" in which he himself thought, listened and wrote? So many years after his death, would we hear that "voice," however accomplished our knowledge of German? Are we "tuned" to his cadences of time and place as well as language? Or are we, in fact, moved into a deeper understanding of Rilke and of where Rilke takes us through those English-language translations that unfold him freshly for us?

To be free to read him close to the way he heard his own poems *and* in contemporary translation would surely be ideal. What is clear, however, is that English-language readers do now and increasingly will remain dependent on translators. And in that context it seems fair to say that if we had no translations in English other than those of Leishman, Babette Deutsch and other brave but obscuring pioneers, the fascination with Rilke in English-language countries would surely be far less than it now is.

The parallel with the thirteenth-century Sufi poet Rumi is clear here. The popularity of Rumi's poetry in English owes little to his worthy early translators and much more to contemporary, liberty-taking "versions" of his ecstatic brilliance from American contemporary writers—few of whom would lay much claim to Farsi. But if this takes us straight back to the notion of representation rather than translation it also takes us onward to the more delicate issue of whether some translators, in some poems, have "surpassed" Rilke, to return to Steiner's point.

At the primary levels of creation and reception, this is absurd. No translator is likely to be the poet Rilke was. And yet central to the challenge of "translating" is a successful retuning of the writing for contemporary ears. When that "works," it moves the spirit of the original creation along from one century to the next, from one culture to another. This is not a question of language only, or of rhythm and tone, although all three count. It is also, surely, a question of relationship? What is the reader seeking through their reading? What is the reader bringing of himself or herself to meet and vivify the words on the page? What is the reader willing to find—and finding? Sometimes the retuning fails dismally. ("OK"—and that's from Bly—does not work in a Rilke poem. It distracts rather than refreshes.) But even this, while it may take us away from Rilke, reminds us that a text is not static. It does not freeze on the page. Each reader's gaze warms it.

There is a moving passage in one of Rilke's letters to Herr Kappus, the eponymous "Young Poet," immortalized in *Letters to a Young Poet*, where Rilke alludes to the shifting depths of comprehension that occur as the relationships of reading and writing develop. Rilke is describing having copied out Kappus's own sonnet, then he writes, "And now I give you this copy because I know that it is important and full of new experience to come upon a work of one's own again written in a strange hand. Read the lines as though they were someone else's, and you will feel deep within you how much they are your own."[11]

In those few lines the power of the transaction, the *covenant* between writer and reader, is revealed, as well as its fluidity and vitality. This is less an intellectual covenant—though the "intellect" may be highly delighted—than it is a covenant of heart, instinct, soul, embracing and emphasizing what it means to be consciously human.

"Learning by heart" is something specific to poetry. That process itself comments upon how singularly embodied (taken deep into one's being) reading poetry is or can be. Poetry is the form of writing most like music, and not because in its debilitated forms it depends on rhymes and the predictable rhythms that come with rhymes. That Rilke is now read so relatively widely and enthusiastically in English is testament to Dante's "motion of spirit" and the willingness of some of Rilke's translators to embrace that. Rilke's focus is not authoritative "truth." That is far too static. Rather, it is a motion toward truth, a quest for the real with all the ambiguity such a word implies. The spiritual intensity of that, along with his equally intense repudiation of conventional religious thought, drives Rilke's relevance for contemporary readers, I am suggesting, but the reader's *reception* is also revealed as something essentially active.

It is George Steiner who points out that "What a truly inspired (very rare) act of translation offers . . . is something *new that was already there.* This is not mysticism. . . . [Some texts] are left, in some palpable sense, richer, more fulfilled than before. They have come into possession, perhaps for the first time, of what was already theirs. . . . Where it is wholly achieved . . . translation is no less than felt discourse between two human beings, ethics in action. This is also part of the harvest of Babel."[12]

The "something new" to which Steiner refers is surely as much about timeliness and tone and especially meaning *in the context of time and place* as it is about words. Fidelity to surface meanings is not enough. Literalism does not do it. It is the life *within* the words that counts.

~

William Gass is author of the sometimes dazzling *Reading Rilke: Reflections on the Problems of Translation*. There is a lot of Gass in the book as well as Rilke but I had no difficulty in falling for its charms. It is as much a fiery demonstration of textual analysis, and testament of love and exasperation (with Rilke), as it is about reading, translation and its problems. It contains Gass's own translation of the *Elegies*, the central text he analyzes in terms of translators' success. In a tough moment Gass complains that "Many translators do not bother to understand their texts. That would interfere with their own creativity . . . they would rather be original than right."[13]

By contrast—although in many ways these two gifted critics have much in common—in his introduction to Stephen Mitchell's translation of Rilke's *Selected Poetry*, literary critic Robert Hass makes a strong case for some contemporary translations "improving" the text.

(It seems appropriately humorous that two prominent critics who swing between particularly dramatic extremes in their admiration and frustration in regard to Rilke should be called Gass [William H.] and Hass [Robert]. In Rilke's work a brilliant use of teasing, echoing internal rhymes constantly recurs. Here, with these two names, it is the sibilant double *s* that stings as well as softens. In these few lines from the Tenth Elegy, it is clear that in its *daß* form that double *s* even looks like the cello that would ideally sound it out: *Daß ich dereinst . . . /Daß von den klar geschlagenen . . . / . . . daß das unscheinbare Weinen . . .*)

Writing about the poetry from *Das Stunden-Buch* (*The Book of Hours*) in particular, Hass offers the view that "they sometimes seem more interesting in English translation than they really are." In the original German, Hass observes "tinkling regularity of the meter" and "neat finality of the rhymes" and contrasts this, in the context of this part of his discussion, with Robert Bly's "vigorous, unrhymed, unmetered translation."[14]

It would nevertheless be a huge claim to suggest that any of Rilke's poems have, in English, come into "what was already theirs" *as though for the first time*. Losses must also be acknowledged. British critic Judith Ryan notes that "Current fashion prefers translations to be unrhymed, but this method ignores an essential feature of much of Rilke's work: he adored esoteric rhyme words."[15]

What can be said is that the variety of translations, and the increasing freedom translators demonstrate and that perhaps readers demand, means that through the best of the translations in English we can potentially discover something within Rilke that is powerfully of this time, as well as for it.

~

Walter Arndt is a relatively "later" translator. His *The Best of Rilke* appeared in 1989, several years after the translations of Robert Bly, Stephen Mitchell and others, and more than fifty years after the earliest translations of Rilke's work were appearing in English.[16] Arndt comments scathingly on several of his translating predecessors, including

Leishman, Herter Norton, C. F. MacIntyre and Jessie Lemont. He singles out Mitchell for special scorn when he calls him a "pains-faking paraphrast" who reveals a "cheery what-the-hellitude,"[17] thus demonstrating that reading Rilke doesn't inevitably make you a kinder person.

Some of Arndt's criticisms of "translators" who do not have an intimate and ideally "mother-tongue" knowledge of the language from which they are purportedly translating are legitimate. I was never less than conscious of those painful limitations myself. Yet Arndt's possibly more "accurate" translation of "The Swan"—one of Rilke's *New Poems*—makes a telling contrast to that of Robert Bly's, which I have also included below.

Arndt is a native German speaker and a German scholar; Bly is neither. But is that what is most at issue here? Reading this same poem concurrently provides a provocative commentary to the questions I am raising: *How* are we reading, and what are we *seeking* when reading Rilke in English?

First, Rilke via Arndt—"The Swan":

This great toil: to go through things undone
Plodding as if tied by foot and hand,
Recalls the uncouth walking of the swan;

Death, the loss of grip upon the shelf
Whereon every day we used to stand,
Mimes the anxious launching of himself

On the floods where he is gently caught,
Which, as if now blessèdly at naught,
Float aside beneath him, ring by ring;
While he, infinitely sure and calm,
Ever more of age and free of qualm,
Deigns to fare upon them like a king.[18]

Now Rilke via Bly—"The Swan":

This clumsy living that moves lumbering
as if in ropes through what is not done
reminds us of the awkward way the swan walks.

And to die, which is a letting go
of the ground we stand on and cling to every day,
is like the swan when he nervously lets himself down

into the water, which receives him gaily
and which flows joyfully under
and after him, wave after wave,
while the swan, unmoving and marvelously calm,
is pleased to be carried, each minute more fully grown,
more like a king, composed, farther and farther on.[19]

And finally Rilke's original "Der Schwan" from *Neue Gedichte* (*New Poems*):

Diese Mühsal, durch noch Ungetanes
schwer und wie gebunden hinzugehn,
gleicht dem ungeschaffnen Gang des Schwanes.

Und das Sterben, dieses Nichtmehrfassen
jenes Grunds, auf dem wir täglich stehn,
seinem ängstlichen Sich-Niederlassen—:

in die Wasser, die ihn sanft empfangen
und die sich, wie glücklich und vergangen,
unter ihm zurückziehn, Flut um Flut;
während er unendlich still und sicher
immer mündiger und königlicher
und gelassener zu ziehn geruht.[20]

It does seem almost farcical that Arndt should choose the word *plodding* so early on. And should I also confess how I laughed out loud when reading, startling the two ancient, handsome cats that sit with me in my study as I write (sometimes actually on top of my computer desk, refusing to accept that there is no room), soothed by the sound of the keyboard and not expecting guffaws?

It is true that no translation could authentically capture Rilke's internal wordplay and dazzling "sound" play and render them into English: *"immer mündiger und königlicher"* is already a croon. The power of sound in Rilke's writing is exhilarating and affirms how acutely he must have listened as he wrote, listening for the sensuality of the words themselves, singly and especially in combination, words that sing in the mouth as well as the ear, while also reaching for tone and meaning.

German can be the most precise and sympathetic, the most intimate as well as the most serious (and sometimes harsh) of languages, and in Rilke's hands it is much more.[21] For all the considerable gifts of contemporary translation, we lose much of that original beauty in English and even more of Rilke's sense of rhythm and play and extreme plasticity of language. Raymond Hargreaves reminds us of what we are missing when he says, "There is such a perfect blend of vision and idiom in Rilke's poetry you believe German was designed as his peculiar medium."[22]

This makes tone and meaning more crucial in translation, not less.

So what is the meaning here, as we look at the swan? It is not a snapshot only. Our gaze is not with or on the swan. It is with what contemplation of the swan through Rilke's eyes *allows*. We look at the swan and we gaze at death. We look at the swan and see the truth: we too will die.

Death, "life's averted half," the "intimate Friend,"

is one of Rilke's constant themes, especially the inextri-
cable relationship of death to life and the seeking of an
unconditional acceptance of both. *Leben und Tod: sie sind
im Kerne Eins (Life and death are in essence one).*

> *Lord, give each one of us our own death,*
> *a dying that emerges from each life,*
> *from the way we loved,*
> *from meanings we made.*
> *And from our needs.*
>
> *For we are nothing but bark and leaf.*
> *That great Death that each of us has within*
> *is the fruit, around which all else turns.*[23]

Rilke wrote often about death, dreading it yet unable
to cease picking at it and its inviolable place in human
consciousness.

> Death is not beyond our strength; it is the measure
> mark at the vessel's rim: we are *full* as often as we
> reach it . . . I will not say that one should *love* death;
> but one should love life so magnanimously, so with-
> out calculation and selection that spontaneously one
> constantly includes with it and loves death, too (life's
> averted half), which is, in fact, what happens also,
> irresistibly and illimitably, in all great impulses of
> love! Only because we exclude death in a sudden
> moment of reflection, has it turned more and more
> into something alien, and as we have kept it in the
> alien, something hostile.
> It is conceivable that [death] stands infinitely closer
> to us than our effort would allow (this has grown

ever clearer to me with the years, and my work has perhaps only the *one* meaning and mission to bear witness, more and more impartially and independently, more prophetically perhaps, if that does not sound too arrogant—to this insight that so often unexpectedly overwhelms me)—our effort, I mean, can *only* go toward postulating the unity of life and death, so that it may gradually prove itself to us. Prejudiced as we are *against* death, we do not manage to release it from its misrepresentations . . .[24]

And again:

Death stands there, a bluish concoction
in a saucerless cup.
Curious place for a cup:
it stands on the back of a hand. You recognize,
only too well, the spot where the handle broke off
on its glassy curve. Dusty. And "Hope"
in exhausted letters on its side . . .[25]

Rilke's affirmation of the closeness of death as well as the unity of life and death or, more accurately, of the worlds of dying and "not-dying" (temporal and eternal) is a witnessing or affirming that itself transforms what death means. It is one of the most prominent of his spiritual themes and he writes about it with typically alluring unconventionality.

Critic Geoffrey Hartman, writing in the 1950s, notes, "Rilke's emphasis on the death-experience of the young, present in his earlier poetry, haunting in [his single novel] *Malte Laurids Brigge*, and leading to the fine evocation of death-in-children ('der Kindertod') in the Fourth *Duino Elegy*." Hartman comments that this emphasis is "quite unparalleled in intensity."[26]

A quick psychological response may be to point to Rilke's own birth. This took place a year after the birth and death of an infant sister and while his mother's mourning for her lost daughter was acute. This affected the infant and adult Rilke profoundly. There is something else to add, however. From a spiritual perspective it is possible to suggest that Rilke is also, and not so simply, emphasizing that death is not present at the end of life; rather, it is present *throughout* life. It is the shock of thinking about young people and death in the same moment that makes this truth most vivid.

~

In "The Swan," we witness death's closeness. Rilke achieves this through that familiar yet fresh image of the swan lowering itself into the water. Allegorical, sensual, evocative of the inward "pause" that a moment of authentic gazing allows: the poem offers all this as well as insight into the depths of the truth of impermanence and our struggle with it. In life we are doomed to "clumsy living," the poem reminds us; leaving life, we may move with greater grace, the poem promises. Death is not an abstraction. It belongs in an absolute sense to the world of experience and for me the *experience* of reading these lines (translated by Bly):

> *And to die, which is a letting go*
> *of the ground we stand on and cling to every day,*
> *is like the swan when he nervously lets himself down*
>
> *into the water, which receives him gaily*
> *and which flows joyfully under*
> *and after him, wave after wave . . .*

is markedly different from the *experience* of reading these (translated by Arndt):

Death, the loss of grip upon the shelf
Whereon every day we used to stand,
Mimes the anxious launching of himself

On the floods where he is gently caught,
Which, as if now blessedly at naught,
Float aside beneath him, ring by ring . . .

As one reads Bly's Rilke, meaning emerges. I feel "touched" as I read, with all that this familiar term entails. When we are *touched,* it is an inner experience. It connects us to the idea, to the poem and especially to ourselves. And how is that to be achieved? How is any outward "thing"—whether it is a poem or a swan—to become the means by which the reader's as well as the writer's inner vision shifts and something and someone is *touched?*

Another more familiar Rilke poem, this time from the 1902 *Book of Images,* has something to say, not about death now but a more truthful understanding of life and, implicit in that, about the power of poetry to move us from where we were, before reading, to where we now are, after reading.

Whoever you are: in the evening step out
of your room, where you know everything;
yours is the last house before the far-off:
whoever you are.
With your eyes, which in their weariness
barely free themselves from the worn-out threshold,
you lift very slowly one black tree
and place it against the sky: slender, alone.
And you have made the world. And it is huge
and like a word which grows ripe in silence.
And as your will seizes on its meaning,
tenderly your eyes let it go . . .[27]

How exhilarating the invitation is to "step out of your room"—the familiar locus of your conscious mind *where you know everything*—to see things/life with greater interest and freshness. Rilke is infectious when writing about life as well as death. Life is most exciting, he makes clear, when you don't already know "everything," when the stale recedes and you let the new shock. This poem calls us to lift our gaze from "the worn-out threshold," from the familiar, to see the black tree "slender, alone" and to discover "in silence" (and in our own loneliness): "You have made the world."

It is imagination that is praised here. With our inner gaze we can lift a tree, place it against the sky: slender, alone. We may be motionless in our chair. We may be doing "nothing" but reading. Yet a tree moves. And not only does a tree move, a human consciousness moves/creates. As "your will seizes on its meaning," *you have made the world.*

What does it take to achieve this? At least, Rilke seems to be saying, it commits us to an acceptance of the inevitability of change and—accepting that—to a more conscious respect for the complex processes of inwardness. And how are these twinned processes best understood? Rilke turns us away from analysis to listen.

"We are the bees of the Invisible," Rilke writes, again to his Polish translator. The "Invisible" should not be confused with the "not-present"; the "Invisible" is absolutely present, just as the unseen is absolutely part of the All. Rilke continues: *"Nous butinons éperdument le miel du visible, pour l'accumuler dans la grande ruche d'or de l'Invisible."* ("We are continually plundering the honey of the visible, so that we might store it up in the great, golden hive of the Invisible.")[28]

And, I would add, we also plunder the sweet honey of the invisible, in order that we might survive the visible.

～

As both idea and experience the "invisible" resists lit-
eralization. That's a tough call in a world where public
discussion is insistently literal. Whatever is tentative and
genuinely original takes a poor second place to what has
already been repeatedly chewed. Abandoning the surface
of things takes something more than curiosity or need for
depth; it takes trust in inwardness.

> *I believe in all that is not yet said.*
> *I want to set free my most intimate feelings.*
> *All that which no one has yet dared,*
> *may become for me a necessity.*
>
> *If this is audacious, my God, forgive.*
> *But I only want to say this to you:*
> *I want my noblest strength to become an instinct,*
> *without anger or hesitation—*
> *just the way that children love you.*
>
> *With this flood, with this flow*
> *into the beckoning arms of the open sea,*
> *with this expansive return,*
> *I want to make my confession and proclaim you*
> *as no one has yet done.*
>
> *And if this is subservience, then let me*
> *make my prayer obediently, bringing it*
> *earnestly and without duplicity*
> *before your shrouded face.*[29]

"[Reading Rilke] can be a shock for readers used to public
literature," Robert Bly writes in one of his commentaries.
"Most American writers begin proudly, even aggressively,

in the outer world . . . but Rilke begins elsewhere. When I first read Rilke, in my twenties, I felt a deep shock upon realizing the amount of introversion he had achieved, and the adult attention he paid to inner states."[30]

This "inwardness" is not a constant experience. Nor is it inevitably a safe and happy destination. Rilke himself wrote, "The terrible thing about Art is that the further you progress in it the more it saddles you with the extreme, the all-but-impossible."[31] One does not achieve a degree of inwardness and then stay there. Seeking must repeatedly be risked. *Vulnerability* must be risked. Michael André Bernstein suggests that, in Rilke's early years of writing, his inwardness and his yearning "remained purely self-referential: affirmations of a desire that had no object beyond itself. Even the moments of despair had too much mere self-display."[32]

Bernstein identifies 1913 as a likely point of change. (The *New Poems* were written around 1907–8. The *Elegies* and *Sonnets* were largely written in a short burst in 1922, although the *Elegies* had been started a decade earlier and remained suspended until the moment of extreme and necessary inspiration returned.) I value Bernstein's work yet want to suggest that alongside Rilke's inarguable self-focus was a highly developed seeking of and for transcendence, a genuine reaching *within* that was accurately mirrored by a reaching *out* to a power far beyond his own, and to a confident sense of a world or worlds that included but also extended beyond himself. I see readers' interest in his early work as testimony to this, and that it is evident in his work from at least as early as 1899 when the mixed but sometimes transporting *Book of Hours* was being written, and writing for the *Book of Images* had already begun, and from his Florence and Schmargendorf journals, written in 1898 at the age of twenty-three.

Nevertheless, as illustration of his point, Bernstein quotes from a poem written in the dark hours of 1913. In this poem, says Bernstein, Rilke "speaks of *'Innigstes unser'* (innermost thing of ours) as that which 'exceeds us,' and acknowledges that in order to know what is within, a person must reach a moment . . .

> when the inner surrounds us
> as the most practiced distance, as the air's
> other side . . ."[33]

The very notion of *air's other side* is brilliantly disturbing.[34] My mind darts: *Where?* In the same essay Bernstein speaks of the "union of simplicity and transcendence" that I see as vital to what draws readers into participating in—not just "reading"—Rilke's writing, even when what they meet is sometimes opaque or despairing. Bernstein describes something contagiously fresh: "Rilke seems to come upon and name his own inwardness not like the expression of an already known and permanently assured possession, but like a sudden discovery, a gift accepted in a spirit that contains both gratitude and an objective assessment of its lineaments."[35]

～

"Inwardness" is not a state of mind only. It is an experience and it changes experience. I believe those of us discovering Rilke and returning often to him know this instinctively and respond to it. The "embodied" physicality of Rilke's understanding and expression of inwardness is emphasized by an analogy he used in 1919, seven years before his death and at a time of fretful frustration in his creative life (and massive grief in the life of Europe as a whole, reeling from the effects of the "war to end all wars"). Rilke writes, "I need the same kind of uninterruptedness and inwardness which a mineral has in the interior of a mountain when it is turning into a crystal."[36]

That "uninterruptedness and inwardness," leaving essential room for inspiration as well as doubt, had already years before created the context for what may well be the most famous passage from Rilke's most famous prose book, *Letters to a Young Poet*.

Rilke, then himself still a young poet (though having published since his teens, already a confident and prolific one), is speaking to the aspirant poet to whom the letters in that book are addressed—and also to himself:

> Here, where an immense country lies about me [Rilke is writing from Worpswede, flat, "empty" countryside near Bremen] over which the winds pass coming from the seas, here I feel that no human being anywhere can answer for you those questions and feelings that deep within them have a life of their own; for even the best err in words when they are meant to mean most delicate and almost inexpressible things . . . I want to beg you, as much as I can, be patient toward all that is unresolved in your heart. Try to live the questions themselves like locked rooms or books that are written in a foreign tongue. Do not now seek the answers; they cannot be given to you now because you would not be able to live them. And the point is to live everything. Live the questions now. You will then, gradually, without even noticing it perhaps, live along some day into the answer.[37]

Living in the presence of questions that have a "life of their own" was, for Rilke, *living*. Or, perhaps more precisely, he was able to live in a quite profound state of Keatsian

"negative capability"—of "being in un-certainties, Myster-
ies, doubts, without any irritable reaching after fact or
reason"—that allows for the most essential of his, yours
and my questions to fill out and gain meaning. Space and
spaciousness, the Open—which I discuss later—together
with a necessary open-endedness allowing for extravagant
inversions of thinking and imagery in the presence of highly
structured writing were more than abstract ideas for him.
They gave energy to the *call* of writing and all that call
brought forth—also in the reader. It was his confidence
in the value of this that held him to his task during bleak
times: that it was nothing less than the *deep parts of [his] life*
that were to be poured out, allowing him (and us) to *see
farther into paintings.* That confidence is surely also part of
what captivates Rilke's readers. *Forward* is the direction in
which most readers also want to be heading.

> The deep parts of my life pour onward
> as if the river shores were opening out.
> It seems that things are more like me now,
> that I can see farther into paintings.
> I feel closer to what language can't reach.
> With my senses, as with birds, I climb
> into the windy heaven, out of the oak,
> and in the ponds broken off from the sky
> my feeling sinks, as if standing on fishes.[38]

From a place of coiled stillness so rare that it is tempting to
call it unnatural this profound "forwarding" comes. Standing
at his high, polished desk, the desk itself carefully positioned
within a room within a castle, or perhaps a tower or a
reliably grand and comfortable hotel, his pens and paper laid
out upon the desk so obsessively that this picture alone tells
a story—a pen for letters and unwelcome bills, a separate

pen for poetry—his small, thin, weakish body poised, tense, inwardly listening, his too-big head lowered, his dark suit and tie office-immaculate, his shoes glossed, fresh flowers arranged in a not-too-near vase, Rilke writes. Or waits.

Rilke regarded the source of some of his finest poems as beyond his own familiar self. He valued work highly but did not believe that he could rely on giftedness and "effort" alone. Receptivity and "readiness" were essential to his complex processes of creation and were, as reflections of a heightened sense of inwardness, unimaginably physically and emotionally demanding. Reception should not be confused with passivity; the contrary is true. Writing about the *Elegies*, which Rilke regarded as his greatest achievement, his biographer Wolfgang Leppmann says, "The poet did not think of himself as their creator but their receiver: the vessel into which they were poured or the prism in which the rays of inspiration were refracted and dispersed. . . ."[39]

The work that came, that felt "given," sometimes in a rush, sometimes only after years of waiting, electrifies the reader, forces a response, but despite the self-focus that sometimes distances even the most patient reader, that response is not primarily to Rilke, nor even to his subject matter. More often, the response is to "the questions," or to where the questions take us. That is Rilke's genius.

"THE NATURE OF POETRY"

"Poetry has been a beleaguered castle on a cliff for a long time," writes William Gass, "and my castle had four towers: Yeats, Valéry, Rilke, and Wallace Stevens. Their period produced some of the greatest lyric poetry our European culture has ever seen—perhaps its last gasp." Of Rilke specifically Gass writes: "[His *Elegies*] gave me my innermost thoughts, and then they gave those thoughts an expression I could never have imagined possible for them. Furthermore, the poet who thought and wrote those things, for all his shortcomings, actually endeavored to be worthy of his work."[1]

After years in Rilke's company, sometimes entranced, occasionally distanced, even appalled, before being re-entranced, I was constantly aware that this is a poet "worthy of his work." We speak of writers' "gifts," meaning their talents. With Rilke it is more accurate to think of gifts in terms also of "what is given." Reading Rilke is to receive abundantly.

Nonetheless, the density and volume of Rilke's writing

mean that the most careful critic remains something of a beginner (or perhaps should). This is what Rilke recommended. And surrendered reading also demands that: repeatedly setting down or aside the burden, even the veils of our preconceptions and approaching *this* moment, *this* reading, *this* poem with freshness.

I was gripped most by the writings that reflect upon or demonstrate Rilke's complex, ambivalent but ceaselessly yearning relationship not to God only (though sometimes that), but also to the idea of God, to his need for God, his anger with and bitterness toward God, his tenderness for God, his desolation without God. This "God" is rarely the God of creeds and cathedrals, although it is sometimes the God of portents, of the Psalms, "wind" and Holy Spirit. Unfinished, vulnerable and dependent, created in large part through relationship and especially through relationship with creator-artists, this is also not the God of literalists.

In 1914, elated by the expectation of a grand love, Rilke wrote to the pianist Magda von Hattingberg ("Benvenuta"): "Am I permitted to feel the world, breathe its air, certain that it contains you . . . as I know that God is contained in it, whom I know, whom I have experienced as boundlessly in the bliss of my work as you have in your music?"[2]

Boundless, but this is a God that must repeatedly be sought in and through inwardness.

> *I have many brothers robed in cassocks,*
> *in southern cloisters sheltered by bay trees.*
> *I know how they fashion their Madonnas humanly,*
> *and I often dream of early Titians and*
> *how the god shimmers through them.*
>
> *But when I bend down into myself:*
> *My god is dark, and like a clump*
> *of a hundred roots that drink in silence . . .*[3]

~

"When I say: God, that is a great conviction in me, not something learned"—Rilke writes in his 1922 fictional creation "The Young Workman's Letter"—"It seems to me, the whole creation speaks this work, without reflection, though often out of deep thoughtfulness." Then, still in his "young workman" persona, Rilke chides those who might think this means somehow lessening a full-hearted appreciation of *this* life: "What folly to direct our thoughts to a Beyond, when we are surrounded here by tasks and expectations and future prospects!"[4]

The intensity of poetry, and of seeking not the familiar theistic "God" but something further out (and further in), unite to tremendous effect in much of Rilke's writing. Here is the seeking of a firsthand, evolving sense of the awesome, untamable power of the spiritual within our more familiar material world. Poetry, at least in the hands of Rilke, forms language from such seeking, forms it out of silence and returns it to silence. Indeed, as my appreciation grew, I increasingly came to see how the medium of poetry itself plays exquisitely to Rilke's strengths. Throughout his lifetime of intense writing Rilke demonstrates what poetry makes possible not just for and within the poet, but also for and within the reader. The paradoxes of poetry reflect his individual sensibility with a touching accuracy: intensity giving way to spaciousness; the sensual giving birth to the spiritual—and vice versa; "still life" transforming the activity of "seeing"; the universal arising out of the strikingly personal.

Reading Rilke with care can lead to a heightened appreciation not of Rilke only but also of poetry. And not just of poetry, either, but of what Yeats called "supreme art." Defying the emerging gospel of modernism, Yeats defined such art as "a traditional statement of certain heroic and religious truths, passed on from age to age, modified by individual genius, but never abandoned."[5] For Yeats, for Rilke, for many readers, it would seem that art truly cannot be separated from religion, by which I do not mean the institutions of religion, but the dark-deep—*like a clump/of a hundred roots that drink in silence*—Rilke would say *instinctive* impulses and desires we call *religious*.

The twentieth-century German philosopher Hans-Georg Gadamer reminds us that "Like all other kinds of experience, aesthetic and religious experience seek expression in language. If we bear in mind their original Greek meaning, the words *poetry*, literally a making through the word, and *theology*, literally speech about divine, make the point."

Nonetheless, we should not confuse poetic and religious speech. Gadamer again: "Anyone who is familiar with Greek theology and poetry knows very well that it is quite impossible to distinguish between the language of poetry and that of the mythological tradition. For it was precisely the poets themselves who mediated that tradition. A question posed in the form 'poetic *or* religious language?' is even less appropriate when we confront the Indian or Chinese traditions of thought, for there we cannot even ask whether we are dealing with poetry, religion, or philosophy."[6]

Those who read "religious speech," or Eastern or Western scriptures as poetry, or some poetry and perhaps Rilke's as "scripture," will take up Gadamer's insights with gratitude. We are back to Bede Griffiths's "higher mode of thought," which is not dependent on intellectual skill or refined aesthetic appreciation but on something more challenging to our conditioned minds: the submitting to or "letting in" to which I am repeatedly returning. In Rilke's writing I easily find the unifying movement that Gadamer describes between aesthetic and spiritual experience, curtailing any need to ask: "Religious or poetic language?" What we are swept into, in Rilke's work, is experience: increasingly mindful and no less affecting when it has the confidence to remain tentative.

It is of course possible to write "beautifully" and without sustaining content. Voice and language are *not* everything. But when voice, style and content merge, as they do sublimely in Rilke's writing, a synergy is created that carries extraordinary power. The poet is then "speaking" not to the intellect only, but also to the imagination, senses, even the soul of the listener/reader. Rilke frequently achieves what great music also can, breaking through the carapace of presumptions and defenses to go to what is quite accurately called "the heart of the matter."

Rilke's own comments are helpful.

To be someone, as an artist, means: to be able to speak one's self. This would not be so difficult if language started with the individual, originated in him and would then, from this point, gradually force itself into the ears and the comprehension of others. But this is not the case. Quite on the contrary, language is what all have in common, but which no single person has produced because all are continuously producing it, that vast, humming, and swinging syntax to which everyone feels free to add by speaking what is closest to his heart . . .

In order to shape prose rhythmically, one has to immerse oneself deeply within oneself and detect the blood's anonymous, multivaried rhythm. Prose is to be built like a cathedral: there one is truly without name, without ambition, without help: up in the scaffolding, alone with one's conscience.[7]

Historian of philosophy J. H. Randall Jr. suggests that religion is like art in that it "furnishes no supplementary truth, but does open whole worlds to be explored." This idea is already rich. There is more. "Very early in every great religious tradition, reflective men came to see that the ordinary ideas entertained and used in worship, prayer and ritual could not be 'literally' true . . . God could not be 'really' the animal, or natural force, or carved image, the imaginative picture in which the average man conceives divine. He could not be even the highest human image, the 'Father,' or the kind of 'person' who in the present fashion seems appropriately approached in terms of the 'I-Thou' experience [particularly as described by Martin Buber]. Important and even indispensable in religious practice as are these ways of imagining divine . . . All ideas of God, like all other religious beliefs, are without exception *religious symbols*."[8]

⁓

Poetry uses and *is* the language of symbols. And symbols are the primary language of emotions. The philosopher John Armstrong, in *Love, Life, Goethe,* quotes Goethe: "I am longing for grapes and figs." Armstrong comments, ". . . but his real longing was for what he might become in a sunny climate; who he might be if he could feast on southern fruit." We hear Goethe again: "Can I learn to look at things with clear, fresh eyes? How much can I take in at a single glance? Can the grooves of old mental habits be effaced?"[9]

Symbols help us to efface "the grooves of old mental habits." They can bypass cognitive ruts, especially when they are startling. They *carry* and evoke emotion. Emotion is, in poetry, both cause and effect. We call writing poetic when it breaches the linear whether or not it is formally "poetry."

"A poet participates in the eternal, the infinite, and the one . . . It is as it were the interpretation of a diviner nature through our own; but its footsteps are like those of a wind over the sea, which the coming calm erases, and whose traces remain only as on the wrinkled sand which paves it," wrote the "atheist" (as Camille Paglia called him) English poet P. B. Shelley in his famous 1821 essay, "A Defense of Poetry."

We call a moment poetic when it takes us "elsewhere" from the "where" of the familiar. Sitting in my study one muggy Sydney summer's day, a day as far unlike the bracing crispness of a Swiss winter as I could imagine, reflecting on Rilke's final winter in his final (modest, not very comfortable) château—in Muzot[10] in the Valais region of Switzerland—I opened up *Learning Human* by another poet, the contemporary Australian Les Murray. And I found this to tell me more about Rilke and why I read and need poetry: *the only whole thinking.*

> *Religions are poems. They concert*
> *our daylight and dreaming mind, our*
> *emotions, instinct, breath and native gesture*
>
> *into the only whole thinking: poetry.*
> *Nothing's said till it's dreamed out in words*
> *and nothing's true that figures in words only . . .*[11]

I find Murray's poem stunning, perfect, and find it amusing that "stunning" is the word that returns each time I read it. To stun means, of course, to be knocked into a dazed state. In that state, time pauses. *Nothing's true that figures in words only* may be another way of talking about the Rilkean "pause"—for the pause is everywhere in a Rilke poem, even when his lines race. It is within the pause that reflection is achieved, or what we now call mindfulness. The pause may be "inside" words as well as between them. In the pause, authentic self-inquiry is authored and "speech about the divine" evolves, to quote Gadamer again. In fact, it is possible to suggest that the very idea of seeking and reading a poem can be experienced as a willingness to pause, both quickening and deepening life.

> *My life isn't this hurtling hour,*
> *in which you see me scuttling.*
> *I am a tree, standing in front of so much . . .*
>
> *I am the pause between two notes*
> *that may somehow always be out of harmony*
> *because Death's note wants to win—*
> *But in the dark interval*
> *they reconcile, trembling.*
> *And the Song remains beautiful.*[12]

Within months of Rilke's death in 1926, his greatest love, psychoanalyst and writer Lou Andreas-Salomé, was writing of a poetry where "the heavenly realm of the Almighty belongs to those who do not at first expect it, but rather have mastered it, and who know one urgent, inviolable, and imperturbable necessity—the unity of life and death."[13]

This was not Rilke's only unifying drive. His biographer H. F. Peters draws attention to a useful phrase from Heidegger, "resolute decision," describing the strength to accept life *as it is*. Peters suggests that unless Rilke had made that choice, he might have written "beautiful poetry" only.[14] Later in her account Lou writes: "The soul's rapture and corporeality were to become for Rilke one and the same."[15]

Since she was writing so soon after Rilke's death, Lou's interest may have been to make explicit the unifying themes of life and death, seen and unseen, lament and celebration, in Rilke's work, and also to show that Rilke's was the synergistic power of true poetic *thinking* (not simply language). Her remarks allow the possibility that in Rilke, poetry and theology—if we can take up again Gadamer's sense of theology as "literally speech about the divine"—come powerfully together *because* he is freely "religious" in the sense of "dwelling" with what is most inspiring and mysterious, and *because* he is unafraid to call on the deepest stories of what it means to be fully human, including understanding death as well as life, and "the soul's rapture" as well as the impermanent and often painful "corporeal."

My life isn't this hurtling hour,
in which you see me scuttling.

Most crucially, it may be because his are the words and silences of symbols and not of literalism: because they are the words of authentic poetry.

~

Lou Andreas-Salomé was herself a remarkable person: "a *femme fatale*. Men longed for her, suffered for her, and it is possible that one or two even died for her."[16] Rilke loved her intensely and remained in awe of her until his death.

"Your heart, God knows," Rilke would write to Lou in 1911, "was in all truth the door through which I first came into the open; now I always return from time to time and place myself against the very door-post on which we used to record my growth, long ago. Leave me this fond habit and love me."[17]

Born in Russia into a distinguished family of German Protestant descent, Lou is famed for her close friendships with Nietzsche, who was desperate to marry her when she was a dazzlingly independent, questioning girl of eighteen, Paul Rée (one of those who arguably "died for her") and Sigmund Freud, as well as with Rilke. In her own right she was a formidable intellect, a pioneering psychoanalyst and feminist and a confident and widely published novelist and writer.

In the same tribute to Rilke from which I quote above, Lou looks back to reflect on her second trip to Russia with him in 1900, the year he turned twenty-five. Rilke was then still discovering Russia (especially his inward creation of it) "as a redemption for him." As crucial for his "redemption" and integral to it, he was deepening the relationship that he and Lou would share at different levels of need and intensity to the end of Rilke's life.

The meaning that prerevolutionary Russia had for Rilke, as well as the role that Russia played in developing Rilke's inner vision, emerges clearly in a letter written in 1904 from Rome when he described it to Lou like this: "Russia was reality and at the same time the deep, daily insight that reality is something distant, coming infinitely slowly to those who have patience. Russia, the country where people are lonely people, each with a world in himself, each full of darkness like a mountain, each deep

in his humility, without fear of humiliating himself . . .
People full of distance, uncertainty and hope: people
becoming something."[18]

It is hard not to think he was finding a way to describe
himself—for all his complex closeness and, at this time,
sexual intimacy with Lou—as, "full of distance, uncer-
tainty and hope . . . becoming something." It was also
Russia that gave Rilke what he described in a letter of
1923 as "the brotherliness and darkness of God, in whom
alone there is fellowship. That was how I named him then,
the God who had dawned upon me, and I lived long in
the antechamber of his name on my knees."[19]

> . . . Sometimes I pray: Please don't talk.
> Let all your doing be by gesture only.
> Go on writing in faces and stones
> what your silence means . . .

The "gestures" of God are everywhere in Rilke's work
and yet his poetry would suggest that such "gestures"
are, more simply, everywhere. From Paris in 1914, Rilke
wrote: ". . . within the Christian church ways to God of
most blissful ascent and of deepest achievement can be
trodden." That is not all, however. "But this conviction
and experience does not exclude in me the certainty that
the most powerful relationships to God, where there is
need and urge for them, can develop in the extra-Christian
spirit too, in any struggling human being, as all Nature,
after all, where it is allowed to have its way, passes over
inexhaustibly to God. . . ."[20]

> . . . Often when I imagine you
> your wholeness cascades into many shapes . . .

Nonetheless, this "everywhere-ness" does not make for easy visibility in the world of Rilkean seeing, for:

> . . . *You run like a herd of luminous deer*
> *and I am dark, I am forest . . .*[21]

It is typical of the reversals in Rilke that in these few lines we have God writing *in faces and stones* (even while the poet is writing God), and a God who is cascading into a *herd of luminous deer* while *I* remain God's ground: dark, forest(ed). And at quite the same time as our ideas about God are turned on their head, our ideas about ourselves refract and spin.

An appreciation of a limitless world emerges, a world of inwardness and imagination linked with the world(s) of "outside" so that the conventions of "outside" and "inside" become virtually meaningless. This should not suggest that Rilke was indifferent to "outside." On the contrary, throughout his life he was immensely sensitive to his immediate surroundings and the effect they had on his feelings. After discovering, with Lou, the physical *place* that was Russia, Rilke wrote to his friend Helene Voronin, "As soon as I have learned and mastered the language, I shall feel myself entirely a Russian. And then I shall bow low before the Znamenskaya Chapel (which I love before all others), three times in suitable reverence."[22]

The giddy exhilaration that Rilke is expressing becomes touching if we remember that Rilke was not yet in his mid-twenties and was inspired as well as sometimes tormented by love, and feeling in the presence of the mature, magnificent and widely desired Lou that his gifts as a poet were rapidly "ripening" (as were his gifts for hyperbole). His letter continues: "If I had come on

this earth as a prophet, I would preach all my life that
Russia was the chosen land over which lies God's massive
sculptor's hand as though in a provident delaying action:
everything it needs is to come to this land . . ."[23]

The poetry that was the gift from that journey began
as *Die Gebete* (*The Prayers*), written in 1899 in Berlin but
with Russia still strongly present. These *Prayers* emerged
through the persona of a Russian monk, an icon painter.

We dare not paint you in our own fashion,
you twilighting one from whom the morning rose.
Out of our old paint boxes we take
the same strokes and the same rays of light
with which the saint concealed you.

We build up images in front of you like walls,
until by now a thousand walls surround you.
And our pious hands veil you
as often as our hearts see you clearly.[24]

The prayer-poems of *Die Gebete* are passionately expres-
sive of the monk's, and perhaps Rilke's, desire for God
and fascinated exploration of what God might be and
become—especially when the *old paint boxes* are set aside,
and *our pious hands* are no longer veiling. The view sought
here is through the eyes of the heart, the only eyes capable
of seeing the *twilighting one from whom the morning rose.*

Das Buch vom mönchischen Leben (*The Book of Monastic
Life*) emerged from that inner and outer pilgrimage and
is what we know as the first part of *Das Stunden-Buch*, his
widely translated, read and loved *Book of Hours.*

The question of inspiration is vivid here, and of a God
still "speaking." Rilke believed those first prayer-poems
"came to him" from somewhere that was not within his

ordinary or even his "writing" consciousness, as other poems had and would, and he did not intend to publish them. It is legitimate to ask: Came from where? But in the context of Rilke's embracing of the nonduality of the seen and unseen, and the *natural* power of the invisible within the visible, it is not a question to answer confidently.

The Book of Hours arose from and offers a rare depth of inspiration. *Inspiration* may not entirely suffice here. This is a work of art that seeks God. It never "lands" God, nor needs to. Within it, God is both sought and seeker; both needed and needy. This does not diminish the "goodness" of God; it increases the seeker's intimacy with God *and* with the world in which we live and seek.

This feat of Rilke's—to seek a God who is at once presence and absence, solace and abandonment, created and, though rarely, creator—is as disturbing as it is astonishing. "The monk's role . . . is one of artist, creator, and source."[25] It may also be confusing.

Lou comments: "One should not be deceived by the fact that the God in his *Stundenbuch*[26] [*Book of Hours*] is not identical to the God he found in Russia; along with the attitude of pious trust in God's protection, the book also presents a reversal of this situation, one in which man becomes a God-creator, a God-constructor, who must now take *Him* under *his* protection. His devotion is not estranged here by presumption; instead it is so infinite that all emotions, from quaking humility to gentle tenderness, flow together. . . . 'God' creates himself in [Rilke's] poetry under the impetus of *all* human feelings; in fearless trust God is experienced as a harmonious and ordering principle."

Lou is developing the Nietzschean idea that, as Robert Hass reminds us, defines the "task of art" as "god-making."[27] She quotes Rilke:

We work at building you with trembling hands
piling one atom upon the other.
But who can ever finish you,
you great cathedral[?][28]

Such moments of intimacy are extreme by any measure
other than Rilke's. They should be taking our breath away.
Here, awe is present (in our "trembling hands"); so is dogged
persistence. But it is when Rilke speaks to God as unfinished
cathedral that our presumptions are exposed. These lines from
The Book of Hours continue a profound litany of reversals.

What will you do, God, when I die?
I am your pitcher (what if I shatter?)
I am your drink (what if I spoil?)
I am your garment and your craft
and when I go, so does your meaning.

It is a constant theme within the scriptural traditions that the
Infinite transcendent works in the everyday world through
us; that we humans are "His" spiritual instruments; that
we are branches to His vine. This is a supreme idea: that
the divine works through us and cocreates with us. This is
meta–intimacy, but also an idea we may have real difficulty
taking seriously, yet not know how resistant we are until
we also hear:

When I'm gone, you'll have no house
where words, near and warm, might greet you—
and I, satin sandals that I am,
fall from your aching feet.

The godly foot receives but also loses the satiny embrace
of the writer.

Your weighty robe will fall from you.
Your gaze, which I now warmly welcome
on my cheek as if that were a pillow,
will come searching ceaselessly for me
until it falls, while the sun itself is setting
into a womb of foreign stones.

And then, poet as petitioner now:

What will you do, God? I am afraid.[29]

~

Those first prayers were written in Berlin between Sep-
tember and October 1899. Two years later, over a period
of eight days in Westerwede, Rilke wrote *Das Buch von
der Pilgershaft* (*The Book of Pilgrimage*) that would become
the second part of *The Book of Hours*. The third part is *Das
Buch von der Armut und vom Tode* (*The Book of Poverty and
Death*), also written in eight days, this time in Viareggio
in Italy, in 1903. The prayers and prose commentary that
had begun the *Book of Hours* triptych were cut and revised
by Rilke and the three books became one when they were
published in December 1905.

In a variety of translations *The Book of Hours* is,
for many contemporary English-language Rilke readers,
the most God-soaked, personal and personally inspir-
ing of Rilke's work. For some readers, I suspect, this *is*
Rilke, yet still it takes us not just into Rilke but also
beyond him. Judith Ryan calls Rilke's *Book of Hours* a
"meditation on creative powers in general." She goes on:
"Constructing the divine also constructs the voice and
the mode that will become inimitably Rilke's: a personal
tone modulated by a virtuoso command of rhetoric,

expressions of intense anxiety combined with grandiose self-assurance. . . ."[30]

It may seem grandiose to address God as an equal. It may seem perverse to reflect openly on God's needs for our imperfect love. When I read aloud the poem immediately above (*What will you do, God, when I die?*) at a conference recently, a man stood up at the end of my talk and lectured me on how Rilke could only be a "flagrant narcissist," and therefore unworthy of our serious attention. He was outraged by what he believed the poem makes explicit, but when it comes to Rilke, and particularly his relationship to and with the mysterious divine, any one-size-fits-all diagnosis is far too simple.

"A DIRECTION OF
THE HEART"

Writing about *The Book of Hours* and the time of heightened relationship and inner change that was the context for its genesis, Lou Andreas-Salomé says: "It was conceived there [in Russia] from the most immediate experience of the hours, verse for verse, prayer for prayer, suspended through days and nights that were filled with inexhaustible devotion—as perhaps has never before been revealed in poetry or prayer. It was as if both only needed to 'be' because they were one and the same."[1]

It is in part the focus or "one-pointedness" of poetry that takes it close to prayer. Thomas Merton lived most of his adult life as a Trappist monk, willingly if not always cheerfully bound to his Kentucky monastery through his vow of stability and spending many hours of each day building the inner rhythms demanded by contemplative prayer. Like Rilke, he was a prolific writer and a poet, so it is particularly interesting that it is he who has suggested that "contemplation has much to offer poetry. And poetry, in its turn, has something to offer contemplation . . . the first thing that needs to be stressed is the essential dignity of aesthetic experience."

Merton defines this as ". . . something that transcends not only the sensible order (in which, however, it has its beginning) but also that of reason itself. It is a suprarational intuition of the latent perfection of things. Its immediacy outruns the speed of reasoning and leaves all analysis behind."

Encouraging the jump away from the limitations of familiar thinking, Merton elaborates: "It is, in itself, a very high gift, though only in the natural order . . . To many people the enjoyment of art is nothing more than a sensible and emotional thrill . . . They like paintings of dogs that you could almost pat. But naturally they soon tire of art, under those circumstances. They turn aside to pat a real dog, or they go down the street to an air-conditioned movie."[2]

Reading Rilke is unlikely to precipitate the need to pat a real dog. The "dignity of aesthetic experience" is, more often than not, fully realized in his work. This means that when the opportunity to pat a real dog comes along, it may be a different experience because of reading Rilke.

This same vital theme of prayer-poetry—and where each points within and beyond the self—is revisited by Lou some years later in 1934 in another essay about Rilke, published after her death as part of a longer and more general memoir, *Looking Back* (*Lebensrückblick*). Lou is recalling a moment when she and Rilke were in Russia and had been traveling up the Volga River for several weeks. The pair found themselves about to board different steamboats, and Lou reports Rilke as saying, "'Even if we had been on two different boats we'd still be going up the same river—for a single source awaits us both.'"³

That theme is heightened further by Rilke in one of a series of strikingly intense letters written in 1914 to Magda von Hattingberg. Describing his years at military boarding school, Rilke confides:

> . . . I felt a bond of trust between [God] and me, and had conversations with him in which, I am sure, I did not hold back with recommendations for bringing about the downfall of the military school. But as one grew warm with God in this urgent intercourse, the strangest, most incomprehensible thing happened: One could not win him over for any annihilation or degradation of the surrounding circumstances, for as soon as one started speaking to him, *the military school was no longer there.* Just as, in later life, one may become so powerfully absorbed in contemplation as to lose all sense of one's body . . . so did the boy's need, *by its instinctual attachment to the divine,* transcend its own motives and become—outside, in space, as it were—a pure unconditional relation, an independent, magnificent experience of soul. ⁴

This instinctual attachment to the divine, so concentrated that even the horrors of military school were *no longer there,* heightens Rilke's words from "The Young Workman's Letter," quoted earlier: "When I say: God, that is a great conviction in me, not something learned." Nevertheless, these parallels between prayer and poetry, and to what each allows in terms of a deepening relationship to *life itself,* should in no way point to any conventional notions of religiosity or even religious belief in Rilke or, indeed, in Lou.

Deeply influenced by Freud, perhaps by Nietzsche, and certainly by her own characteristic self-questioning, Lou's first book was called *In the Struggle for God* (*Im Kampf um Gott*), yet she was even less of a believer than Rilke, or certainly not in the "God" of her Protestant formation. H. F. Peters, biographer of Rilke and (separately) of Lou, writes of religion as being a theme that occupied them both "deeply." He comments, "They were both extremely fond of the Bible,[5] especially of the Old Testament. And when they were alone together [in the early years] in the privacy of Lou's rooms, Rilke sometimes read to her . . . and he could feel the current of sympathy that his words aroused in Lou's heart."

> *So many angels search for you in the light*
> *and thrust their brows toward the stars*
> *and want to know you in every brightness.*
> *But it's like this with me: whenever I write of you,*
> *they turn their faces away and distance*
> *themselves from the folds of your garment . . .*
>
> *. . . Altogether dark is your mouth from which I drifted,*
> *and your hands are ebony.*[6]

"Belief" is not a useful word here. There is too much fixedness in it and perhaps too much light. There is loss in these poems as well as union; frustration as well as craving.

> *How is it that my hands fail in the painting?*
> *If I attempt to paint you, God, you hardly notice.*
>
> *I feel you. On the hems of my feelings*
> *you begin to hesitate, as in the presence of many islands,*
> *and your eyes which never blink—*
> *if I come into your presence.*

You no longer inhabit the heart of your own shining
where all the lines of angel-dance,
the distant ones, exhaust you like music—
you dwell in the farthest house.
Your entire heaven listens from my depths,
because in my brooding I kept silent about you.[7]

Peters again: "Starting from the premise that all gods are man-made, Lou's concern was with the retroaction, as she called it, of these manmade gods on those who believe in them."[8] Yet what was also true was that Lou could not leave the idea of God alone. As for Rilke, "God" was more than ceaseless activity; it was seeking itself.

~

Rilke famously called religion "a direction of the heart," a phrase I treasure. (If only that was all religion was—with space for other "hearts" also to move freely!) The French philosopher Gabriel Marcel suggests that it was *God* that Rilke called "a direction of the heart," which would, indeed, capture the energy and incompletion of this finite/infinite relationship.[9] The best evidence I could find for this was a passage in the penultimate section of Rilke's only novel, *The Notebooks of Malte Laurids Brigge*, where the narrator writes: "I had sometimes wondered why Abelone did not use the calories of her magnificent feeling on God. I know she yearned to remove from her love all that was transitive, but could her truthful heart be deceived about God's being only a direction of love, not an object of love? Didn't she know that she need fear no return from him? . . . Or did she want to avoid Christ?"[10]

Direction of love is a phrase that will also ring true for many contemporary readers. And yet that's not all

God is or was for Rilke. Judith Ryan writes confidently that "in Rilke's poetic transposition of Lou's ideas, God is in essence a projection of human consciousness. . . ." Ryan goes further. "Though inspired by the spirituality Rilke believed he found in Russia, *The Book of Hours* in fact presents a heretical anti-mysticism. God becomes a metaphor, not for the creative act, but for the art object."[11]

I can't agree. Ryan is attributing to Rilke a view of God quite widely held in these postmodern times. God as a creation of the human mind, as an "objective correlative for art,"[12] as Ryan puts it, has been powerfully argued, including by esteemed philosophers Don Cupitt and Lloyd Geering.[13] But this is not the God nor the trailing vapor that I find as I peer with Rilke and into Rilke's work, even knowing that I am doing so through the thicket of my own desires and projections.

Perhaps the least presumptuous thing to suggest is that Rilke and Lou were each driven by powerful religious *feeling*, no small thing, and that through their many individual changes in self-perception and ideas about God it was this religious feeling and the yearnings such feeling express and arouse that remained a constant.

Near the end of his life Rilke describes in a letter to Ilse Jahr something of his inner journey and also shows how aware he is that Ilse wants from him a depth of conviction or consolation that he cannot, in truth, provide. The "books" to which he is referring are those that became the single *Book of Hours*. He writes, "It may be also that you do not turn so much to who I *am*—perhaps you address and rejoice with him who I *was* twenty years ago, when I wrote those books that have grown so close to you and become yours. . . . Now you would hardly ever hear me name him [God], there is an indescribable discretion between us, and where closeness and penetration once were, new distances stretch out as in the atom which the new science also conceives as a universe in little. The Tangible slips away, changes; instead of possession one learns the relativity of things, and there arises a nameless-ness that must begin again with God if it is to become perfect and without deceit."[14]

This paragraph may seem disappointing to those readers who long—as one senses Ilse Jahr did—to "preserve" or anoint the selective "*Book of Hours* Rilke," who has become unusually dear to them. And yet, those readers never entirely lose him. There *is* a continuity of yearning and seeking throughout Rilke's writing life. It's not so hard to trace. What's more, and perhaps less predictably, I can also see how those same lines could give countless contemporary readers not less but *more* confidence that in Rilke's writing they can feel met and sometimes assuaged. After all, the "indescrib-able discretion" of which Rilke writes so delicately allows for the mourning of "the Tangible." The Tangible leaves its traces; yet for many readers even traces of the old may be too much. Giving up "possession" means giving up any hint of God-clinging. That is a kind of freedom.

> Losing also is ours: and even forgetting
> gathers a shape in the permanent realm of mutation.
> What we release can circle; and, though we are seldom the center,
> each of those circles enrings us in its absolute curve.[15]

To risk losing takes courage, even when knowing a little of the *absolute curve*. We feel weariness in Rilke's letter and, again, in the poem above, written in 1924, two years from death, *the permanent realm of mutation*. Making demands on our own inner experience, we may feel a mirroring weariness and wariness within ourselves. Yet Rilke is surely saying, if we are not to lie to ourselves, then we certainly cannot afford to lie about this: *not this.*

What we release can circle; and, though we are seldom the center,
each of those circles enrings us in its absolute curve.

Uncertainty about the "thingness" of God is not an extinguishing of spiritual fire (. . . *forgetting/gathers a shape* . . .). It may not mean loving less or less personally. It is not purgatory, either, with the paradise of conviction on the other side. It is itself a kind of arrival.

~

In the notes to their exemplary translation of Rilke's *Diaries of a Young Poet*, Edward Snow and Michael Winkler describe Lou and Rilke as "two worldly God-seekers with an emotionally charged interest in theological questions."[16]

Those two, and particularly Snow, who has translated more of Rilke's poetry into English than any other contemporary scholar, have a formidable knowledge of Rilke's work. Nevertheless, I do wonder whether Rilke was ever "worldly." "Carnal" sometimes; fussy and obsessive always; affected by physical environment and atmosphere as much as by people, but not "worldly" in the sense of driven by or willing to manipulate the ideas and values of the world around him. I would also challenge the idea that it was theological questions in any formal sense that possessed Rilke and, to a lesser extent, drove Lou. "God-seeking" and "emotionally charged" are nevertheless apt. This is true despite Rilke's immense ambivalence about the "what" of God as well as the "who."

Ellen Key, a prominent Swedish feminist renowned for the strength of her opinions, was a friend of Rilke's for some years and an enthusiastic promoter of his work. When she used the term *God-seeker* to describe him it disturbed him greatly. J. F. Hendry comments: "Despite his entreaties, Ellen published an essay in 1911, 'Rainer Maria Rilke: a God-Seeker,' that made him extremely uncomfortable."[17]

"God, now become unutterable, is stripped of all attributes and these fall back into creation, into love and death," wrote Rilke in 1923.[18]

"Unutterable" and not a "personal" God in any generally accepted sense, the God so often to be found in Rilke's poetry is nevertheless achingly "near" and vulnerable. ("While the Bible says that man is lost until God's love finds him, Rilke implies that God is lost until man's love finds Him," writes H. F. Peters.[19])

Living with this key phrase *God-seeker,* and letting it rest in my own mind, I came to see it as a "fit" for myself and central to why I read Rilke and, more significantly, chose to spend these years thinking and writing about him and about why any of us might read the kind of poetry he sometimes gives us. I also feel deeply the (desirable) "negative capability" of all that this phrase implies: accepting some degree of uncertainty or unfolding, and the questing that goes with it. Just as clearly, I see why the phrase itself was too definitive for Rilke. There was too much "claim" in it for one who had no choice but to "circle" the divine in some state of confusion. Rilke had previously told Key that ". . . it fixes my religious development at a stage beyond which it has in part already progressed."[20] Being "fixed" was, for Rilke, imprisonment.

An earlier letter that Rilke wrote in 1915, when living in Munich, offers one among many possible examples of these crucial shifts and reversals in his thinking. This time he is in part reflecting on his novel, *The Notebooks of Malte Laurids Brigge*, which mirrors some of his most unresolvable and sometimes tormenting inner questions. He refers to this when he asks, rhetorically: "How is it possible to live when after all the elements of this life are utterly incomprehensible to us? If we are continually inadequate in love, uncertain in decision and impotent in the face of death, how is it possible to exist?"[21]

Rilke is, of course, posing questions made poignant by the "meaninglessness" of mass violence and death at that time of war. Unsurprisingly, "God" does not provide neat or easy answers. In the same letter, Rilke writes:

> Does it perplex you, my saying God and gods and for the sake of completeness haunting you with these dogmatic terms (as with a ghost), thinking that they must immediately mean something to you? But assume the metaphysical. Let us agree that since his earliest beginnings man has shaped gods in whom here and there were contained only the dead and threatening and destructive and frightful, violence, anger, superpersonal, tied up as it were into a tight knot of malice: the alien, if you like, but already to some extent implied in this alien, the admission that one was aware of it, endured it, yes, acknowledged it for the sake of a sure, secret relationship and connection . . . *Could one not treat the history of God as a part, never before broached, of the human mind, a part always postponed, saved up, and at last let slip . . .*[22]

Again, such lines may seem at first to support Ryan's view of Rilke's God being a "metaphor for the creative act." They may also seem at odds with some of Rilke's best-loved poetry. I think they are not. Poet Denise Levertov writes of "Rilke's lifelong maintenance of a balance between his innate and intense religious emotion and his equally definite rejection of theological monopolies, especially of conventional Christianity."[23] This is an elegant summary, although rather than "balance" one could suggest that his writing gives the sense of someone magnetized by God even in God's frequent absence, an experience likely to be strikingly familiar for readers who share Rilke's "religious emotion" and his "definite rejection of theological monopolies."

The following poem is for them. It seems at first to be uncertainty's hymn, but that may be illusory. Perhaps it is, rather, the faithful seeker's hymn because surely there is something marvelous, even noble, about "persisting" when the props of conventional faith cannot be leaned upon and yet one still continues *circling*.

> *I live my life in widening circles*
> *which spread out to encompass all things.*
> *I may not bring the last one to completion,*
> *but that will be my attempt.*
>
> *I circle God, the ancient tower,*
> *circling and circling for thousands of years,*
> *and don't yet know—am I a falcon, a storm,*
> *or an immense song?*[24]

Rilke's early biographer, the aristocratic J. R. (Jean Rudolf) von Salis, knew Rilke personally toward the end of the poet's life, having landed on Rilke's doorstep at Muzot in April 1924, when he himself was only twenty-two and Rilke was almost fifty. Von Salis writes of Rilke's spirituality "concentrated in the magnificent vault of the clear forehead and in the wide-open mauve-blue eyes," which contrasted somewhat with his "excessively large" mouth, small chin and a "drooping, thin mustache"—but also "one of the most expressive [hands] that I have ever seen . . . With a little more strength it might have been the hand of a painter or sculptor."[25]

It is striking that von Salis, an intelligent and empathic observer, speaks confidently of Rilke's "profound belief in the existence of God," along with his "rejection of the Christian faith," and regards Rilke's later works as "witness and monument to the fidelity with which he carried out his survey of the soul's inner space, 'inner-world-space' (*Weltinnenraum*) . . ." He also says that although "Rilke was not so unpolitical as he appeared to be," nonetheless, "Not the outer, only the inner ways of men were important to him."

Perhaps the most telling of von Salis's remarks—particularly in relation to the *Elegies*—is that Rilke was "no mystic aiming at union with a transcendent God but a worshipper and singer of the earthly and creaturely."[26]

> *Voices, voices. Listen, Oh, my heart, as hitherto only*
> *holy men have listened, listened so the mighty call*
> *lifted them straight from the ground, although they kneeled on,*
> *these magicians—and paid no attention,*
> *they so utterly listened. Not that you could bear*
> *the voice of God—far from it.*[27]

The Italian philosopher Federico Olivero, also writing shortly after Rilke's death, goes so far as to describe Rilke as an "agnostic," without any "certainty of faith on which to found his hopes."[28] That is too cerebral a description for contemporary ears. A strong whiff of rational indifference

hangs around the word *agnostic*. None of that seems appropri-
ate to Rilke. Is it possible, then, to say that Rilke was both
hoffnungsvoll and *hoffnungslos* (filled with hope and emptied
of hope)?

Certainly "seeking" and "God" were to preoccupy
him throughout his life, despite that "increasing discretion"
between Rilke and God quoted earlier. In fact it had been
Lou's essay "Jesus the Jew"—in which, prophetically in the
light of Rilke's interests, it is Christ's solitariness which is
praised—that had first captured Rilke's attention. Rilke
was then twenty-one, slight, intense, highly self-conscious,
beautifully mannered and spoken, and the author, among
many other poems, some of them far from good, of the
then-unfolding *Visions of Christ*.[29] Lou was thirty-six.

But moving forward, and still adding to these glimpses
of Rilke's inner world, comes this statement from Lou. She
is addressing Rilke directly as "you" (or, more precisely,
addressing her inner image of him, as he had died eight
years earlier) when she writes: "When I think of these
things, I could spend the rest of my life telling us both
about them, as if in this way, for the first time, the nature
of poetry might be revealed—not as works, but as incarna-
tion, not text, but body, and it is this which is life's 'miracle.'
That which rose in you, almost without intention, as
'prayer,' remained within the person at your side [Lou]
to the end of her days as an unforgettable revelation. It
enveloped any person with whom you came in contact;
it remained corporeal, disclosing at your touch how it
partook of the divine; and the childlike, unselfish way
in which you accepted it so trustingly ensured each day,
each hour, its intimate perfection."[30]

Lou's interpretations were highly subjective even during
Rilke's own lifetime. In Lou's case, they were conditioned

not only by her personal experiences of Rilke, and his considerable demands on her, but also in the later years by the newborn Freudian psychoanalytic theories through which she enthusiastically came to interpret the world, her patients and those closest to her, including Rilke. Lou is nevertheless the woman who arguably knew Rilke best. Rilke thought so.[31] A poignant statement from the last days of his life starkly demonstrates this dependence. He was dying of a particularly painful form of leukemia but still assumed that the source of his illness was psychological. Having written to Lou two weeks before his death, for the first time in a year, describing pain that "unloosens me. Day and night," he "implored his doctors to 'ask Lou what is wrong with me. She is the only one who knows.'"[32]

For all the limitations as well as insights that flow from an ideological view of the world and humanity, Lou emerges through her own writing, as well as through Rilke's attitude toward her, as a woman with more than enough emotional self-possession to be capable of changing her opinions and her mind. It is poignant and convincing, therefore, when, toward the end of this posthumous "letter" to him, she returns to the time of Rilke's Russia-passion, his Lou-passion, and the time of his creation of *The Book of Hours*, and says, "The spirit arrived in yet another sense than you suspected in the storm of your emotions. To me it was like an Ascension of the poetical *work* above the poet as a *man*. For the first time the 'work' itself—what it would become through you, and what it would require of you—seemed to me to be your rightful lord and master."[33]

Lou's descriptions may seem inflated to a contemporary reader, but as everyone who lives with Rilke on the

page must at least sometimes feel, Rilke and Lou emerge
as people with a larger-than-life vision. That *largeness*
invites us in.

Ah, not to be cut off,
not by such slight partition
to be excluded from the stars' measure.
What is inwardness?
What if not sky intensified,
flung through with birds and deep
with winds of homecoming?[34]

Those brief lines reflect a vision I find sublime. I imagine
the words written out and pinned to many notice boards,
or written on countless cards to be sent to lovers. The
vision is pure Rilke. The infinity of inwardness, bringing
nothing less than a *sky intensified, /flung through with birds
and deep/with winds of homecoming* to one's own sometimes
parched, sometimes desolate being, gloriously emphasizes
the "intimate immensity" of Rilke's work, as Bachelard
describes it. Quoting Rilke, now: *"Le monde est grand, mais
en nous/il est profond comme la mer."* ("The world is vast, but
in us/it is deep as the sea.")[35]

Yet our appreciation may grow more, not less, when
we allow ourselves to remember that sublime writing is
not effortlessly achieved. There may well be enchanted
moments, and Rilke had many of those. But his constancy
was also tested. In 1911, reflecting on the writing of *The
Notebooks of Malte Laurids Brigge*, that "difficult, difficult
book," Rilke wrote: "As soon as I tried in those days to
look out beyond that work, I saw myself on the far side
of it doing something quite different, never writing again.
Now I have hesitated after all to try something else . . .
Can you understand that? And tell me whether one of

these is arrogant and which one: to 'give up' work, to step aside as though something had already been accomplished, or, through all the aridity, to persist in it because all that it realized was indeed scarcely even the beginning of that to which one deemed oneself boundlessly committed?"[36]

As a younger poet—already "boundlessly committed"—and finishing in an outburst of creativity his book of short stories, *Das Buch vom Lieben Gott und Anderes* (*The Book of God and Other Things*), later called *Geschichten vom Lieben Gott* (*Stories of God*), Rilke had written this in his journal:

> O nights, nights, nights,
> long I would like to write,
> and always, always, over pages bend and fill them
> with those tenuous signs that are not written
> by my weary hand,
> betraying that I myself am but a hand of One who
> does such wondrous things
> through me.[37]

There was fidelity in Rilke, above everything to poetry and, with greater ambivalence, to the *One who/does such wondrous things*—and whose "hand" Rilke at least sometimes felt himself to be. Twenty years after writing that journal entry, and despite the "distances" between himself and God that he had described so eloquently to Ilse Jahr, Rilke wrote to the closest confidante of his final years, Nanny Wunderly-Volkart, "Ultimately there is only *one* poet, that infinite one who makes himself felt, here and there through the ages, in a mind that can surrender to him."[38]

HUSBAND, FATHER,
LOVER—POET

In his early twenties, and already in his own mind nothing but a poet, Rilke wrote: "There is still much about me that I dislike; and yet I feel already that these qualities are *foreign*, contingent, not really connected to me. From this comes a certain confidence, a certain strength. Whether I will succeed some day in going about entirely in my own clothes—I do not know. At any rate, I want to start off by becoming naked, then everything else will take care of itself."[1]

   This "nakedness" seems to have demanded quite a high price. At least from this distance it would seem that Rilke's outer life was one of not fitting. After he left Prague at the first opportunity, moving to Germany, France, Italy and Switzerland as well as back and forth from all those places, it was also a life of never settling. Rilke disliked the description "German poet"[2] but was more uncomfortable still to be described, by reason of his birth in Prague—then capital of Bohemia and part of the Austro-Hungarian Empire—as an "Austrian poet." In fact, "loathing of Austria was one of the oldest, most deep-seated and permanent of all his loathings."[3] Rilke himself said that "Everything happened to be against my having a fatherland" and spoke of total "*Heimatlosigkeit*."[4] And if that homelessness seems sad—and there were certainly ways in which it was sad and also caused sadness for others—then it may also seem apt. Nothing about Rilke's imagination or achievement can be limited to one rooted, external "place." None of it readily "fits" either, at least not into the models with which most of us are familiar, even with all the allowances we would normally extend to those most exceptional of all writers: poets.

~

René Karl Wilhelm Johann Josef Maria Rilke was born to a German-speaking family in Prague in December 1875. When he was a baby and little boy, Rilke's pious, emotionally hungry and intrusive mother, Sophie, or Phia, dressed him in girl's clothes and called him René when she wasn't calling him Sophie, "Fräulein," or Margaret. Her longed-for infant daughter had died the year before René was born. He did not become Rainer Maria until his early twenties (when he also transformed his handwriting), influenced in this significant turn toward "masculinity" by that utterly formative relationship with Lou Andreas-Salomé.[5]

Rilke's father, Josef, a socially ambitious "failed army officer" who eventually worked for a private railway company, tried and failed to make a soldier of his delicate, exceptional son. When, in 1884, his parents could no longer even pretend to be able to bear to live with one another, and the suffocating but familiar home in the "cramped, rented apartment"[6] they had created together was being disbanded, René lived for some time with his mother, then was sent, in 1886, to a military boarding school chosen at least in part because his fees could be subsidized. But that economic factor was not all that mattered.

At that time, for the dominant German minority living a militarized imperialist dream of superiority to the Czech majority they lived among, the archetypal image of the "soldier" would have had multiple layers of meaning. "Rilke loathed and disowned his native country and his native city, Prague," writes E. C. Mason. It was a place Rilke called a "miserable city of subordinate existences" and, in Mason's words now, "unmitigated philistinism."[7]

From an early age René Rilke learned French from his mother. At school he learned "passable" Czech but nevertheless lived in an almost entirely German-speaking world of home, family, friends and school—a world riven with its own internal snobberies, classifications, fears and failures, as well as its unexamined "superiority" to the life literally taking place next door. In the context of his father's thwarted ten-year military career and the disappointment that followed, the archetype of the "little soldier" gained additional power.

From a twenty-first-century and relatively child-focused perspective, it is difficult to comprehend that Phia and Josef could have looked at their small, dreamy son—a keen writer of "verse" from the age of nine—and seriously believed that military school could transform him into the robust fellow they, and particularly Josef, longed for him to be. Yet they did, with Josef perhaps hoping that René might live out the career dream that he, Josef, had been unable to realize, and his mother perhaps fantasizing about her son providing the status and security, even the glamour, that her husband could not.

In his early twenties, after the two journeys to Russia with Lou, and now at Lou's urging Rainer (more "manly" and "German") rather than René, Rilke adopted another kind of uniform to intensify another kind of dream, or, even more painfully when seen from the outside, another kind of "becoming." "Passionately in love with Russia and everything Russian,"[8] this time he chose the clothes of his idealized inner "Russian" that announced to the outer world his deepest identifications.

In 1900, the first phase of his relationship with Lou was in decline. The relationships with painter Paula Becker and sculptor Clara Westhoff, and his idealization of their artistic community in rural Worpswede, were about to launch. This is a crossroads moment. Rilke is described as reading his own poetry, "Seated romantically between two icons and flickering candles. Wearing sandals and his Russian tunic, he read in his quiet, melodious voice that made a ritual of the occasion."[9]

Such studied moments, replete with talismanic props and heavy overtones—and there are many—make Rilke easy to mock. They may even make it tempting to dismiss him or his work. And yet, writing and thinking about them, I was never less than aware that it was precisely these apparent incongruities that create some of the fascination Rilke provokes. More crucially, I was never less than grateful that from the same period as Rilke's fancy dress and portentous reading, as the century turned and Rilke was still only in his unfinished midtwenties, comes poetry that takes the reader directly to God, or to their desire for God.

You, Neighbor God, whom I often
rouse with loud knocks in the long nights,
I do this because I rarely hear you breathing,
and know: You are in the great room, alone.

And when you need something, no one's there,
no one to bring drink to your outstretched hand.

I eavesdrop constantly. Give some small sign.
I am so near . . . [10]

That image of God so close as to be "neighbor" strikes a note of compelling intimacy. Readers who have been discovering Sufi mystical poetry and especially Coleman Barks's, Daniel Ladinsky's and Robert Bly's English-language adaptations over recent decades, may have become somewhat used to that thrilling shock of the near. Readers of the Hebrew Bible are also used to God guiding and chiding like the Father they believe Him to be. But still, bringing God down from on high and right into the room next door nevertheless shocks and *works*: works especially in the way it both satisfies and provokes questions within the reader: *Where is God for me? Where am I for God?* It also works as writing: rocketing away from the shores of the known. That same intimacy—taste as well as sound, and again the nearness of "neighbor"—resonates in this, another of so many favorites:

> *. . . I named You the neighbor of my nights*
> *and all my evenings' deep secrecy,—*
> *and You're the one none could conceive*
> *had You not been thought out from eternity.*
> *You're the one in whom I've never erred,*
> *the one I entered like a well-known house.*
> *Your growing now goes on beyond me:*
> *You are Becoming's essence, all-evolving.*[11]

Here, as in many other places in Rilke's work, readers are not called to love their human neighbor as themselves;

they are called to a mere-wall-away neighborliness with the divine: *I rarely hear you breathing/and know: You are in the great room, alone.* Or, closer still in the second poem above, now not even a wall between ourselves and God: *[You are] the one I entered like a well-known house.* And, like us humans, the divine "You" is poignantly unfinished: *Becoming's essence, all-evolving.* Implicit in everything that he writes, Rilke promises and points to more.

~

In one of his most influential lectures on art, Swiss expressionist painter Paul Klee spoke of an art of the "inner eye" that passes beyond manifest appearances to "the womb of nature, at the source of creation, where the secret key to all lies." Klee—born just four years after Rilke and passionately interested in transcendentalism—said in the same lecture, "Chosen are those artists who penetrate to the region of that secret place where primeval power nurtures all evolution . . . But not all can enter." Those who can enter "help to lift life out of its mediocrity. For not only do they, to some extent, add more spirit to the seen, but they also make secret visions visible."[12]

Making "secret visions visible," Rilke's poems are nevertheless not an escape from this world but an invitation to stand more squarely *upon* the earth, to experience the world and ourselves-in-the-world as participants in the poetry and not spectators to it. The more we read Rilke and the more of Rilke that we read, we grow in confidence about that unity within the world(s), a classic theme of mysticism. The poem that follows is just one of many that expresses this. Calling as it does to One *space [that] spreads through all creatures equally—/inner-world-space,* it is especially affecting to know that it was written as war was about to devastate and fracture Europe.

> *Everything beckons to us to perceive it,*
> *murmurs at every turn "Remember me!"*
> *A day we passed, too busy to receive it,*
> *will yet unlock us all its treasury.*
>
> *Who shall compute our harvest? Who shall bar*
> *us from the former years, the long-departed?*
> *What have we learned from living since we started,*
> *except to find in others what we are?*
>
> *. . . One space spreads through all creatures equally—*
> *inner-world-space. Birds quietly flying go*
> *flying through us. Oh, I that want to grow,*
> *the tree I look outside at grows in me!*
>
> *It stands in me, that house I look for still,*
> *in me that shelter I have not possessed.*
> *I, the now well-beloved: on my breast*
> *this fair world's image clings and weeps her fill.*[13]

Rilke's confidence in *inner-world-space* is beguiling.

> *. . . One space spreads through all creatures equally—*
> *inner-world-space. Birds quietly flying go*
> *flying through us.*

This echoes the Sufi poet Kabir: "What is inside me also moves inside you." And from Gaston Bachelard: "The two kinds of space, intimate space and exterior space, keep encouraging each other, as it were, in their growth." A little later, Bachelard quotes Rilke: "'Through every human being, unique space, intimate space, opens up to the world. . . .'"[14]

World, space, inner, outer: recurring unifying images bring us more thoroughly *into* life, making good sense of Rilke anthologist Ulrich Baer's comment that Rilke "did not want his writing to be put under glass like orchids made of silk but instead hoped it would be read irreverently, spoken not only by professional custodians of high culture, but breathed deeply into the messiness of life that no one can avoid."[15] Yet for all that, Rilke did a fine job of avoiding "the messiness of life" where he could: "Rilke did not go to his daughter's wedding for fear of losing his concentration."[16]

~

Rilke had married the gifted, somberly beautiful sculptor Clara Westhoff in April 1901. He had returned from that second fateful journey to Russia with Lou only nine months or so before, and there seems little doubt he was still enthralled by her. He was also dependent upon Lou's eloquent, generous "wonder, admiration and love. Her whole being responded: her heart to his music. . . ."[17] But Lou was married, approaching forty (Rilke was twenty-five) and, although her marriage was at least as unconventional as everything else about her—she had agreed to marry her brilliant but histrionic husband when he stabbed himself with a pocket knife, but not to be sexually intimate with him, ever—there was no question of Lou wishing to marry Rilke or any of the lovers who followed him. Post-Russia, when Rilke went to Worpswede in the summer of 1900 and met Clara there—one of a number of artists living in a "colony" in the countryside near

Bremen—Lou already needed considerably more freedom than Rilke seemed eager to give.

It seems unlikely that Clara was ever a great love. Rilke may have been more captivated by her friend the Expressionist painter Paula Becker (later, Modersohn-Becker), who would die a few days after giving birth in 1907, and was memorialized by Rilke in his 1908 "Requiem" (*"I have my dead, and I have let them go,/ . . . Only you/return; brush past me, loiter. . . ."*).[18] It could even be that the two young women were most lovable or fascinating in combination: "In September, 1900, Rilke quite suddenly changed his residence [from Worpswede] to Berlin, but he still kept up an assiduous correspondence with the 'two sisters of my soul.'"[19]

One of many Clara/Paula/Rilke stories is that Rilke gave Clara a first gift of oatmeal and Paula a favorite book by Jens Peter Jacobsen. There's a hum of truth in that and we can feel sorrow for the possibly too-little-loved Clara. If not a great love, however, Clara seems to have been in many ways a great woman. "She is grand and splendid to look at—and that's the way she is as a person and as an artist," Paula wrote in her journal.[20] Ernst Nordlind, a contemporary, commented, "Her entire being radiated kindness and she was everybody's friend. . . . As with her husband, her experiences had been transmuted into wisdom."[21] Talented—a former pupil of Auguste Rodin—discreet, encouraging and intelligent, she was one of very few significant women in Rilke's life who did not write about him or discuss in public her feelings for him. I applaud that—even while acknowledging how interested I have been in those other more disclosing commentaries.

Their one child, conceived before their relationship was firmly established, was Ruth, the girl whose wedding

Rilke was too busy to attend and whose husband and child Rilke never made the time or effort to meet. What adds to the poignancy of this is that Ruth and her husband, Carl Sieber, devoted themselves to Rilke's literary heritage, and Carl—like Ruth—was encouraged to call him "little Daddy," but they never met. Writing to Carl in 1921 after his engagement to Ruth, Rilke acknowledges that he "let [Ruth] forgo the really familial" but reassures Carl that his daughter, a girl of "quiet and strong talents," had "felt from childhood that this did not happen out of lovelessness . . . but because the exclusive call to the *inner* realizations of my life was so great that work on the *external* ones, after a brief attempt, had to be abandoned."[22]

Clara and Rilke shared a home for less than two years. There is some evidence they considered leaving Germany for Russia. "My wife doesn't know Russia," wrote Rilke in March 1902 to the publisher Alexander Suvorin, "but I have told her so much about it that she is ready to leave her native land, which has become as alien to her as to me, and join me in making the move to your country—which is my own country spiritually. Ah, if only it turned out that we could live there for good! I believe this is possible—possible because I love your country, love its people, its suffering, and its greatness: *love is the power and the ally of God.*"[23]

Instead they went to Paris, though not to live together, and Paris would remain Rilke's "headquarters and the center of his life until the outbreak of war in 1914."[24] Clara and Rilke did not divorce; neither married again. Rilke regarded her as temperamentally "more a disciple than a wife" and admitted "it was bad luck that she ended up with me; for I could not properly nurture either the artist in her nor that part which yearns for a wifely role."[25]

The two shared occasional holidays, periods of time

together in the same city (though rarely under the same roof), and, predictably, corresponded for many years. Their letters are warm and thoughtful generally, and their correspondence on art is exceptional. Clara's intelligence and knowledge were the catalyst for a remarkable series of letters that Rilke wrote to her on Cézanne. Commenting on those letters, Heinrich Wiegand Petzet suggests they demonstrate an awareness on Rilke's part that Clara "possessed a quality which the poet only very rarely encountered . . . she was his equal."[26] In the final years of his life, however, Rilke made increasingly fewer efforts and in his last weeks in 1926 refused Clara's entreaties to see him.

"When Clara, hearing he was not well, asked to visit him in November [a month before he died], he made it clear that he would refuse to see her even if she came, that indeed he would flee across the nearest border." And when it came to his funeral, in deep snow on 30 December 1926, "Neither Clara nor Ruth was encouraged to attend."[27]

But that's to dash ahead. Before Ruth's birth and the brief period in which Rilke actually lived with Clara, Rilke had conjured up this domestic idyll in a letter: "In the little cottage there would be light, a soft, shaded lamp, and I would stand at my stove and prepare a dinner for you: a lovely vegetable or grain dish [Rilke was a vegetarian] and heavy honey would gleam on a glass plate, and cold butter, pure as ivory, would quietly stand out against a colorful Russian tablecloth. . . . And there would be roses around us, tall ones bowing from their stems and reclining ones gently raising their heads. . . ."

Similarly languid paragraphs follow before Rilke brings quite a different note to the letter: "Premature dreams: the cottage is empty and cold, and my apartment here [Berlin] too is empty and cold."[28]

~

Two famous passages about intimacy and solitude are often used as examples of Rilke's wise insight. In the context of his *actual* relationship with Clara, and his *actual* relationships with the many women who followed Clara, one could see them as quite painfully self-serving.

> In marriage, the point is not to achieve a rapid union by tearing down and toppling all boundaries. Rather, in a good marriage each person appoints the other to be the guardian of his solitude and thus shows him the greatest faith he can bestow.[29]
>
> It is good, too, to love, because love is difficult. For one human being to love another is perhaps the most difficult task that has been entrusted to us: the ultimate task, the final test and proof, the work for which all other work is mere preparation. That is why young people, beginners in everything, are not yet *capable* of love. It is something they must learn. . . . Loving does not first mean merger, surrender or uniting with another person. . . . Love calls to the individual to ripen, to become something in himself, to become world in himself for the sake of another person. Love is a vast, demanding claim on us, something that chooses us and calls us to vast distances.[30]

Rilke's numerous relationships with women were marked by intense initial activity, a fairly extreme and eventually predictable pattern of high idealization, generally on both sides, and then almost total withdrawal on Rilke's part, other than the "vast distances" and distanced version of intimacy that letter-writing allows.

It is exhausting to read about these affairs: so many

women and such little variation on the theme of Rilke's compulsive, stylish, enchanting, needy calls; the women's eager, flattered responses; his rapid retreat into whispers, then silence (other than the scratching, sometimes the sublime scratching, of a pen); their confusion, disappointment and irritation but generally also, and sometimes amazingly, continuing interest and loyalty—as though each is thinking that he must not be judged by the standards of ordinary men. (He is a *poet*.)

Jane Hirshfield is both a poet and a contemporary critic. She usefully points to the "shadow in poetry in the specifically Jungian sense" and the uncomfortable lack of congruence that is sometimes all too evident between the quality of what the writer produces and how the writer lives. Hirshfield asks, "How often some new biography is published and the reader finds herself baffled: how is it that poems so loved and admired could have been written by a person so deeply, cruelly flawed?"[31]

Rilke is not on her list of examples—though he might have been. Instead Hirshfield speaks of "the misogyny and bigotry of [Philip] Larkin's letters . . . [Wallace] Stevens's racism . . . [Ezra] Pound's and [T. S.] Eliot's anti-Semitism [and also] the cruelty and carelessness toward others that mark the stories of many recent poets." Most tellingly, and here Rilke stays in the foreground, Hirshfield says, "These flaws are not necessarily unconscious. Commenting to Kingsley Amis, Larkin once wrote, 'I have always taken comfort from D. H. L[awrence]'s "You have to have something vicious in you to be a creative writer." ' "[32]

Vicious? Possibly. And conscious? Almost certainly.

As one reads the many biographies, and thinks about the life of Rilke, it is hard to escape the sense that here is a man—not just a *poet*—who despite his rare gifts remained limited by his emotional needs, needs he saw in brilliant Technicolor while those of others remained, at best, a grainy black and white.

I attempted at one point to collate from the stack of Rilke biographies that looms in my study a list of women with whom he had some kind of attachment—if we can call almost never seeing someone in person an "attachment." I wanted to put this list of relationships alongside a list of all the places he lived and, alongside that, and perhaps making sense of it all, a list of what he wrote and when. The first two lists, however, defeated me.

Yet the questions did not. Rilke's inner and outer restlessness—that constant changing of people to love and places to live—were extreme. Was he unable to settle, or to engage in a sustained way with other people and their needs because he was consumed by his art? Or was he consumed as well as driven by his art because "everyday life" and, most particularly, intimate or demanding relationships were psychologically hazardous for him? Many opinions are offered in the Rilke literature. And they can only be speculative. Nevertheless it would seem reasonably safe to say that Rilke, for all his unceasing self-focus, was truly convinced that he was serving a cause greater than himself. It also seems safe to suggest that Rilke felt not just more competent but more complete as a poet than he ever did as a son, husband, lover or father.

Writing to Ellen Key in Sweden from Paris in 1903, Rilke inquires rhetorically, "Ought we not perhaps to seek refuge in some peaceful handcraft and no longer have any fear for what ripens into fruit deep within us, behind all stir and agitation?"[33]

Ripening is a word I have come to love, reading Rilke. It is a prominent Rilkean theme appearing both implicitly and explicitly throughout his work, sometimes accompanied by the sense of decay that follows any peaking of perfection. Inwardly ripening is a powerful force and an intensely desirable one: it companions seeking. In the same letter to Ellen Key, Rilke speaks of "ringing in the silence," the futility of forcing such ringing, and the incomparable pleasure when such a moment comes. "Sometimes it is there and I am the master of my depths, which open out radiant and beautiful and shimmering in the darkness," he writes. And then Rilke emphasizes how such moments cannot be "willed" but only welcomed. "It is not that I have said the magic Word, God says it when it is time, and it is meet for me only to be patient and to wait and suffer my depths trustingly which, when they are sealed, are like a heavy stone many days of the year. *But then Life comes and wants to use me somehow,* me and my stone . . ."[34]

> *Unknowing before the heavens of my life*
> *I stand in wonder. O the great stars.*
> *The rising and the going down. How quiet.*
> *As if I didn't exist. Am I part? Have I dismissed*
> *the pure influence? Do high and low tide*
> *alternate in my blood according to this order?*
> *I will cast off all wishes, all other links,*
> *accustom my heart to its remotest space. Better*
> *it live in the terror of its stars than*
> *seemingly protected, soothed by something near.*[35]

The sense of being "used" by Life, God and particularly Art is central in Rilke's self-perception and writing. It is another way of talking about surrender: *Not my will but thine be done.* At the very least it gave a central point to his own part in the universal *rising and the going down,* to the highs and lows of inner and outer. It also made him only marginally available to be "used" by those who loved him, even when his own need of them was intermittently extreme.

~

It was the relationship with the older, revered and supremely self-confident French sculptor Auguste Rodin that affirmed Rilke's desire to place work above all else. This quite obviously suited Rilke psychologically. Work was always to be his safest place. But it also suited him creatively as it allowed him to write poetry even in the apparent absence of direct inspiration (something being wholly "given"). It changed his relationship to the world of "things" outside himself and was internally generative for him in quite specific ways, allowing him to create through the work of looking and inquiring, and being fully present.

The story of the relationship that began in 1902 between the non-German-speaking sixty-two-year-old Rodin and the then less-than-French-fluent twenty-six-year-old Rilke has been retold many times.[36] Rodin had been Clara's teacher for a time. Clara fostered Rilke's awe of him and their shared delight when he was commissioned (despite his self-proclaimed lack of "scholarly" skills) to write a monograph on Rodin.[37]

"With that move, [Rilke] became a European, and a city poet as well, living on the edge of poverty," writes Robert Bly.[38] But it was surely because Rilke was eager to hear the famous lines glorifying work that they "took" in Rilke in the way they did. What's more, they remained potent long after the relationship between the two men had collapsed under the weight of significant differences in personality and style. *"Il faut travailler, rien que travailler"* is what Rodin apparently urged upon Rilke, explaining how new works came into being (although Rodin, like Rilke, was always to find time *pour beaucoup d'amour,* alongside "It is necessary to work, nothing but work").

This explicit affirming of work wasn't a new idea and probably not new to Rilke either. Goethe is credited with saying, "No blessing is equal to the blessing of work. Only lifelong work entitles a man to say, 'I have lived.'"[39] Nevertheless, when Rilke was writing, "work" was rare in the wealthy "leisure" classes and the idea of constant work would generally have been perceived differently then from now. It was considered essentially middle-class to pursue a profession (army, medicine, the law); lower-middle-class to be "in trade," however rich this made you; and "working class" to work for—and need—wages.

Today we see a remarkably similar set of stratifications in the world of writing, with those forms of writing assumed to depend intrinsically on inspiration at the top of the pile and those that depend on research—obvious "work"—as well as inspiration somewhere further down, or anyway less idealized. This is reversed in the world of academic writing, where "literary" writing that is original rather than being itself the "object" of research has little currency in the scramble to establish grants, tenured positions, etc. In other words, a career may be built writing *about* a poet, but rarely *as* a poet.

With poetry, the confusion between inspiration, talent and hard work is certainly intensified. The inspiration, as well as gifts of insight and language, that poetry (and poets) needs is mystifying to non-poets and to many poets.

Is it possible to take the idea of work seriously, yet produce something rarely bigger than a leaf that has virtually no financial value? Can the many hours be justified by the few words, however apt or gorgeous? On the other hand, is a poem less "poetic" because one is getting on with the disciplines of writing, observing, *dwelling* in work, perfecting it and also readying oneself for it, rather than waiting for inspiration to arise, or fall?

This is a spurious dichotomy in any case. All original work requires inspiration and imagination *and* demands unquenchable tenacity and patience. Having written novels, nonfiction books, talks, articles, reviews, columns—virtually everything but poetry—I know that each medium demands something different but, in my experience, none depends entirely on inspiration or can do without craft. Craft (patient whittling, shaping, reshaping, discarding, assessing, criticizing, perfecting) brings unconscious instincts as well as imagination to fruition, while inspiration lifts and guides craft. Craft is where one has more conscious control and where experience may count for something, but if the work is merely "conscious" and "experienced" it remains flat, utilitarian, uninspiring as well as uninspired.

Rilke knew all this and far more. Edward Snow describes it: "As his enthusiasm for the sculptor's work increased, so did his dissatisfaction with his own . . . the energy and dedication with which [Rodin] immersed himself in the actual process of *making* seemed to Rilke a rebuke to his own lyric dexterity and slavish dependence on inspiration. . . . [He] set about acquiring an entirely new set of working habits—forcing himself to write every day during regularly scheduled hours, wandering about Paris practicing the art of observation. . . ."[40]

~

The massive commitment to work (and the degree of surrender to inspiration) that Rilke achieved is evidenced by his extraordinary output—its quality as well as volume.

The single-volume German edition that I have of his collected poetry has been published using very small type on the thinnest of paper yet it is still formidable at almost 900 pages long. Then there are the eleven thousand extant letters, many as long and thoughtful as an essay—and who knows how many more Rilke letters sit in drawers, cupboards, or family collections, or were carelessly discarded years ago? Then there are his journals, the novel (which cost him a great deal of anguish), plays, stories and multiple translations of other poets' work . . . And yet, for all that, some readers will clearly feel an ambivalence that disturbs them as they witness personal relationships and responsibilities—the foundations of ordinary life for most people—being sacrificed quite so ruthlessly to art or the idealization of art, even art such as Rilke's.

This ambivalence can and does easily tip into moral judgments or plain distaste. J. D. McClatchy, for example, calls Rilke a "selfish poseur" and wonders if he "isn't being sold as the Kahlil Gibran of the intellectual set."[41]

But Rilke never was "most people." English critic John Bayley captures this: "The irreverent modern mind is sometimes exasperated by what seems Rilke's self-dedication, the seriousness with which he took himself."[42] This "exasperation" extends even to some readers who are poets.

W. H. Auden, for example, born thirty years later than Rilke but dying almost fifty years later in 1973, considered his own work to be a religious "calling." While he followed that calling ardently, Auden was not a Rodin or a Rilke. In *Auden and Christianity*, Arthur Kirsch notes, "Auden steadily insisted on the limits of poetry." Kirsch quotes Auden as saying that the Greeks "confused art with religion" because they were "ignorant of the difference between seriousness and frivolity," and writes that Auden believed, or anyway stated, that "'along with most human activities art is, in the profoundest sense, frivolous. For one thing, and one thing only, is serious: loving one's neighbor as one's self.'"[43]

That statement is more than a little self-serving. Auden was notoriously selective about which of his "neighbors" deserved his loving attentions. Elsewhere he calls Rilke (who must really have gotten under his skin) "The Santa Claus of Solitude." But the Auden–Rilke story doesn't end there. After walking around for days thinking, "That can't be all," and turning over in my mind my earlier statement that it is poets who appreciate Rilke *most*, I discovered these lines from Auden:

> *To-night in China let me think of one*
> *who for ten years of drought and silence waited,*
> *until in Muzot all his being spoke,*
> *and everything was given once for all.*
>
> *Awed, grateful, tired, content to die, completed,*
> *he went out in the winter night to stroke*
> *that tower as one pets an animal.*[44]

Auden's poem is biographically somewhat off the mark. Rilke wrote often about death and was in many ways obsessed with the intimate relationship of life to death, but at barely fifty-one he was not in the least content to die.[45] The poem itself edges dangerously toward banality. (Not a good night for Auden.) What is striking, though, is that twelve years after Rilke's death, in China but with his mind leaning toward a Europe preparing again for war, Auden was thinking of Rilke: "awed," "completed."

~

Rilke's not-so-private life is certainly not above moral discussion. On the contrary, some critics have spun years of work out of exactly that. Yet anything beyond a glance in Rilke's direction shows that the paradoxes around him are extreme. They may even partly account for some of our contemporary interest in him: such a "spiritual" writer (who is also provocatively, lyrically sensual—brilliantly exemplifying that the spiritual can indeed be rediscovered in the sensual); such a "wise" writer (who like so many found wisdom easier on the page than off it); such a "sensitive" writer (who nonetheless found it all too easy to ignore the sensitivities and needs of other people).

Another poet, this time Galway Kinnell introducing his *The Essential Rilke*, notes: "A number of readers and critics . . . reverse the conventional wisdom—that an artist's human deficiencies, as well as any attendant human wreckage the artist might leave behind, are simply the price that must be paid for great art—and find that certain often-dismissed human flaws in fact damage the art. These more skeptical readers see Rilke less as an authority on how to live than as a sufferer telling in brilliant confusion his own strange and gripping interpretation of what it is to be human."

Kinnell goes on to offer an alternative view: that Rilke was "not naïve about his failure as a lover," implicitly demonstrating that simplistic thinking (limited person/ great poet) *itself* becomes a choice for any reader.[46]

That was certainly my experience. Immersed in the biographies, I could sometimes feel impatient, distanced and exhausted. Without exerting myself, I could feel critical— and *entitled* to my criticism—of his behavior toward women, his snobbishness and selfishness, his appalling lapse of taste and sense in writing what amounted to "odes to war" (which he later regretted) when war broke out in 1914, a hypochondriacal preciousness and addiction to spas that hasn't weathered well, and especially his cavalier behavior toward Clara and Ruth, about whom I grew to feel absurdly protective.

What would save me and renew my eagerness for this work was not reading more about Rilke, but closer and more open-minded reading of his work. In his work he was deeply connected, unquestionably committed and utterly faithful. And, reading again, I was never less than grateful.

These dichotomies seem similar to those explicitly dreaded by Auden, who, according to English playwright and critic Alan Bennett, ". . . was wise to want no biography written." In fact, Bennett continues, "the more one reads about [Auden], the harder it is to see around him to the poetry beyond, and he grows increasingly hard to like. . . ."[47]

I believe it is possible to think about Rilke's internal dilemmas as well as the external dramas they caused without finding him "increasingly hard to like." They may even add texture to each reader's individual experiencing of his poetry, rather than detracting from it, because they certainly show Rilke as a more complex and incomplete, even vulnerable figure, mirroring in that way our own sense of fragile incompleteness and *unfolding*. It also seems fair to suggest that while some people do think about Rilke and read and quote him as a "guide to life," or as a sage, on the whole it is not more of the ordinariness of "ordinary life" that Rilke's readers are likely to be seeking.

"As recent headlines suggest, 'ordinary life' seems more than ever before to be deeply unpoetic, obsessed with speed, size and one-click efficiency: it's a life in which relatedness to the world is being reduced to 'interactive marketing,'" writes contemporary critic Daniel Mendelsohn. "What the Internet conglomerates can't deliver, though, is meaningful self-knowledge—how to be at home in 'our interpreted world,' as Rilke puts it in the First *Elegy*."[48]

I am moved that in mourning the superficiality of many aspects of contemporary life, it is Rilke's First Elegy that Mendelsohn should cite. Like Mendelsohn, I believe that a life starved of symbol, mystery, depth and at least intimations of wholeness is, indeed, "deeply unpoetic," ignorant of shadows and of bliss. *Life comes and wants to use me somehow*, wrote Rilke. And while "life" is, in our time, indeed frequently and sometimes relentlessly "interpreted" or raked over, this is often done with devastating shallowness. Mendelsohn is *right*: a different kind of existence and attitude toward existence is evoked in Rilke's First Elegy. The first of its extraordinary verses flows and follows.

> *Who if I cried out would hear me amid the hierarchy*
> *of angels? And even if one of them were to take*
> *me suddenly to heart, I'd waste away because of*
> *that stronger presence. Because beauty is nothing*
> *but the beginning of terror which we can just endure,*
> *and we are amazed by it precisely in its calm spurning,*
> *and for the way it threatens to destroy us. Each and every angel*
> *is fearsome.*

Impossible to read quickly, fearsome to analyze, this poem nevertheless offers something immediate and irresistible. In the absoluteness of its being—if one can say a poem has "being"—it provides a devastating comment on the "deeply unpoetic life" where most of us live.

And so I gather myself together and swallow the alluring call
held in this dark whimpering. Oh, who is it we are finally able
to need? Not angels, not other people,
and the clever animals immediately notice
that we aren't at home, aren't trustworthy
in the world we have managed. That leaves us, perhaps,
some tree on the slope we've seen daily,
over and over; yesterday's street still remains for us,
and the warped loyalty of a familiar habit
that gave us pleasure and thus remained and didn't leave.
Oh, and the night, the night, when the wind filled with universe
wears away our face: for whom won't the night linger, the desired
and yet gently disappointing night which stands before each
heart as a heavy burden? Is the night any easier for lovers?
Oh, these hide themselves, together, from their fate.
Don't you know this yet? Cast the void from your arms
into the spaces we breathe, so that the birds might
feel this billowing air intimately in their flight.[49]

In the same self-confessing letter of 1921 where he is explaining himself to his daughter's future husband, Carl Sieber, Rilke had suggested that some people might be able to manage "*inner* realizations" and "*external* ones," but that he could not. He continues: "I may be reproached that my strength and my concept did not suffice to accomplish *both*; I have nothing to oppose to such censure save the silent indication of those domains into which I have thrown all my abilities, waiting to see whether in the end I am indicted or acquitted."[50]

It is again helpful when John Bayley places Rilke's view of his choices in context, explaining that his "self-dedication" was "typical of the artistic attitudes of the time," just as some of his personal decisions, including his idealizations of peasant life, his lifelong vegetarianism and his occasional séances, were reflective of attitudes then influencing many intellectuals. Bayley continues, suggesting that such artistic attitudes could be highly mannered, "But in Rilke it is not so, just as it is not so in [his contemporaries] Proust or Joyce, or in the art of Cézanne. Each of these geniuses had solved in his own way the old romantic dilemma: their concentration brought into coincidence the world and the self, the outside world and the personal vision as the unified work of art."[51]

~

Can we expect greatness of "great" writers? Are we *entitled* to that? And on what basis do we rest our entitlements? Are our ideals crushed or is it our feelings that are disappointed when our most loved writers' "clay feet" go up to their knees? Does their writing become less "great" in our perception and reception of it when it is not matched by ideal conduct? Or are these questions relevant only with writers who lay explicit claim to greatness through wisdom, as Rilke emphatically did not?

The English moral philosopher and novelist Iris Murdoch—who was married to John Bayley, whom I have just quoted—takes this complex discussion forward. She refers to Kant's suggestion that "the good artist is a sort of image of the good man, the great artist is a sort of image of the saint. He is only a sort of image, since in his whole person he may be a dreadful egoist."

An acclaimed writer herself (but shy and publicity-averse), Murdoch continues, "Artists have their own specialized temptations to egoism and illusions of omnipotence. Art is power. We are specialists in morality . . . and it is difficult (impossible) for the whole man to be virtuous. But inside his work, and 'in so far as he is an artist,' to use the device employed at the beginning of [Plato's] *The Republic*, he can be humble and truthful and brave and inspired by a love of perfection."[52]

Murdoch then turns to consider Rilke specifically, and his taking up of Rodin's *Il faut travailler, rien que travailler* dictum. She writes, ". . . the good man, if we can find him, is probably not an artist. . . . The egoism of the good artist or craftsman is 'burned up' in the product. . . . At the highest level this is practical mysticism, where the certainty and the absolute appear incarnate and immediate in the needs of others."[53]

I find Murdoch's views quietly convincing. My sense is that they can help us toward a less moralistic way of thinking about Rilke and perhaps also a less static, idealized way. This is a writer who deserves to be more than an "icon," fixed forever in the eye of the beholder.

> *I read it out, out of your word,*
> *from the history of gestures with which*
> *you surrounded what is becoming with your hands,*
> *shaping it all with warmth and wisdom.*
> *You said* life *loudly and* death *quietly,*
> *and repeated again and again:* being.
> *And yet murder preceded the first death,*
> *and a rip tore your ripened circle,*
> *and a cry burst forth*
> *and ripped out the voices*
> *which had first gathered you,*
> *in order to say to you*
> *in order to carry you*
> *on bridges over every abyss.*

And all that they stammered since
are fragments
of your old name.[54]

There is something else stirring here, too, which makes me think that our conclusions about Rilke should not be hasty—and that we do our own reading a disservice if we slip into that. Later in the same discussion, Murdoch quotes French poet Paul Valéry (a poet much admired by Rilke, who translated his work): "At its highest point, love is a determination to create that which it has taken for its object."[55]

I have read Valéry's sentence many times. Each time it opens up an immense sense within me of how formative—and expressive—the choices are that we make in our thinking and creative work. This strikes me as perhaps the most crucial "biographical" analysis I need to make.

Let me share a personal example before returning to Rilke. I wrote one of my own books, *Forgiveness and Other Acts of Love*, at a time when I desperately needed to focus on the highest qualities that could sustain me when life itself felt both fragile and dangerous. I discovered through writing that book, and in countless moments since, that what I claimed there was, in fact, true: what we pay attention to will grow stronger in our lives. What our "subject matter" is, what our obsessions are, shape us and may eventually describe us. To a remarkable degree, we reflect the objects of our attention and, conversely, the objects of our attention reflect the direction in which we are choosing to gaze.

This point is abundantly illustrated in Rilke's life. Examples are everywhere in this book alone, but the one that follows seems to me to be exemplary. Some scene-setting first. The Valais is the area of Switzerland where Rilke spent his final years. Always highly attuned to landscape, he described this as ". . . not only among the loveliest of landscapes I have ever seen, but also, to an amazing extent [offering] manifold reflections of our inner world."[56]

It was from there that Rilke wrote the following poem to the Russian poet Marina Tsvetayeva, with whom he exchanged passionate letters for part of his final year. The poem includes these transporting lines:

Oh the losses into the All, Marina, the stars that are falling!
We can't make it larger, wherever we fling ourselves, to whatever
star we may go! In the Whole, all things are already numbered.
So when anyone falls, the perfect sum is not lessened.
Whoever lets go in his fall, dives into the source and is healed . . .
. . . Waves, Marina, we are ocean! Depths, Marina, we are sky.
Earth, Marina, we are earth, a thousand times April . . .

. . . Praising, my dearest—let us be lavish with praise.
Nothing really belongs to us . . .
. . . As angels draw marks as a signal on the doors of those to be
*   saved,*
we, though we seem to be tender, stop and touch this or that.
Ah, how remote already, how inattentive, Marina,
even in our innermost pretense. Signalers: nothing more . . .[57]

What kind of man is it who could write such a poem while, in his own words, ". . . sitting on a warm (though not yet warmed for good, unfortunately) wall and riveting the lizards in their tracks by intoning it?"[58] A man exultant with praise of the All is, in my experience, a rare being. This doesn't make him, or our assessments, necessarily simple or coherent. Yet is it not true that whoever we are, our writing, reading, praying can remain more subtle, intuitive, imaginative, sensual and refined than "we" are, or than our everyday self is? And is it also not true that as we write or read, we are not only "working" on our writing or reading but, and crucially, permitting it to work on us?

~

M. D. Herter Norton, an early translator of Rilke, suggests, "If a man is a deep writer, all his works are confessions."[59]

To a great extent, subject matter *describes* the inner world of the writer, both what is conscious and less conscious and, in his work, there is no doubting that Rilke was "humble and truthful and brave and inspired by a love of perfection," in the Platonic way that Murdoch quotes. In his emotional and moral conduct, the picture is more complicated, yet Valéry's remark has singular value.

Thinking about Rilke now, you can "read" the biographical details and I will continue to provide them. You might prefer one interpretation to another, perhaps because it correlates more closely to your own worldview or to the image of Rilke you already have. You can read his letters. You can read his poems. What you can also do is "read" his images and subject choices and make something of them. In fact, you can read the recurring words, phrases, ideas, emotions and leitmotifs—what he evokes as well as speaks to—as an inescapable portrait of his inner reality. And, in addition, in thinking about Rilke and his subject choice in this way you can also understand something about your own self that goes considerably beyond your critical or "readerly" interest.

Does this seem all too obvious, that we will indeed choose how to think—and what, over the course of a fleeting life, we will most faithfully think about? It seems undeniable, though, that writers, readers and critics in general tend *not* to look routinely at their intellectual choices as a potent source of self-understanding. Certainly many of us routinely consider how our choices are "read" by other people. We are often highly sensitive to those issues with all their implications of admirability and status. Yet how those choices might even more truthfully illuminate the processes and drives of our own inner world is often, I suspect, far less obvious to us.

Understanding *ourselves* better as readers, we have a chance to appreciate Rilke with fewer obstructions. It is worth listening closely to another poem from Auden, written in 1940 in memory not of Rilke but of that other complicated man and poet W. B. Yeats, who died in 1939.

> . . . *You were silly like us; your gift survived it all:*
> *The parish of rich women, physical decay,*
> *Yourself. Mad Ireland hurt you into poetry.*
> *Now Ireland has her madness and her weather still,*
> *For poetry makes nothing happen: it survives*
> *In the valley of its making where executives*
> *Would never want to tamper, flows on south*
> *From ranches of isolation and the busy griefs,*
> *Raw towns that we believe and die in; it survives,*
> *A way of happening, a mouth . . .*[60]

Those spare, tremendous lines *poetry makes nothing happen: it survives/In the valley of its making* are worth a book themselves. Poetry makes nothing happen; poetry greets and shapes everything. Rilke describes it: "We must allow every impression and every germ of emotion to mature by itself, in the dark, indescribable, unconscious realm that cannot be attained by our reason, and we must wait in deep humility and patience for the [birth] of a new enlightenment: that is the only way of life for a poet, for comprehending as well as for creating. . . . To be a poet means . . . to ripen slowly like a tree that does not urge on its sap. . . . Patience is everything."[61]

There is uncertainty within Rilke, and there are multiple inconsistencies about him. What also remains compelling is that, to the end, what was sacred was real for Rilke and that the mystery was permitted to remain mysterious.

To return to the key Valéry quote I gave above: in his writing, Rilke does *not* consistently demonstrate that "love [was] a determination to create that which it [had] taken for its object." His life was too ambiguous for that. Yet if we look detachedly at his subject matter, then we see that the influence of a love that goes beyond the personal is almost always close at hand if not actually guiding his hand. That insight remains, for me, utterly convincing.

THE MAKING OF A POET

In a lavishly insightful and often tender series of letters that was eventually collected and published as *Letters to a Young Poet*, Rilke is ostensibly directing his thoughts toward a younger man, Franz Xaver Kappus, the eponymous "young poet." Kappus had been at the same military school Rilke attended, though a few years later, and he began writing to Rilke in 1903 about his own writing efforts. Describing that beginning, Kappus recalls, "I unreservedly laid bare my heart as never before and never since to any second human being.

"Many weeks passed before a reply came. The blue-sealed letter bore the postmark of Paris, weighed heavily in the hand, and showed on the envelope the same beautiful, clear, sure characters in which the text was set down from the first line to the last. With it began my regular correspondence with Rainer Maria Rilke. . . ."[1]

The letters that Rilke wrote back from 1903–8 make wonderful and often surprising reading for anyone remotely interested in the "fabric-making" that is writing. They are sensual, anti-moralistic and frank. They were also encouraging, although for Kappus encouragement was not enough. "If Rilke followed Kappus's career after the correspondence died, it could only have disappointed him: the fledgling poet became a war correspondent and eventually a writer of inconsequential novels."[2]

Kappus's "inconsequential" writing life, though, is not the point here. It is Rilke who holds our attention. To a great extent, and quite typically of his letter writing to people he did not know personally, Rilke was largely presenting himself to himself. Kappus held up a timely mirror but the face reflected back was Rilke's own. This does not mean that Kappus played no part. His needs and questions, his openness, and their points of connection *mattered*; readers have every reason to be grateful to him. But the letters can also be read as a kind of inner memoir from a young man—Rilke—whose own childhood was chronologically close and psychologically and spiritually closer still.

Reflecting on his correspondence with Kappus, and perhaps on what that specific exchange of letters allowed, Rilke said this to Clara: "In childhood we have used up too much strength, too much grown-people's strength—that may be true for a whole generation. Or true over and over again for individuals. What shall one say about it? That life has unending possibilities of renewal. Yes, but this too; that the using of strength in a certain sense is always increase of strength also . . . all strength that we give away comes over us again, experienced and altered. Thus it is in prayer. And what is there, truly done, that is not prayer?"[3]

~

Half a lifetime later, in 1924, unwell but certainly unaware he had just two years left to live, Rilke would write to his only child, Ruth, describing a brief moment in his childhood when it had seemed that the restricted, disappointing life of his childhood in Prague could be replaced by something resembling an "increase in strength," something far more exciting, romantic and appropriate to the Rilke family's sense of itself than the cramped, rented flat in Prague.

"What exciting weeks we went through when, very late, much too late, I must have been about eight, he [Josef Rilke, who would then have been forty-five] tried to exchange his position as [private railway] official for that of manager of an estate . . . The anticipation and hope in our home was great. Not only were the financial advantages and health considerations to be taken into account in the change, but the large baroque castle of the Sporksch, in Kuka, was empty, and had been assigned to the new manager. Insofar as I understood anything of the obscure affair, I let myself go in my passion for carriage-drives and sledging, high rooms and long white corridors. . . ."[4]

There is something doubly poignant here. First, it is sobering that Rilke is telling this story to a twenty-three-year-old daughter with whom he virtually never lived, whose financial needs he had only intermittently been concerned with and whose emotional needs must have been an almost complete blank to him, so consistently did he neglect them. Homeless himself, and unwilling or unable ever to establish a home, Rilke had not provided a home for Ruth at any time, never mind a castle. At the same time, this glimpse of all that the "castle" promised (especially an escape from the "cramped, rented flat" in

Prague, the disappointing marriage of his parents and the failure that hung over them all) illuminates some of the futile desiring that dominated René Rilke's earliest experiences of family life. Perhaps it also makes some sense of the adult Rilke's apparent need for fine hotels, long "cures" in the most fashionable spas, plush drawing rooms and extended stays in grand houses and castles during much of his later writing life.

Is this pursuit of physical comfort at odds with his virtually inviolable sense of himself as an artist?[5] Is it at odds with his poetic drive?

In a letter Rilke wrote to Ellen Key from Italy in 1903 he demonstrates what seem to be fairly typical contradictions between insight and obtuseness. The letter starts with a dramatic, exaggerated account of his noble origins on his father's side, already a sad flagging of grandiosity. He then says, "Of my mother's family I know nothing."

This cannot be true. His wealthy maternal grandparents and other members of his mother's family were known to him and, when needed, were kind to him. Were there Jewish ancestors in his mother's family?[6] For most contemporary readers it would be a serious black mark to think that this might concern him, but since he was a product of his time and place, it is possible, although here, too, there should not be a rush to easy conclusions, as he certainly had close friends and lovers who were Jewish. Leppmann, in fact, one of his biographers, claims that Rilke "had affairs with numerous Jewish women."[7]

So was it the absence of even a trace of nobility in his wealthy maternal lineage that obliterated all else? Or was it that his mother's life did not extend for him in any meaningful way back into the years before he was born?

"My parents' marriage was already faded when I was born," he told Ellen Key. Then he describes his parents' inability to see him, their real child, in a way that is painful to read: "She [Phia Rilke] was a very nervous, slender, dark woman, who wanted something indefinite of life. . . . Actually these two people ought to have understood each other better, for *they both attach an infinite amount of value to externals;* our little household, which was in reality middle-class, was supposed to deceive people and certain lies passed as a matter of course. I don't know how it was with me."

The poet of the inner world himself came to attach an "infinite amount of value to externals," or was unable to shed this family habit. But perhaps those paradoxes were too raw to be fully conscious. Within the context of the contradictions I am tentatively exploring here, Rilke's last sentence seems especially strange: *I don't know how it was with me.* Strange because Rilke then goes on to state clearly how it was with him: "I had to wear very beautiful clothes and went about until school years like a little girl; I believe my mother played with me as with a big doll." Not a great fate for a boy. And then, back to Phia: "She wanted to pass for young, sickly and unhappy. And unhappy she probably was too. I believe we all were."[8]

Rilke's parents separated when he was nine. His mother's life did not take a greater turn toward reality. "Determined to start a new and more fulfilling life," writes Eric Torgersen, "[Rilke's] mother took to dressing all in black, like widowed ladies of the Hapsburg nobility."[9]

～

As one spends time in Rilke's company, it becomes easy to see that this master of the poetic image was inwardly haunted by a number of significant internal images that shaped his developing consciousness. They included but were not confined to the "little girl," the daughter his mother wanted but who he could only briefly be; the "little soldier" and the "professional soldier," this time failing father as well as mother (and disappointing himself); the "not-Czech," but not *quite* German either, growing up in Prague; the ambitious social aspirant; the young intellectual segueing into young poet; the "Russian" who wasn't Russian; husband/father—soon gone; the lover—more fulfilled and fulfilling in absence than presence; and, not least, "the poet."

Images of powerlessness and victimhood are also part of Rilke's makeup. I use the term *victimhood* reluctantly. Nevertheless, Rilke did see himself as a victim of his own childhood and this reverberated throughout his life. In his mid-forties, Rilke wrote to Major General von Sedlakowitz, a former teacher at his Military Academy at St. Pölten in Lower Austria. The powerlessness he describes is stark: "When in my more reflective years . . . Dostoevski's *Memoirs of a Death-House* [*Memoirs from the House of the Dead*] first came into my hands, it seemed to me that since my tenth year [his year of enrollment at St. Pölten] I had been admitted into all the terrors and despairs of the convict prison! . . . But Dostoevski, when he endured the unendurable, was a young man, a grown man; to the mind of a child the prison walls of St. Pölten could, if he used the measure of his helplessly abandoned heart, take on pretty much the same dimensions."[10]

The mind of the child, René, was never lost to the mind of the man, Rainer Maria. Rilke's experience at the lower and upper military academies where he boarded for five years from shortly before his tenth birthday, as well as the loss of the home and his parents' marriage, which at least somewhat precipitated his enrollment two years later at St. Pölten ("What will we do with the boy?"), was psychologically and socially devastating. He would allude to it throughout his life.

More significant still is the ignorance the decision shows on the part of Rilke's parents as to the inner makeup of their son. In 1922, Rilke wrote that "only by the most antagonistic, rebellious deviation [at the age of ten] was I able to take possession of my blood and spirit."[11] And again, in a 1924 letter, he writes of a "more than life-sized experience of loneliness" among five hundred boys. Yet in the same letter, and remarkably forgivingly, he says that when he eventually came home from the senior academy his father, the disappointed soldier himself, "needed the support of all his great love for me in order to concede that the officer's profession might not be the most fitting for me."[12] But that generosity did not extend to his mother and even in relation to his father seems to have been somewhat qualified.

This story, too, has roots in the earliest days of Rilke's life. From the beginning he seems to have been the object of his parents' strong, unrealistic projections. While this in itself is not so unusual, what made the situation more harmful was that he was the only surviving child (the earlier dead daughter could only worsen the situation by remaining "perfect" as well as dead), and was also exceptionally sensitive. His "helplessly abandoned heart" was abandoned early: by the mother who wanted to experience his dead infant sister through him, the nurses who in his first year of life "came and went like the hours of the day,"[13] and by the father who wanted to see in front of him not an introvert and emerging poet but a "brave little soldier."

The effects of some of this were extreme. Rilke remained so disturbed by his mother's presence that he avoided seeing her through most of his adult life, although she continued to wash his gloves and he continued to write her reasonably affectionate and thoughtful letters.[14] The following example was written in 1920 when Rilke was forty-five, Phia sixty-nine.

> Once more at our blessed hour [6 A.M., the time when Josef Rilke would ring the bells on Christmas morning], most loving remembrance of Christmas days of longest ago, and the wish that now, after such bad times, there may be granted you celebrations each year more quiet, more peaceful, and finally too in a little home of your very own again!
>
> . . . What I wish for you, dear Mama, is that on this evening of consecration, the remembrance of all distress, even the consciousness of the immediate worry and insecurity of existence may be quite checked . . .
>
> . . . But this is the night of radiant depth unfolded—: for you, dear Mama, may it be hallowed and blessed. Amen—René.[15]

Lou the analyst, never slow to analyze Rilke, believed that part of the reason for his visceral distaste for his mother was that the hysteria he feared and despised in Phia was something he also feared and despised within himself.[16] This may be true. Rilke's obsessive need to control his physical and emotional environments was mythologized even in Rilke's relatively early writing life as something essential to his noble calling. It is not myth only that he made an elevated virtue of solitude. Neurotic avoidances became "sacrifices" willingly made in the service of poetry and himself as poet. Knowing the levels of toughness and tenacity that a commitment to writing actually does need, I can see some psychological strength in that. Yet at least as powerful as the fear that he was more bound to his mother through their mutual weaknesses than he would ever have wished was the equally unwelcome reminder that as a person with his own vulnerable inner reality, as a child and man, he remained unseen.

Writing to yet another intelligent, sympathetic friend, Princess Marie von Thurn und Taxis-Hohenlohe, a crucial patron as well as friend, and owner of Duino Castle, Rilke suggests that no one has ever "shaken" him "utterly" [as a lover] perhaps because he was unable to love his "pleasure-loving, miserable" mother. At nineteen Rilke had told his then-fiancée, Valerie von David-Rhônfeld ("Vally"), that his mother had loved him only when she could "parade" him.[17] This assertion raises more questions than it settles, not only because he is trespassing into Lou's territory, analyzing his insufficiencies in the light of his childhood, but also because he is skating past the sustained love he felt for Lou, at the very least. Perhaps another quote from the same letter is more self-knowing: "All love is exertion for me, something achieved, *surmenage*, only in relation to God have I any ease, for to love God means to enter, to walk, to stand, to rest, and to be everywhere in the love of God."[18]

That letter was written in 1913. The poem that follows was written in 1921, yet strikes a similar note. Here we have the contrasting rhythms of darkness and light, of acknowledgment and denial, powerfully juxtaposed. But here also the "praising poet" reveals something of the wound, if not the thorn.

> *O tell, poet, what do you do?*
>   I praise.
> *But what about the lethal and monstrous?*
> *How do you survive and take that in?*
>   I praise.
> *But what of the nameless and anonymous,*

how do you continue to call out to them, poet?
    I praise.
Where does your right to be real come from
in such dress and in every mask?
    I praise.
And that the stillness and impetuousness
know you like star and storm?
    Because I praise.[19]

I find it impossible to think about Rilke's early years without also considering the childhood of Ruth, the daughter born in December 1901 a week and a day after her father's twenty-sixth birthday. Rilke's imaginative power, and his equally powerful capacity to disengage from the realities of everyday life, are again nakedly demonstrated in a letter written in 1907 when Ruth was six and, however intelligent, far too young to comprehend what her scarcely known father was telling or intending.

Rilke is remembering riding lessons that he had when he was sixteen or seventeen and how, after half a dozen lessons, he "still could not do anything!" Despite that, perhaps even in reaction to it, Rilke confides that he "could not keep from fantasizing. I pretended that it was the close of a day of battle. I was wearing a dusty, dark-colored uniform with a high collar and a single decoration, a star . . . Possibly there was even a wound, in my shoulder, but I had not deigned to give it a glance."

Again, the fantasy continues at some length, and then: "Some dog or other raced into the hall, my horse shied, and as you can imagine what followed no longer corresponded to my fantasies . . ."

Finally, and now with real humor, Rilke says,

presumably still addressing himself more than Ruth: "The dear Lord surely must have been in doubt whether to take away my imagination or the riding lessons . . . he [God] thought it over and left me with my imagination, just to see if I might not learn to make better use of it as I grew older. If one day I could convince him of that—do you suppose he would give me back the riding lessons?"[20]

In considering Rilke's childhood years (and Ruth's), and the effect those crucial years had on his personality and *Weltanschauung* as well as his work, what emerges is a striking absence of reliable emotional ties, a reluctance or inability to form such ties in adult life, a vast sense of inner dispossession, and a breathtaking talent for turning each and all of these "losses" into poetry that lays bare his experiences even while his "reach" as poet is to solidify and transform them.

Critic Brian Phillips reinforces this: "Rilke believed that his poetry resulted from the interior transformation of the perceived world within the organ of his soul, and he lived his life as an attempt to prepare himself to accomplish the transformation."[21] As they move to the page, it is those transformations *within the organ of his soul* that the reader meets. Two examples follow.

> *They still say* mine *and claim possession, though*
> *each thing, as they approach, withdraws and closes;*
> *a silly charlatan perhaps thus poses*
> *as owner of the lightning and the sun.*
> *And so they say: my life, my wife, my child,*
> *my dog, well knowing all that they have styled*
> *their own: life, wife, child, dog remain*
> *shapes alien and unknown,*
> *that blindly groping they must stumble on.*[22]

Isn't it like breathing, this constant interchange
between attachment and relinquishing,
when something barely was, and, vanishing,
is recollected in a nearby face?

World and face: how they displace each other,
and seldom look alike—neither winning . . .
I found the distant slopes fulfilling
yesterday. Today I need not bother

with looking up, or speaking.[23]

What each reader finds on the page is not less affecting when, like so many of Rilke's own catalytic experiences, it reflects that *world and face* "displacing" each other as self and concepts "melt" into solitary, ineffable processes of becoming. Being and "not being" do not merge: that already implies too much separation. As in so many of Rilke's most affecting poems, it is duality itself that is left behind and nonduality that is hailed. What's more, *this constant interchange/between attachment and relinquishing* is promised to be no more difficult than *breathing.* This is a holy moment: *Rest in it*, Rilke invites.

Writing to Rilke from her home in Göttingen, in his last months in Paris in that momentous year, 1914, Lou cherishes the poetic power that arises within him, that is "delivered" by him to the page, to be "received" there by the reader.

"*You* are in pain," writes Lou. "*I*, through your pain, feel bliss.

"Forgive me for that."[24]

WHAT ARE POETS FOR?

In whatever way twenty-first-century readers are discovering or rereading Rainer Maria Rilke—a few uplifting lines at a wedding, consoling words at a funeral, a discovery of a fresh translation of *The Book of Hours* or *Elegies*, or writer's comfort from *Letters to a Young Poet*—they do so at a brief moment in history that it is tempting to call, among many other valid possibilities, the "age of psychologizing." Viewing people and events through the prism of a relatively or explicitly psychologically based "cause and effect" paradigm seems unexceptional and even predictable to many contemporary readers.

Discussions about books and writing, personality and texts that have become commonplace in a variety of settings would suggest that, with varying degrees of consciousness and self-consciousness, some version of psychological analysis is quite routinely used by the contemporary reader. Whether she is curled up reading her book in Toorak,

Toronto or Toulouse, that reader is more likely to be a woman than a man—and is more likely to care about the psychological context of what she is reading than its historical or political frameworks. I am not suggesting that this is how people *ought* to read. But if I am even somewhat correct then this means that the risks of a more "surrendered" way of reading remain especially potent when thinking about reading Rilke and, crucially, what we may be reading *into* Rilke. How are our own images, projections, assumptions, yearnings and desires determining what we find on the page?

Rilke is a poet who sharpens our perceptions of the *surfaces* of things while writing at singular depth about the "inner*ness*" of things and people. Precisely because his subject matter is, broadly, inwardness, reading his work allows his readers to participate in a range of discoveries (some made in the dark). They include Rilke's ideas; our responses to his ideas; our ideas about poetry (what is it *for?*); our ideas about writing and "knowledge" more broadly. And yet to gain most from reading Rilke, we need to read with as few presumptions as possible—and that is a tough ask! We *like* our presumptions; we may even believe them or believe in them. Nonetheless, we persist.

A wry teaching from the Jewish tradition reminds us that we do not see the world as it is; rather, we see the world as we are. The multiple acts of reading—of reading text, author, our own self—can be similar. How we read reflects how we are—and shapes it. And this conscious and unconscious process—bringing the past to the present moment in quite specific ways—is likely to be heightened when reading Rilke because of both the depth of his work and its subject matter, touching as it does, and meeting as writing rarely does, some of our deepest hungers. But if the hungers are great that we bring to reading Rilke, it is also legitimate to suggest that the projections through which we read Rilke may be equally fierce.

Michael André Bernstein captures the dangers that come with psychological theorizing, and especially from squeezing a complex human being and his work into a paradigm that may be as limiting as it is revealing. He writes, "Rilke's inwardness intrigues and moves readers so powerfully . . . largely because it speaks from a view of the self that confronts the most fundamental questions of life, desire and mortality without drawing on any of the levelling tropes or dubious scientisms of traditional psychology. This is also why biographies of Rilke are usually so unsatisfying: they can tell us nothing about inwardness because it is fundamentally neither a narrative nor a psychological category at all."[1]

The biographies of Rilke *are* fundamentally unsatisfying, as carefully and elegantly written as most are. (Ralph Freedman spent fifteen years on his, the longest and most recent, and the first adjective he applies to Rilke is *tortured*.) Biography is an inadequate medium through which to discover Rilke, or Rilke's or our own inwardness. There is inevitably too much "middleman" in it—one of Rilke's pet hates. As I attempt to show more fully in the second section of this book, "inwardness" is a concept that is, above everything, a moment-by-moment experience. It is also, of necessity, highly subjective and, in a curious way, monological. To what extent are your internal experiences of "self" and "other," even "inside" and "outside," like mine? Do you feel love as I do? When I say "lonely" or "afraid," do you know what I mean? When you say you love this poem or that phrase, do I hear it as you would?

This is classic Rilkean territory: moving the anxious
need for answers aside; allowing ever more meaningful
questions to arise—and be *lived*. Bernstein continues,
"Rilke's inwardness is the absolute antithesis to any form
of normative psychology, just as his ideas of love as endless
leave-taking go against every conventional notion of
intimacy . . .

"It is not the specific tenets of his personal metaphysics,
but rather Rilke's whole language and tone, his basic way
of framing questions, that implies an immensely suggestive
alternative to any psychoanalytic idea of the self. It begins,
as any persuasive alternative must, with a deep respect for
the ultimate impenetrability of the human heart."[2]

That "impenetrability" of Rilke's human heart—the same
heart that could all too readily feel needy or bereft—is
highly relevant here. An Austrian critic, writing in 1951,
already noted that the Rilke critical literature "towers
over Rilke's Orphic work like a mountain range."[3] Would
Rilke have been appalled? It is quite possible, although
more likely he would have ignored it, keeping his attention
on what he regarded as sustaining.

Reflecting on that "mountain," and some of its least
predictable features, Rilke's biographer H. F. Peters care-
fully suggests that the difficulties some critics have with
Rilke (or with any one of a number of Rilkes, stretching
from *The Book of Hours* through *New Poems* to *Duino Elegies*
and the *Sonnets*) is adapting to his "method." "Unless the
critic accepts Rilke's way of looking at the world, unless
he is able to view it through the undivided consciousness
of a child, he cannot evaluate Rilke's poetry because he
does not understand it."

His words echo a familiar warning: "I tell you the

truth. Unless you become as little children [free of limiting constructs] you will not enter the Kingdom of Heaven [realize the unitive truth that is already present]."[4] This might suggest that what blocks reception exists within our conditioned mind, even while much of our conditioning genuinely seeks to liberate us.

Peters believes that Rilke "transcends logic and opens a door into the vast realm of the unconscious." He continues: "The more intellectual a critic is the less likely is he therefore to understand Rilke. This explains the seeming paradox that many first-rate minds are baffled by Rilke's poetry while quite unlearned people have no difficulty with it at all. It also explains Rilke's popularity and what has been called the 'Rilke cult.' Now it would of course be absurd to say that you have to be simple-minded to understand Rilke. The complexity and subtlety of his work is too well-known for that, but it is of a kind that demands intuitive rather than intellectual understanding. . . ."[5]

Rilke's own views, expressed in one of his early letters to Franz Kappus, the "Young Poet," point to the gap between critical and intuitive ways of thinking and the potentials of the latter. Rilke urges Kappus to "read as little as possible of aesthetic criticism." He goes on:

> . . . Such things are either partisan views, petrified and grown senseless in their lifeless induration, or they are clever quibblings in which today one view wins and tomorrow the opposite. Works of art are of an infinite loneliness and with nothing so little to be reached as with criticism. Only love can grasp and hold and be just toward them. Consider *yourself* and your feeling right every time with regard to every such

argumentation, discussion or introduction; if you are wrong after all, the natural growth of your inner life will lead you slowly and with time to other insights. Leave to your opinions their own quiet undisturbed development, which, like all progress, must come from deep within and cannot be pressed or hurried by anything. *Everything* is gestation and then bringing forth. . . .

. . . Being an artist means, not reckoning and counting, but ripening like the tree which does not force its sap. . . . [6]

The call is for a quiet confidence in the slow *ripening* of one's capacity to know, even in the presence of confusion. Reception is critical in reading: I make this point repeatedly. *It is no less critical in writing.* In his lectures on Rilke given in 1944, French philosopher Gabriel Marcel speaks of Rilke's supreme "creative receptivity," especially in relation to matters "eternal." Marcel writes, "What Rilke teaches us better than anyone, and what I think such writers as Nietzsche or Kierkegaard have generally either never known or in the end forgotten, is that there exists a receptivity which is really creation itself under another name. The most genuinely receptive being is at the same time the most essentially creative."[7]

One of Rilke's simplest and most tender poems affirms this.

You darkness that I come from,
I love you more than the fire
that rings the world,
because it shines
only for a single orbit,
and of this creature knows nothing at all.

But the darkness holds everything together:
forms and flames, animals and myself,
all thrown together,
humans and powers—

and it could be that a great strength
moves all about me where I am.

I believe in nights.[8]

Reading Rilke ignites the wondrous possibility that *a great strength/moves all about me where I am*. I, too, can *have faith in nights*. What is no less true is that from the moment we are born and placed in a high-tech cradle or on a bed of straw we are the vessel of ideologically, socially and culturally driven projections and interpretations. The "vessel" itself is not empty. Those projections and interpretations work on and in us. They shape our ideas, interpretations and prejudices. They shape our relationships. They are essential to the self we are continuously becoming and, significantly, to the self we believe we can become. A neutral reading is scarcely possible. Instead, clarity is needed about what gives context to and drives an individual's questions or interpretations, or forbids other questions from arising.

Multiple factors—many out of sight—contribute to how we became the reader that each of us is, and how we have become conditioned to see what we see and to miss so much else. We can make room for "space"; "convincing" has to be neither absolute nor resolute. This potentially rescues us from what Karl Jaspers calls "the arrogant faith in reason."[9] Space is deep "inside," but also "reaches out." And, as Rilke again shows, birds can fly through it.

What birds plunge through is not that intimate space
in which you feel all forms intensified.
(There, in the Open, you'd be denied yourself
and vanish on and on without return.)

Space reaches out from us and translates each thing:
to accomplish a tree's essence
cast inner space around it, out of that space
that has its life in you . . .[10]

An example of what can emerge from an open-minded—
not uncritical—exploration is given by Mark Burrows—a
historian of Christianity as well as a Rilke scholar and
translator—in an article that points to the potential rewards
of an allegorical reading of biblical scriptures, rather than
"following the canons of historical criticism." A compelling
question seems implicit: How far can we go—or allow our-
selves to be taken—when we bring to that reading Keats's
ideal of "negative capability," or the "quiet undisturbed
development" that Rilke speaks of in the quote above
("*Everything* is gestation")?

Burrows writes: "To interpret allegorically is to read
expectantly. . . . The practice of allegorical reading *requires*
the reader's receptivity to the text's continual ability to generate
meaning in the present. Such an interpretation need not, of
course, be uncritical. It might rather express something of
the encounter Paul Ricoeur has called a 'second naïveté,'
a discovery of meaning on the other side of a critical
engagement with the text."[11]

An "open mind" is an illusion dear to many of us. How
rich it would already be simply to recognize the ways in
which our minds are "not open"! As I sit at my computer,
rereading Burrows's remarks and thinking about both trust

and anticipation as necessary to openness in reading, I am reminded of a particular kind of coloring book that I had as a child. If one splashed water liberally onto the page, bright colors would emerge. The page held the colors *within itself* so that at first all I could see were black outlines on a white page. As I applied water (literalizing my attention and enchantment), the colors were revealed and the page was transformed. So, too, was my perception of it. Something was revealed as I watched and I felt *wonder.*

In the opening paragraphs of his celebrated 1946 essay on Rilke, "What are poets for?"—a guiding question in my own work on Rilke—Heidegger quotes the poet Hölderlin and mourns the fleeing of the gods from our world: "The default of God means that no god any longer gathers men and things unto himself, visibly and unequivocally. . . . The default of God forebodes something even grimmer, however. Not only have the gods and the god fled, but the divine radiance has become extinguished in the world's history. . . . The turning of the age does not take place by some new god, or the old one renewed . . . Where would he turn on his return if men had not first prepared an abode for him?"

Dare one suggest that *preparing the abode* and restoring *divine radiance*—or, as Burrows suggests, "pointing toward it in 'the distances' as Rilke does"[12]—is what these rare visionary poets are *for?*

"To be a poet in a destitute time," Heidegger continues, "means: to attend, singing, to the trace of the fugitive gods. This is why the poet in the time of the world's night utters the holy."[13]

Uttering the holy—and willingly hearing the holy: It

may also be that affirming this preparation and witnessing this "restoration," in part through careful reading and the surrendered engagement of spirit as well as mind, is what we readers of such poets are *for*. "We are in need of poets who can bring the world back to life so that it is once again weighted with significance," the American philosopher Rick Anthony Furtak plainly states.[14] That is an astonishing statement. Do we dare take it seriously?

Gaston Bachelard asserts that a philosophy of poetry "should not simplify, should not harden anything." A philosopher and writer of rare beauty himself, Bachelard has this to suggest in *The Poetics of Space*: "We should have to say that poetry, rather than being a phenomenology of the mind, is a phenomenology of the soul. . . . The word 'soul' is an immortal word. In certain poems it cannot be effaced, for it is a word born of our breath. . . . The word 'soul' can, in fact, be poetically spoken with such conviction that it constitutes a commitment for the entire poem. The poetic register that corresponds to the soul must therefore remain open to our phenomenological investigations."[15]

Bachelard's image of the *poetic register* feels revelatory. More, the poetic register must *register* to gain its power. It depends on us; we may come to depend on it. Indeed, the invitation of deep reading makes explicit and knowledge-full the inevitable flow of relationship and relational space between what inspires and who is inspired; what is written and what is read, as well as how it is read. None of that happens outside an ontological reality. *Real people write; real people read. Real people are changed by reading and writing.* They are profound acts, determining what is known and what can be known.

Heidegger expresses something similar, if more abstractly. "The poet things [*sic*] his way into the locality defined by that lightening of Being which has reached its characteristic shape as the realm of Western metaphysics in its self-completion." He then asks a series of questions that have great meaning in this work and for this time. "Is Rainer Maria Rilke a poet in a destitute time? How is his poetry related to the destitution of the time? How deeply does it reach into the abyss? Where does the poet get to, assuming he goes where he can go?" Heidegger begins to answer those questions.

> Rilke's valid poetry concentrates and solidifies itself, patiently assembled, in the two slim volumes, *Duino Elegies* and *Sonnets to Orpheus*. The long way leading to the poetry is itself one that inquires poetically. Along the way Rilke comes to realize the destitution of the time more clearly. The time remains destitute not only because God is dead, but because mortals are hardly aware and capable even of their own mortality. Mortals have not yet come into ownership of their own nature. Death withdraws into the enigmatic. The mystery of pain remains veiled. Love has not been learned.
>
>   . . . Meanwhile, even the trace of the holy has become unrecognizable . . .

Heidegger then asks another question, this time rhetorically: "Who today would presume to claim that he is at home with the nature of poetry as well as with the nature of thinking and, in addition, strong enough to bring the nature of the two into the most extreme discord and so to establish their concord?"[16]

The long way leading to the poetry is itself one that inquires poetically. This insight returns us to twin issues of primary significance in how we read Rilke's work: our ideas about reading (the "how" and the "what") and our ideas about the man himself.[17] Rilke is part of that "long way," both in how we think about him and more particularly how we respond to his capacities to "bring the world back to life so that it is once again weighted with significance" (and "divine radiance"). Yet how are we to interpret this?

Where are we placing ourselves, as participating readers, "along the way"? On what assumptions are we building our reading and responses to the work as well as to the "innate person" of whom Lou spoke? Theories can open space and emphatically close it. What may be more personally challenging is to maintain the surrender to which I keep returning. Gadamer spoke of a need for freshness and, as an old man, of ". . . all our efforts to understand . . . [that] must each time be taken back again and again . . . beginning each time anew."[18]

The idea of "beginning again" is also vital to Rilke. He makes this clear in one of a magnificent series of letters to the artist Baladine Klossowska, for some years from 1919 his lover and "Merline": "At the onset of every work, you must recreate that primal innocence, you must return to that ingenuous place where the Angel found you, when he brought you that first message of commitment: you must seek through the brambles for the bed in which you then slept; this time you won't sleep: you will pray, wail—anything; if the Angel condescends to come, it will be because you have persuaded him, not with your tears, but by your humble decision always to start afresh: *ein Anfanger zu sein!*"—to be a beginner.[19]

The adventure is clear. Those choosing to read at the limits are challenged not by refined and subtle poetry only, but more nakedly by innocence. We are challenged to come close enough to what the poet intends to begin anew, to play our own small part in witnessing with Rilke, and through the driving desires of our own souls, the restoration of the divine in these destitute times, or at least retracing the holy.

We are workers: apprentices, journeymen, masters,
and we build you, you immense central nave.
And sometimes it happens that an earnest traveler arrives,
penetrating our hundred spirits like a brilliant flash,
showing us, trembling, a new hold.

We climb the swaying scaffolds,
the hammer hanging heavily in our hands
until the hour kisses us on our brow,
which, shining as if it knowing everything
comes from you, like the wind from the sea.

Then I heard it: the echo of many hammers sounding
one blow after another through the mountains.
Only as it grows dark do we relinquish you,
and your approaching contours fade.

God, you are immense.[20]

LOOKING WITH ALICE
AND JAMES

To my knowledge, neither the contemporary Swiss analyst Alice Miller nor the contemporary American analyst James Hillman has written directly about Rilke. Yet the theoretical stance of each of these widely read writers quite dramatically highlights how our reading is shaped by assumptions, prejudices and perceptions, so much so that each of us is reading/creating something of our own "Rilke," and interpreting our own reading processes similarly subjectively.

I was reminded of this recently when a well-educated German woman asked me what I was working on. Sensing danger, I mentioned Rilke and mumbled something vague about my interest in how or why we might read him. (I didn't mention how reading Rilke might open our eyes wider to learning more about ourselves.)

"Ah, the *Romantic* poet," the woman said, rolling her eyes, telling me through this gesture that serious people should be long past reading Romantic poetry and, at the same time, how "cute" or perhaps predictable it might be that English-language readers would latch on to a German-language *Romantic* poet. That Rilke is not a Romantic poet, or that this is only one among several possible categorizations of his work, was not the point. In her made-up mind, that was where Rilke sat.

Rather nervously, I asked the woman if she had read Rilke's work in recent years. She looked amazed at my stupidity and said, still laughing, "We had enough of him at school. We learned by heart 'The Panther' and 'The Carousel.' It is enough!"

A mingling of roles is subtle here. Writer? Reader? Judge? Judged? But it seems indisputable that a writer, a *person*, haunts the intimate space "between" our reading and us. As we read, we create. Out of our own responsiveness, a *version* of both text and author emerge. We also create connections between the past and the present, inner and outer. Doing so, we are influenced by what is on the page and what we believe is on the page. Crowding into the experience is also what we have read previously, how we more generally receive and interpret what we call the "world" and perhaps also whether we are in need of sleep, a walk or a cup of tea.

~

In writing about public figures, and especially writers, the work of psychoanalyst Alice Miller is persuasive. For decades she has been sharing with readers her advocacy on behalf of children, and her ardent conviction that the abuse of children, and most particularly of talented, sensitive children, will determine the adults they become.

Despite her English-sounding name, Alice Miller was born in Poland, is German-speaking and was educated and has spent most of her life in Switzerland. The major figures she has written about include James Joyce, Sylvia Plath, Virginia Woolf, Käthe Kollwitz, Friedrich Nietzsche, Marcel Proust and Friedrich von Schiller, all of whom she believes were victims of tyrants, albeit "well-meaning" ones: their own parents.

In *For Your Own Good*, first published in German in 1980, Miller writes, "The former practice of physically maiming, exploiting and abusing children seems to have been gradually replaced in modern times by a form of mental cruelty that is masked by the honorific term *child-rearing*." Miller describes this "mental cruelty" as "basically directed not toward the *child's* welfare but toward satisfying the parent's needs for power and revenge."[1] The revenge the parents are seeking is often against their own parents. The power they are exhibiting is often produced by revulsion for their own weakness that they see repeated in the child.

The result? "The person is not really himself, nor does he know or love himself."[2]

In her tenth book, *The Body Never Lies*, Miller is directly self-revealing. She writes, "I had to learn to see and judge everything I felt through my mother's eyes and to systematically kill off my real feelings and needs . . . I know now that my parents did not want me . . . They were hoping for a little boy . . . But they got a little girl instead, and for decades that little girl did all she could to compensate them for the happiness they had missed out on. This undertaking was doomed to failure."[3]

The greatest violence that parents can perpetrate against their child, in Miller's view, is not the failure to provide consistent warmth, presence, love and guidance, but the failure to *see the child as he is*. In her own autobiographical statements she makes it clear how agonizing it was to be aware of not being the child whom her own parents expected: they wanted a boy; they got Alice. The cruelties of premature toilet training and rigid obedience were possible because Alice's parents were not attached to her and did not see her as a separate being in need of and deserving love. What they themselves needed (a boy) and what they continued to need (cleanliness, conformity and no complaints) filled their emotional horizon.

The conclusion Miller draws is that in the face of such childhood suffering extensive treatment will always be needed, treatment grounded in total acceptance of the child within the adult and of the veracity of the child's inner "story." Only this will allow the adult to see what had been done to the child who still lives inwardly and *is acted out in so many of their most crucial interactions and relationships.*

In fact, before those injured children can learn to give or accept love—and not simply demand, "spoil" or reject love—they must *experience* the empathy and unconditional love for the child that was not available from the parents when it was most needed. They must experience it from the therapist *and* from themselves. It is only this awakening of compassion as well as truth, Miller believes, that will liberate the person into feeling fully alive and emotionally "awake"—not dangerous to others or to themselves. But she warns that because emotional neglect and unrealistic parent-focused demands are so normalized in Western societies, the essential recognition of the series of truths that must precede any degree of authentic transformation is difficult to achieve. She writes: "Disassociated from the original cause, the feelings of anger, helplessness, despair, longing, anxiety, and pain will find expression in destructive acts against others . . . or against themselves . . . *a child responds to and learns both tenderness and cruelty from the very beginning.*"[4]

Meanwhile, or without treatment, the child starved of love and attachment will reflect *through her choices* the indifference of her parents as to her true self or fate. With pertinence to the many writers whose childhoods she examines, Miller writes: "Inability to face up to the sufferings undergone in childhood can be observed both in the form of religious obedience and in cynicism, irony, and other forms of self-alienation frequently masquerading as philosophy or literature."[5] What's more, until the child/adult learns to recognize and witness her own suffering, she cannot authentically "bear" or bear witness to the suffering of others.

~

This is a careful unpicking of a familiar situation. Through the Miller prism, things don't look good for René/Rainer. Over our reading (interpretation) of him, a pall falls. The facts tell us that he had a vain, pious, immature mother, mourning for a dead daughter, by turns emotionally greedy and selfishly neglectful, angry with her husband, innately pretentious and ashamed of her diminishing social standing, boastful and eager to parade her clever child—but as a girl, a doll, and then as a precocious verse-writer and *not as himself*. This does not lay the foundation for resilience, trust or easy affection in René's adult life.

It may be a stretch to think that in Rilke's internal and external restlessness, his constant turnover of lovers, briefly idealized and then rejected, there is an echo of the earliest years of his life when the many nurses Phia hired came and went with such rapidity that this was noticed even at a time when the convenience of the parents really was everything. Perhaps the greater effect of this was that in addition to not being able to rely on his mother's presence, moods or affection, René was also unable to rely on comforting mother substitutes. Here today; someone else tomorrow. Nor was he able to rely upon a father to step in and save him.

Rilke said of his father, "Whenever he was home, only my papa bestowed upon me love combined with care and solicitude."[6] Nonetheless, René's father wanted a "little man," not the girly-boy who initially charmed his mother, and certainly not the invalid who could not become the soldier his father would have admired. This seems to be a relationship of absence and frustration, riven with ambivalence and a powerful sense of longing and defeat.

> . . . You, father, for whom life
> turned so bitter when you tasted mine—
> that first murky influx of what would feed my drives—
> who kept on sampling it as I grew older, and,
> intrigued by the aftertaste of so strange a future,
> tried looking through my vague upward gaze,—
> you, father, who since your death have been here
> often in my hope, far inside me, afraid,
> forfeiting that equanimity, for my bit of fate—
> Aren't I right? . . .[7]

Illness became Rilke's trump card—until eventually it turned on him. "Illness became René's first profession," says William Gass. "It brought his mother to his side."[8] Through his adult lifetime, punctuated by long visits to spas—havens for the hypochondriacal—illness and "exhaustion" would also bring him sympathy, escape and arguably a degree of erotic attention that sat well alongside the adoration of Rilke the poet.

There was, always, neediness in René/Rainer, yet as Gass notes, far from clinging to others, Rilke "would specialize in dumping."[9] With the exception of Lou Andreas-Salomé, Rilke was the abandoning one through all his adult years, and not of his many lovers only; also of Ruth, his daughter, and Clara, his wife.

It is not Gass but the critic Hass who takes us back to

the making of Rilke: "Rilke came to hate his native city [Prague] . . . There was probably nothing more suffocating than the life of a genteel, aspiring European household of the late nineteenth century in which failure brooded like a boarder who had to be appeased, or like the giant cockroach which was to appear in another Prague apartment in 1915. All his life Rilke carried that suffocation inside him. . . ."[10]

The failure that brooded in the Rilke nest was, of course, manifold and relates strongly to the string of inner self-images I described earlier (none adding up to an easily coherent sense of self). The failure of René to be a girl collided with the failure of René to be a strong and healthy and soldierly boy; the failure of Phia's ambitions for her husband and therefore for her marriage; the failure of Phia to match her envied sister's aristocratic marriage; of Josef to save his loved brother from suicide (when it was clear that he would never get the promotion in the army he most desired); and—most overtly—truly the cockroach in the Prague corner, Josef's failure to make it in the army, the railway or as a husband, father and provider. With so much failure in the air, is it any wonder that the parents' failure of their son remained oblique, although in Miller's terms, described above, certainly no less painful for that.

"Rilke blamed his emotional deficiencies on his irremediable childhood experiences," writes Siegfried Mandel. "Why was he a shy, self-dissatisfied child who could not love other children? His verse-answer to Lou is: *'Because my devotion drove me to my mother/and because her bearing resisted my will,/so it was that love remained inside of me'*. . . . He wanted Lou to play a redemptive role—as an acquiescent mother, a loved one, and as an object of prayer."[11]

In a letter to Clara written in 1907, Rilke announces his rage and pain more starkly still: "I cannot bring home to her the least thing that is real to me. With her false conception of me, she sees inside me such a hole, such an emptiness that nothing retains its validity for her. Who can enter a doll's house on which the doors and walls are only painted?"[12]

This statement becomes more chilling still when set alongside an anecdote told by Magda von Hattingberg ("Benvenuta"), with whom Rilke had a particularly intense love affair in 1914.[13] She writes, "Rilke had received some colored pictures of dolls—I believe from the woman who made them. They looked as though they had been modelled on insane persons or on those sick from taking opium. He showed them to me and I thought them frightful. I was shocked when Rilke said he found them 'moving and beautiful.'"

After a heated discussion about toys and children, Rilke then read Benvenuta an essay he had written on dolls.[14] According to H. F. Peters, who tells this anecdote, Benvenuta became "more and more upset." He quotes her: "Suddenly I had an irrepressible desire to cry, 'Rainer,' I said, 'I cannot listen anymore . . . I don't even know why your hatred of dolls affects me so much, for after all, it is your hatred, not mine—but I cannot go on. I find it horrifying.'"[15]

~

It is Alice Miller's view that "truth" is curative. She writes: "What makes us sick are those things we cannot see through, society's constraints that *we have absorbed through our mother's eyes* . . . The inner necessity to constantly build up new illusions and denials, in order to avoid the experience of our own reality, disappears once this reality has been faced and experienced. We then realize that all our lives we have feared and struggled to ward off something that really cannot happen any longer: it has already happened."[16]

But like Pontius Pilate on a far graver occasion, we must ask, "What is truth?" In the world of any artist, the pursuit of truth remains highly charged. "Truth" will resound at many different levels and cannot depend upon coherence. A person who demonstrates brilliance in one area of their life may remain agonizingly insecure or blind in other areas. In mood alone, never mind in insight, Rilke was sensitive and complex. The evidence of his letters shows that there were times when he was immensely joyful. There were also times when he was intimate only with defeat.

In October 1900, just months before his marriage to Clara and two months before his twenty-fifth birthday, Rilke wrote in his diary: "There comes a time when every past sheds its heaviness, when blood affects us like brilliance and sadness like ebony. And the darker and more colorful our various pasts were, the richer the images will be by which our quotidian life redeems itself . . . All cruelty and force becomes brilliance among grandchildren. All heirs bear deceased fates like jewelry. . . ."[17]

And there is this:

You are abandoning me, you hour.
Your beating wings leave me bruised.
Alone. What shall I do with my mouth?
With my night? With my day?

I have no lover, no house.
No room of my own.
All those things to which I give myself
grow rich, and use me up.[18]

A Milleresque view of Rilke's childhood and adult life is plausible. Taking it up could transform our reading of Rilke. Damage was done; the boy and, later, the man, was damaged. And despite the extreme edge to Miller's arguments, because they are founded in Winnicottian "object relations" they are familiar enough to make sense for many psychologically experienced readers, even to seem self-evident. *And they may be.*

People are, however, far slipperier than theories. Rilke knew this. He did not want to be read as theory, studied as a theory or fitted into a theory. He was fearful of psychoanalysis, despite his own curiosity and Lou's increasing professional interest. When Clara pressed the idea of it on him, he strenuously resisted her. To Lou he wrote, "I know now that analysis would have sense for me only if I were really serious about the strange reservation of *not writing anymore*, which during the finishing of [his novel] Malte I often dangled before my nose as a kind of relief. Then one might have one's devils exorcized. . . . But am I the man for such an experiment with all the consequences of that experiment?"[19]

Stephen Spender and J. B. Leishman speak of Rilke as a prophet "of an intensely personal vision of reality."[20] And in a 1909 letter to Rilke, Lou alludes to this also: "Ellen has just told me that you are not doing very well, and for the moment I cannot picture this at all since I am still feeling the enchanting happiness that fills your poems . . . how exceptionally life has favored you with this possession, Rainer."[21]

There is something else to add here, beyond that diversity of views. I want to suggest that while Alice Miller's grim prognoses are shocking, they also comfort. At a mundane level they fit familiar models of cause and effect:

do this and you will get this result; do that and you will get
something different. But leaving aside the actual pain that
this theorizing refers to and seeks to assuage, does this add
up to more than an attempt to put symptomatic emotions
and behaviors within a reassuringly convincing framework?
Do these theories deepen our reading or our understanding
of the person who wrote what we so eagerly read? Can
they help us better to understand the man who wrote . . .
*Praising, my dear one—let us be lavish with praise./Nothing
really belongs to us?* Can they help us to feel, understand or
inhabit more deeply the words themselves?

There is no doubt that the child René suffered dread-
fully. There is no doubt that the man Rilke caused others
to suffer, sometimes dreadfully. The poet of solitude had
little capacity for intimacy beyond the noncorporeal figures
that filled his inner world. For all that, though, his was a
life of illumination and achievement. That is unassailable.
He is the man who could write:

I am praying again, Awesome One.

You hear me again, as words
from the depths of me
rush toward you in the wind.

I've been scattered in pieces,
torn by conflict,
mocked by laughter,
washed down in drink . . .

. . . I am a house gutted by fire
where only the guilty sometimes sleep
before the punishment that devours them
hounds them out into the open . . .

. . . It's here in all the pieces of my shame
that now I find myself again.
I yearn to belong to something, to be contained
in an all-embracing mind that sees me
as a single thing.
I yearn to be held
in the great hands of your heart—
oh let them take me now.
Into them I place these fragments, my life,
and you, God—spend them however you want.[22]

Conventional thinking would have it that in shame we lose ourselves, or cannot gain a stable sense of self. Rilke is saying something quite different while also voicing a seeking for wholeness that his readers, surely, would echo. Oh, could we not all ask what would it mean *to be contained/ in an all-embracing mind that sees me* not in pieces but *as a single thing?*

I yearn to be held
in the great hands of your heart . . .

Is this a poem? A prayer? Reading becomes, for a moment, sacrament. And from the *Elegies*, symphonic in their power, come these lines from the Third, written more than twenty poem-packed years after the hymn immediately above, by someone you would swear knows as much about love as the orders of angels.

You see, we don't love like flowers, the effort
of just one year; sap from time immemorial
flows through our arms when we love. O girl,
this: that we've loved, within us, not that one person yet to come,
but all the weltering brood: not some single child,
but the fathers who lie like mountain-ruins
within us: and the dried up riverbed
of former mothers——; and the whole
soundless landscape beneath our cloudy
or cloudless fate: all that, *O girl, claimed him first.*[23]

Should we be bewildered or simply grateful?

~

In *The Soul's Code: In Search of Character and Calling,* writer
and once-upon-a-time Jungian analyst James Hillman has
a good deal to say about the cause and effect of what he
calls "the parental fallacy." Recognizing that we make sense
of the world according to our expectations and, indeed,
our fantasies (and read in those ways also), Hillman writes:
"If any fantasy holds our contemporary civilization in an
unyielding grip, it is that we are our parents' children and
that the primary instrument of our fate is the behavior of
your mother and father. . . . The individual's soul continues
to be imagined [and therefore responded to] as a biological
offspring of the family tree. . . ." And: "The myth of the
mother as the dominant in everyone's life remains constant."

Like Alice Miller, Hillman is gazing intently at the child/
parents relationship. But what he sees is notably different.
"The elevation of the parents, of the mother in particular,
to the neglect of all other realities—societal, environmental,
economic—shows that adulation of an archetype can obliter-
ate common sense."

Hillman believes not only that this elevation is false but that it reduces us to a "mere effect": the result of our parents' "causes." And now, proposing something arguably far more shocking than Alice Miller's views given above, Hillman writes, "*We are less victims of parenting than of the ideology of parenting; less the victims of Mother's fateful power than of the theory that gave her that fateful power* . . . This ideology traps women in the parental fallacy and children in mother-blame."[24]

Reading, we have power. We have power to clarify and to obscure, to receive or to impose. But "power," too, is no neutral concept. The "power" of what we read or gaze at also works on us. Deflating the archetypal Mother, and discarding the long shadow she is assumed to cast over our lives, Hillman is not entering into or creating a theory-free zone. His theories may carry less power in part because they are less familiar, but they are fully present. His demolishment of the parental archetypes is itself ideological. In addition he proposes an "acorn theory" of childhood: a neat idea that each of us comes into this life with a potential fate to be discovered, as well as the gifts to grow that fate and to live it fully.

Time-traveling back to the last quarter of the nineteenth century, to provincial Prague and a small, unhappy household living close together in a rented flat, we might, with Hillman's guidance, see Rilke's childhood somewhat differently from a Miller-influenced reading. Those same sorrows, shames, restrictions, desertions, pieties, inadequacies and disappointments are there—yes. And also . . . the chance to learn languages; the mother who taught him French at an early age, read Schiller's ballads aloud to him and believed in his gifts even while parading them, and who encouraged him to write;[25] the father who "really had tried to do what was best for him";[26] the images of Jesus and the saints which he grew to hate, though, as Gass points out, "there are more Virgin Marys, saints and angels in [Rilke's] work than in many cathedrals."[27]

And what of Rilke's "calling," or our own calling to read his work? What of that? It may be more *entertaining* to read a hundred other writers. We heed a call to something beyond entertainment when choosing Rilke. The idea of a call or calling is conventionally thought to be religious. Hillman broadens the context wonderfully: "Extraordinary people display calling most evidently. Perhaps that's why they fascinate. Perhaps, too, they are extraordinary because their calling comes through so clearly and they are so loyal to it. They serve as exemplars of calling and its strengths, and also of keeping faith with its signals . . . They seem to have no other choice . . . Extraordinary people bear the better witness because they show what ordinary mortals simply can't . . . Extraordinary people are not a different category; the workings of this engine in them are simply more transparent."[28]

Rilke's inwardly led calling, and the "call" it evokes in readers, is something I find myself thinking and writing about repeatedly. Writing, I am responding to it, without wishing to manipulate it. Nor am I wishing to give Hillman's ideas greater weight, necessarily, than those of Alice Miller. Each theory is only that: a context for reading, something that corresponds with our biases or challenges them.

J. R. von Salis draws on his personal memories to tell us that "during [the years of living in Switzerland, Rilke] spoke oftenest of his long-dead father . . . His father really had tried to do what was best for him, Rilke would say in conversation, when his stories had made clear how little understanding the growing boy and youth has received from his solicitous but bourgeois-minded parent—and although he had then experienced the father–son conflict in all its painfulness."[29]

Alice Miller would no doubt argue according to her theories that the tenderness that Rilke showed to the memory of his father, and his occasional kind, pious or good-humored communications with his mother, were possible because he had not been "treated" (analyzed).[30] He was still unconsciously aligned with his parents against himself, and this showed in his personal relationships and especially his "failures" at intimacy. *And that may be so.*

For all its attraction, though, a purely psychological explanation is not enough. Rilke could also write this, and did so in his early prayer-poems (*Die Gebete*) when childhood shames and pains were close:

> *I love the dark hours of my life*
> *in which my senses deepen;*
> *in them as in old letters I find*
> *my daily life already lived and,*
> *as in legends, distant and complete.*
>
> *From these hours comes the awareness that*
> *I have room for a second life, timeless and wide.*
> *And sometimes I'm like the ripe and rustling*
> *tree which rises above the dead boy's grave*
> *—gathering him in its warm roots—*
> *and fulfills the dream he had lost*
> *in sorrows and songs.*[31]

The past is not forgotten here, yet the *boy in the past,* the boy in the grave, is also feeding and growing the "tree," the self that rises above the grave, *ripe and/murmuring.*

What's more, because the differences between Hillman and Miller are stark, they provide a warning against conclusions that are convincing because familiar. Taste, sensibility and literary "value" are highly plastic notions. What the Miller/ Hillman theories also emphasize is that theories themselves are never neutral, in their histories or in their effects. As a tiny example, on rereading those two I could not help but observe how stimulated I felt in Hillman's company, even and sometimes particularly when I was disagreeing with him, in contrast to the considerable flatness and heaviness that came upon me each time I pushed myself to reread Miller.

Reading is not disembodied. Those reactions also tell me something. A determinedly psychoanalytic view once felt fresh; it no longer does. And especially it no longer does when the writer and writings in question have long ago escaped the tyranny of the exclusively "rational."

Hillman writes, "Psychopathology prompts sharper psychological insight than do spiritual ideals and formulae. A negative approach sheds the harshest light. . . . When the invisible forsakes the actual world . . . then the visible world no longer sustains life, because life is no longer invisibly backed."[32]

For many years I had a small psychotherapy practice alongside my writing. I have no desire to denigrate the efforts of analysts and psychotherapists working with those who have suffered losses of dignity and self in childhood through parental abuse and neglect. That is not my intention. Nor do I have any wish to deny the validity of a psychological analysis of literary texts. I am deeply "marked" by that tradition myself. Also, I am aware that Rilke himself described his childhood in terms at least as bleak as those that Miller could have chosen: "As a child, when everyone was always unkind to me, when I felt infinitely forsaken, so utterly astray in an alien world, there may have been a time when I longed to be gone. But then, when people remained alien to me, I was drawn to things, and from them a joy breathed upon me. . . ."[33]

Without trivializing such genuine suffering in any way I want nevertheless to show through the "extraordinary person" who is Rilke, to quote Hillman now, how "natural" and therefore seductive it can seem to read/interpret/ analyze a writer in a way that is partisan and reductive. Losses flow from that.

The distance in worldview between Miller and Hillman does more than provide different sets of possibilities. It shows theory to be what it is: a context of ideas that speculate and convince, or not; ways of thinking that are helpful, or not; map-making, not truth-making. Can anything else be claimed?

There is an innately subversive power to Rilke's language and thinking. He will not be *bound*. Hillman reminds us: "As the old Greeks said of their gods: They ask for little, just that they not be forgotten."[34] There is a dimension to Rilke's work and being that is not easily available to theorizing: it may be the place where gods are remembered. To claim a precise or privileged reading of the poetry or of the man is to wander far from his own warnings. "To come to agree with what is great and to allow it to be valid is nothing but an insight: to celebrate it, however, is exuberance . . ."[35]

Straining so hard against the strength of night,
they fling their tiny voice on the laughter
that will not burn. Oh disobedient world,
full of refusal. And yet it breathes the space
in which the stars revolve. It doesn't need us,
and, at any time, abandoned to the distance,
could spin off in remoteness, far from us.
And now it deigns to touch our faces, softly,
like a loved woman's glance; it opens up
in front of us, and may be spilling out
its essence on us . . .[36]

Michael André Bernstein writes of "safeguarding the radical specificity of individual experience from any homogenizing discourse."[37] The *radical specificity* of Rilke remains obvious yet fragile. The seductive powers of *homogenizing discourse* are hard to resist. It is also hard to avoid cliché when saying again that Rilke—the man, the poet—is unusually ambiguous in other people's experience of him. Three brief anecdotes demonstrate this.

The first is told in Nora Wydenbruck's early, affectionate memoir, *Rilke: Man and Poet*. She is quoting Raymond Schwab's firsthand account of a literary gathering in France in 1925, Rilke's last Paris stay. "[Rilke] was talking with his gaze fixed into the void, his head resting on one shoulder, a sad, stooping figure; his neck, his joints, the very ends of his mustache were drooping . . . At first a circle had formed around him in the drawing-room, but little by little people drifted away, fatigued by his loquacity. Rilke was talking to nobody in particular without paying any attention to the effect of his words. . . . I have no doubt that those people, whose names I will not mention, have now become enthusiastic admirers of Rilke. But that day—I have got to say it—they only considered him a bore."[38]

That same story appears in von Salis's *Rainer Maria Rilke,* along with warm descriptions of Rilke's "beautiful voice," "laughter" and the rare pleasure of being in his company—and this:

> There was something curiously touching about the way he came to say goodbye to me in the Sierre pension where I had been staying for a few days. Coming back from a walk I found Rilke in the drawing-room. . . . He was sitting, quite inconspicuously, on a sofa near the door, busy with some writing. "You haven't put your name in my visitors' book," he said, explaining his unexpected presence. "I have marked the day, between my last visitors." Then he showed me the place in the leather-bound book where I must put my name. When this had been done, Rilke turned over the pages on which the names and thanks of many guests were written. Happily and proudly he showed me Paul Valéry's signature. With a quick movement, as though he would prevent me from thanking him, the strange man next handed me a slender book which he had taken out of his attaché case: "I don't think I've given you a copy of my book. . . ." Then he rose, and we went upstairs to my room, where he stayed for a short time, chatting away cheerfully. He would not stay to supper; he had some more work to do at home. From the steps outside I watched Rilke as, with stick and attaché case, he walked briskly through the darkening garden.[39]

The final story gives us a glimpse of an all-day meeting on 13 September 1926, in a park and under "great trees," between Rilke and Paul Valéry. Elsewhere, Ralph Freedman notes that Rilke described this particular day as ". . . exquisite and of incomparable value to our friendship."[40]

The day is again captured by Wydenbruck, and told from Valéry's perspective. "[The two poets] were walking up and down, discussing the "Narcissus" myth, and Rilke took his friend's arm and plied him with questions on the special significance it held for him. "As I spoke," writes Valéry, "he listened to my attempt to create for him alone what did not yet exist and perhaps might never exist, listening as a poet listens to himself, as does someone who stands within and is beset by ideas, temptations, inhibitions, inspirations, stirrings of the will, decisions and renunciations, by all that is the true inner essence of a poem."[41]

A memorable photograph of that day survives. It shows Rilke smiling joyfully, more freely than in any other photograph I have seen. It is Freedman who adds a final poignant note. "At the end of the day Valéry and his wife accompanied Rilke to the landing dock to return to the Swiss side of the lake [Lake Geneva]. "We saw," wrote Valéry later, "how his smile lost itself; a little smoke and . . . Adieu."[42]

Three months later, Rilke was dead.

"I love life, and I believe in it. Everything in me believes in it," wrote Rilke to Ellen Key in 1903.[43] Not other people's theories but his life and writing make it clear that Rilke saw his childhood, as well as the neuroses that almost certainly had their origins in his childhood, as a lifetime burden. But that's not all.

Work of sight is done,
now do heart-work
on the pictures within you, those captives; for you
overcame them . . .[44]

Reading Rilke achieves many things, not least confidence that art, and especially transcendent art, generates and regenerates. It is, itself, *deep seeing* and deep living. Rilke writes not from and to the mind only, but to the soul. To repeat the words of Bachelard: "The word 'soul' is an immortal word. In certain poems it cannot be effaced, for it is a word born of our breath."[45]

Beyond soul's code is soul's search. Driving soul's search is a deeply human, deeply recognizable yearning for the healing fullness of soul's experience.

PART TWO
YEARNING

O Lord, hear my voice when I call.
Have mercy and answer.
Of you my heart has spoken,
"Seek his face."

Psalms 27:7

You, my own deep soul,
trust me. I will not betray you.
My blood is alive with many voices
telling me I am made of longing.

Rilke (Trans. Barrows and Macy)

THE LANGUAGES OF LONGING

When Friedrich Nietzsche's "madman" announced in 1882 that God was dead, few were listening.[1] Twenty years later, Rilke was writing this:

God speaks to each of us as he makes us,
then walks with us silently out of the night.

These are words we dimly hear:
You, sent out beyond your recall,
go to the limits of your longing.

Embody me.

Flare up like flame
and make giant shadows that I can move in.
Let everything happen to you: beauty and terror.
Just keep going. No feeling is final.
Don't let yourself lose me.

Nearby is the country they call life.
You will know it by its seriousness.

Give me your hand.[2]

It is true that in the years preceding and following Nietzsche's proclamation many once-powerful images and ideas about God did collapse. Some had anyway been under siege for centuries. In the decades since, the loss of "God" has accelerated for many, influenced by significant changes in thinking following the devastation of two world wars and continuing "minor" wars; radical changes in technology, education and ideas about social equality and knowledge; increasing mechanization and the dramatic ascendancy of science. This makes it more and not less fascinating that some ideas and especially feelings about God remain strikingly persistent.

It is Rilke, writing in 1921, who suggests that, "God is the most ancient work of art. He has been preserved very poorly and many parts have been added later, in approximations. But it is of course incumbent upon any educated person to be able to talk about him and to have seen his remains."[3]

A similarly striking persistence drives the propensity we can best call "yearning." Often assumed to have love, beauty and truth as its primary objects, yearning—in German, *Sehnsucht* (seeking to *see*)—reaches toward a riskier, more profound experience of life and death than the most satisfying of daily encounters would allow.

Yearning expresses a profound desire that life would have meaning beyond the "seen," other than the exclusively material or rational. It may also describe a wish to avoid the horror of death, seeing death not as an "end" but

THE LANGUAGES OF LONGING

as a leave-taking from familiar mortal, transitory experience. Yearning may lean, too, toward a confidence in an essential unity that underpins all forms of life, sensed even in the face of loneliness. "God carries all things hidden in himself, not this and that, distinct and separate, but as one in Unity. . . . This unity is causeless," wrote the German mystic Meister Eckhart, "it is self-caused. . . . Ego, the word, I, belongs to no one but God alone in his unity. *Vos* (you) means that you are one in the unity. . . ."[4]

Not least, yearning may be a reaching toward love so unconditional and sublime that the only way to describe it is as "divine." Such "reaching toward" is fraught, perhaps courageous. It has an uncertainty to it that Rilke feels and expresses perfectly; it has a defenselessness that even the most earnest but more active "seeking" does not. Yearning stretches beyond the self yet its origins lie deep within the self. This is Rilke's "stretch" precisely.

> These are words we dimly hear:
> You, sent out beyond your recall,
> go to the limits of your longing.

British theologian John Hick expresses something about yearning in a sentence that is masterful in its understatement: "There is an aspect of our nature which responds to the transcendent."[5] We could add: there is an aspect of our nature that yearns for and is compelled *toward* the transcendent, as variously as this may be expressed.

There are few people who cannot, under any circumstances, be moved by something authentically "touching," in ways that are not propelled by emotional and aesthetic considerations only. To be spiritually touched is an inward experience that literally engages our senses. Our bodies echo it. We may involuntarily lean forward; we might cry or laugh, or laugh and cry together; we might feel an inner release, letting go tension we did not know we carried. We may feel exceptionally "open," even dangerously so. Our compassion for others may be awakened, or a little more compassion for ourselves. Our defensive edges may soften. We may feel newly connected or reconnected to life, sometimes in the face of death. I see the effects of this softening and opening with people on a spiritual retreat, more often than not. Yearning, we are touched inwardly: by what?

My sense is strong that it is the yearning reader who is most likely to be drawn to Rilke, then repeatedly drawn back again. The reader in search of "high art" only, as magnificent as that can be, may be discomforted by Rilke, or some of him, in ways that the yearning reader will not be.

Like a bass line that is not always audible, drowned sometimes by the languages of brilliance, the yearning reader hears—or wants to hear—another, inner, darkly sonorous language. This is the language of our roots, our "darkest" self. In much of Rilke's poetry, such language is released by yearning and is expressive of it. The yearning describes an attraction; it is itself attracting. Reading Rilke would suggest that yearning has some of the characteristics of desire and of grief but is distinct from both. Desire generally implies a greater need for possession or at least temporary satisfaction than the more ambivalent—though no less passionate—experience of yearning. And when grief is present, there is certain knowledge that something or someone is lost, while in yearning there is absence, self-evidently—one cannot yearn for what is present. However, in the experience of yearning there is hope, still, of union and reunion. One *may* meet; one *may* be met. Longing survives extreme ambivalence. In fact, ambivalence is prominent in the experience of yearning.

The very nature of yearning—its ragged intimacy, the vulnerability it demands and reveals, the chasm it potentially displays between oneself and the object of one's yearning—invites reflection upon experiences of self and not-self as well as the space between. More specifically, yearning disrupts the familiarity of what we might usually think of as "between."

The Spanish philosopher José Ortega y Gasset brings "between" completely to life for me when he writes, "How unimportant a thing would be if it were only what it is in isolation."[6]

The "thingness" of things is also a theme that Rilke illuminates in radical ways.

Kierkegaard captured this with the phrase "passionate inwardness." Yearning arises from and speaks to that same place, which is of course "no place."

~

Rilke abundantly demonstrates the extreme plasticity of "place" and "space." This is what religious philosopher Rudolf Otto calls, in relation to Meister Eckhart, the "exalted feeling of Eckhartian mysticism . . . floating high above space and time."[7] Such feelings are also familiar to readers of "exalted" Mahayana Buddhist texts and the Hindu Upanishads, as in this glimpse from the Taittiriya Upanishad: "O lord of Love, may I enter into you, and may you reveal yourself to me. The pure One masquerading as the many, you are the refuge of all those who would serve you. . . . Space and entity are the elements. . . ."

I am not comparing Rilke to those writers; nor do I want to make "scripture" from his poetry. What I do want to say is that Rilke achieves a rearrangement of our usual concepts and limitations, using a writing register that is far more often sensual and emotional than it is abstract. It necessitates deep or even innocent looking. Doing this, he sustains a tremendous intimacy with the reader and powerfully shifts the limits of our own self-understanding. Rilke tells us—directly in one famous instance—that we must change ourselves. This is an invitation to the whole person, not to a part. Or to the person who yearns for wholeness: *"You must change your life."*[8]

This phrase may be better translated as *"You must transform your life."* After all, once *transformed*, we cannot go back. "Once was blind, and now I see." Irony is overflowing here: in those "darkest" places we cannot change ourselves; we can only allow ourselves to be changed. This is what Rilke sometimes achieves. Transforming us (if we allow it), though that would never have been his intention—too much utility, far too much "claim"—Rilke shifts the boundaries of world, "life," "self" and "God." Rilke makes promises and breaks them. He laments and celebrates. He woos and is indifferent. He writes consolingly and remains unconsoled. "What, finally," he demands, "would be more useless to me than a consoled life?"[9] Rilke's "God" is given much the same contradictory treatment: a vulnerable neighbor one moment, like a "clump of a hundred roots" the next; "an ancient work of art," then a much-needed "hand," a cathedral, a dreamer. Absent here, breath-close there; as often in darkness as in light.

It must also be said that even an infinitely multifaceted and not-entirely-disappearing God is never solely the point. *Wenn du der Träumer bist, bin ich dein Traum./Doch wenn du wachen willst, bin ich dein Wille . . . (. . . If you are the dreamer, I am your dream./But should you choose to wake, I become your will . . .*)[10] What is also always present with those shifting, brilliant images of and feelings about God are equally brilliant unstable and destabilizing images and feelings about the self.

You see that I want much.
Perhaps I want it all:
the darkness of every infinite instance
and of every ascent experienced as a light-trembling game.

So many live and demand nothing,
relying on the fickle feelings of
enfeebled judgment.

But you delight in every face
that serves and thirsts.

You delight in all who depend on you
as if on a tool.

And you aren't cold, nor is it yet too late
for us to immerse ourselves in your growing depths
*   where life quietly reveals itself.*[11]

"What is it about [Rilke's] poetry that so speaks to us in the postmodern era?" asks the critic Kathleen Komar— who then replies, "I would suggest . . . that at least one aspect of his appeal lies in his attempts to understand how human consciousness can survive its temporal prison and reach out to a metaphysical realm without abandoning this human, physical world."

It is, indeed, *in this life* that the sacred is to be found in Rilke's work. That is surely an experience that has particular meaning for contemporary readers cut off from easy acceptance of dogma, or belief in the glories or terrors of a life to come. The idea of what "this life" is, or is continuously becoming, is under persistent scrutiny in Rilke's work. Just as inside and outside blur as duality recedes, so "before," "now" and "later" are exposed as highly fluid notions. Komar continues: "Rilke is a seeker after wholeness who helps us envision a reunification of our isolated consciousness with something larger and more unified."[12]

Reunification or "identity" in its deepest sense drives the authentic spiritual quest. It is the *grail*: reunification *within* the self allowing for a less limited view *of* the self. And what, in this context, is the self? Not Rilke but Wordsworth wrote, a century earlier:

> . . . Our birth is but a sleep and a forgetting:
> The Soul that rises with us, our life's Star,
> Hath had elsewhere its setting,
> And cometh from afar:
> Not in entire forgetfulness,
> And not in utter nakedness,
> But trailing clouds of glory do we come
> From God, who is our home . . .[13]

Yearning is a kind of homesickness. Rilke calls God (among many other names) "You, the great homesickness we could never shake off."[14] It is worth noting that Rilke had a feeling of "coming home" when he met the unfettered spirituality that so attracted him on those young-man visits to Russia in the company of Lou Andreas-Salomé.

But this is an "adding on" rather than a "giving up." The context and stimuli of the outer world remain vivid, not just in our experience of them but also in our experience of Rilke's world and work. Not least, this outer world is where we live and learn. Our sense of how much our everyday world "matters" grows as we grow inwardly. As we engage more deeply, any sense of disconnection from others, or from the sacred within life or ourselves, diminishes; we are *freed* to care. A mystical understanding of life reaches toward and embraces wholeness, not separateness: cause cannot be divorced from effect; the small cannot be lost in the big. This allows us a deeper understanding than usual of the newly popularized term (and experiences of) *mindfulness.* "Life delineates itself on the canvas called time," writes the Zen teacher Shunryu Suzuki, "and time never repeats: once gone, forever gone; and so is an act: once done, it is never undone."[15]

The circle from outside to inside turns; the outer can be a prompt to know the inner more honestly and fearlessly. To feel more deeply "at home" within oneself and in one's life is no small thing: it is a psychological challenge. To expand one's vision of *within* and *without* is also no small thing: it is a spiritual challenge. In relation to such questions Rilke himself wrote in 1914 that "art is not a making-oneself-understood but an urgent understanding-of-oneself."[16]

Some of Rilke's finest and most immediately coherent poems are hymnic still lifes, capturing and holding a moment of something ordinary "out there" and transforming it "in here" through the power of the poet's gaze. This kind of deep noticing, that involves seeing something freshly and seeing oneself freshly in relation to it, itself provokes a kind of yearning while also expressing it. Yet to attempt to write critically and fruitfully about yearning or seeking, especially when this specifically applies to yearning for and seeking the eternal dimensions of life and living, is to walk with shoes where even light slippers may seem too much.

~

In 1999, the pre–September 11, 2001, world, the American novelist and academic A. G. (Grace) Mojtabai gave a significant paper in which she said, "It has been suggested to me that the positive view I take of religion 'is a minority position among writers.'" She went on to say that she hoped this was not the case (I suspect she hopes in vain), and then described the yearning, the hunger, that is central to my own thinking about Rilke and about reading, yearning and "attending to the holy," more generally.

It is my conviction that there exists today a religious hunger in our country and in our world so widespread that writers ignore or disdain it at our peril. I'm not talking only about the peril of backlash, of censorship, and repression from the outside, but of something even more deadly that eats away at us from within: untruthfulness, shutting out the voices we don't want to hear.

. . . Contemporary Americans may have garbled or lost much of the traditional language of religious belief [or literalized it into extinction] but we haven't lost the yearning for that belief. About this reality, this intractable huge fact, the American literati, for the most part, have maintained a defensive or indifferent silence, or taken satiric note . . .

. . . With my most accomplished students, questions of encompassing vision tend to be repressed as distracting to aesthetic concentration. . . . There's a marked avoidance of those "eternal questions" (why are we here? where are we going? what is a truly human life?), a withering away of any significant sense of greatness. Indeed, the word *awesome* has lately become one of the tamest expletives.[17]

~

Reading Rilke, and thinking about what poetry might be *for*, centralizes that "hunger" and also the "encompassing vision" that Mojtabai eloquently evokes. Ulrich Baer also notes, "Rilke's promise of redemption suspended over the abyss of nothingness which haunts all of modern literature," and writes of "man's thirst for meaning in an age bereft of transcendental assurances."[18] A yearning for the transcendental has profound implications for countless people, individually and socially. To avoid or silence spiritual yearning because it is easily trivialized or explained away in reductive psychological terms is a version of censorship or untruthfulness that, ironically, many general readers are unprepared to accept.

Equally, yearning cannot be confined, either, to religions or religious institutions. "I personally feel a greater affinity to all those religions," wrote Rilke, "in which the middleman is less essential or almost entirely suppressed. . . .

"Where is the church that would not insult me with the stingy pettiness of its depictions and representations? . . . To come in contact with the church today means to become indulgent toward ineptitude, toward the sweet phrase; toward all the vast expressionlessness of its images, prayers and sermons."[19]

~

In Rilke's work, yearning is sometimes, but not necessarily, stated. It is context as well as theme, counterpoint as well as melody. It may on occasions be more powerful when it is driving Rilke's writing rather than showing itself within the writing. And it is not just yearning, either. It is also what the poetry or the poet is yearning *for*. Yearning can be sentimental. One could wish for the "good old days" that never were or for a carefree future that never will be. The Rilkean yearning is of another order and often reaches toward another realm (rarely beyond what we know as life; *within* life). The yearning that is evoked may never be "met" in any conventional sense, or need to be met. It is, itself, *something*.

What's more it is a captivating and highly potent "something," responsive to an infinitely magnetizing "something." Almost eight hundred years ago the Sufi poet Jal-al-uddin Rumi spoke of this interdependent dance of attracting and attraction in this tiny parable: "The thirsty person is moaning, 'Oh, delicious water.' The water is also moaning, 'Where, oh where is the water-drinker?'" Rumi comments, "This thirst in our souls is *the attraction exerted by the Water*. We are Its, and It is ours."[20]

Augmenting our understanding, Rumi brings "the search" to life:

> *Lovers think they're looking for each other,*
> *but there's only one search: wandering*
> *this world is wandering that, both inside one*
> *transparent sky. In here*
> *there is no dogma and no heresy.*[21]

In our own time, Dom Bede Griffiths has illuminated love and our suffering around it. "Love," he notes, "is the total giving of oneself to another."

In the familiar sphere of human relationships, such

"total giving of oneself to another" was impossible for Rilke. His personality did not allow for even the usual simulacra. Passion for his work was something else. There, no intimacy was too great. But perhaps such total giving is anyway less possible and may even be less desirable than we might wish to believe?

Bede Griffiths continues, "It is impossible to give oneself totally to any other human being. It is the illusion of romanticism that the ideal of love can be realized in any human being. This is why all romantic love when it is realistic is tragic. It consists of seeking the satisfaction of *an infinite desire in a finite, defective being.* For human love is really infinite in its capacity."[22] What Griffiths does not say, at least not here, is that human love can be, may in its purest forms always be, also infinite in its source and in its direction. Poetry must be unafraid to sit with mystery or to *be* mystery.

Sing, my heart, about gardens you've never known,
bright and remote, like gardens set in glass.
Water and roses of Isfahan and Shiraz,
sing their praises, second to none.

Show, my heart, that you will always be there.
That they have you in mind, their ripening figs.
That you blend among the blossoms and twigs
with the intensified, near-visible air.

Never make the mistake of believing
you have to renounce in order to be!
Silk thread: you too went into the weaving.

Whichever image expresses your mind,
even a scene from a life of misery,
feel the whole carpet's radiant design![23]

Poetry must also be unafraid of beauty—not consuming beauty, but feeling its power to move the observer, even in the presence of fear and in the direction of incompletion, even where dark *silk threads* mingle with those of silver and gold.

> . . . *But if the endlessly dead awakened a symbol in us,*
> *perhaps they would point to the catkins hanging from the bare*
> *branches of the hazel-trees, or*
> *would evoke the raindrops that fall onto the dark earth in*
> *springtime.*
>
> *And we, who have always thought*
> *of happiness as rising, would feel*
> *the emotion that almost overwhelms us*
> *whenever a happy thing* falls.[24]

In his discussion of beauty, philosopher John O'Donohue has this to say about Rilke's primary art form: "Poetry is where language attains its greatest precision and richest suggestion. The poem is a shape of words cut to evoke a world the reader can complete . . . The poet wants to drink from the well of origin: to write the poem that has not yet been written. In order to enter this level of originality, the poet must reach beyond the chorus of chattering voices that people the surface of a culture . . . the [poet] must reach deeper inward: go deeper than the private hoard of voices down to the root-voice."[25]

The *root-voice*, the *well of origin*, the place beyond the *private hoard of voices* is where Rilke went—and takes those ready to go. What he "excavates" cannot be found at more superficial levels of being and yet—and this is what makes his discoveries sometimes enchanting—there is an ease and naturalness often to what he is writing and to the direction of his gaze.

TERROR AND INSPIRATION

To read Rilke persistently in many ways resembles spiritual practice: faithfully and repeatedly using the familiar to release the fresh. It is easy to imagine that for Rilke himself writing *was* spiritual practice, a constant learning of what it may mean to open to the hidden dimensions of reality. The effect, though, is not always soothing.

> *See how everything unfolds: it's how we are;*
> *for we're the bliss of such unfolding.*
> *What was blood and darkness in an animal*
> *grew on in us as soul and goes on*
>
> *crying out as soul . . .*
>
> *. . . With us eternity is always passing . . .*[1]

Knowledge of the *blood and darkness*, out of which we wrench experiences of soul, can be confronting and confusing. And never more so than when we allow ourselves, trembling, to take seriously the imminence and inevitability of death, and knowledge that time, if not *eternity*, is *always passing*. This familiar life and body will not come again.

"If in the general darkness and incertitude [*sic*] that have descended upon all things human," Rilke wrote in 1919, that year of war and slaughter, "I can still see one paramount task before me, independent of all else, it is this: to use the deepest joys and splendors of life to strengthen our trust in Death, and again to make him, who was never a stranger, more known and felt as the silent sharer in all life's processes."[2]

The disturbing power of beauty in Rilke's work may be underplayed in some translations and commentaries. (Occasionally it is overplayed, as in David Kleinbard's dispiriting *The Beginning of Terror*.) Mark Burrows describes this power as "a consuming presence that is not sweet and lovely but dangerous and costly. . . ." This raises questions about how far readers may wish their yearning to extend. If I can use an almost entirely inappropriate spatial analogy, "way out there" can, with Rilke, seem all too far. Burrows continues: "The poet turns toward what he sees as the *terrors* of beauty—or, to be more precise, Rilke faces a *terrible* beauty. . . . Proximity to the divine one is marked by danger, warnings, and demands—and the proper primary response is fear, and only subsequently the construction of an orderly world of law and commentary."[3]

Earlier Burrows had speculated that "the deepest spiritual posture is that of waiting in the desolations, silences, and absences of the heart. These experiences form the depths of human consciousness . . . evoking the human longing for a presence that eludes us."[4]

Any seeming contradictions of longing and union, presence and absence, beauty and terror, themselves express the inevitable "tides" of the yearning experience. Dom Bede Griffiths evokes "the rhythm of the universe" and says—wonderfully to my mind: "God is not simply in the light, in the intelligible world, in the rational order. God is in the darkness, in the womb, in the Mother, in the chaos from which the order comes . . . darkness is the womb of life."[5]

Such tides make more sense still when remembering that for Rilke "God" is more creation than creator, limited only by our human capacity to imagine and also made more terrifying (and more desirable) by precisely that same imaginative drive. In Rilke's hands confusion itself, like "becoming," has its own mesmeric beauty.

> *You are the future, the immense morning sky*
> *turning red over the prairies of eternity.*
> *You are the rooster-crow after the night of time,*
> *the dew, the early devotion, and the Daughter,*
>
> *the Guest, the Ancient Mother, and Death.*
> *You are the shape that changes its own shape,*
> *that climbs out of fate, towering,*
> *that which is never shouted for, and never mourned for,*
> *and no more explored than a savage wood.*
>
> *You are the meaning deepest inside things,*
> *that never reveals the secret of its owner.*
> *And how you look depends on where we are:*
> *from a boat you are a shore, from the shore a boat.*[6]

The mood of exultation even in confusion—or perhaps acceptance that *how you look depends on where we are*—was never more than part of the story, although no less essential for that. In his 1900 diary Rilke shares far darker impressions that would recur throughout his writing life.

There were times, earlier, when I believed: he [God] is in the wind, but for the most part I didn't experience him as a unified personality at all. I knew only aspects of God. And many of those aspects were horrifying. For even death was only a component of his being. And he seemed to me unjust in the extreme. He tolerated unspeakable things, permitted cruelty and grief, and was massively indifferent. . . .

. . . I argued on his behalf. That his shortcomings, his injustice, and the deficiencies of his power were all matters of his development. That he is not finished yet. "When was there time for him to have *become*?"[7]

In that same period, in the same diary, Rilke writes these lines:

Whoever walks now anywhere out in the world,
walks without cause in the world,
walks toward me.
Whoever dies now anywhere out in the world,
dies without cause in the world,
looks at me.

. . . Before you possessed me,
I didn't exist. But I remain now
when you no longer see me.
Not in the words I write down;
I live on
in all that decays,
blows away . . .
I am growing more alone . . .
. . . I am a picture.
Don't expect me to talk.
I am a picture . . .

I am so old
. . . that I can't grow older.
People sometimes stand next to me at night
and hold the lamp up to my face
and know only: It isn't me . . .[8]

In each of those glimpses of Rilke's inner world, uncertainty is pronounced. It extends to God, back to the self, and onward from the self. What is not in doubt is Rilke's confidence in a significant spiritual dimension to life and within his own being. He does not fail the holy. "What do I owe Russia?" he speculated in 1920. "She made me what I am, of her my inner self was born; there is the homeland of my instinctual being, every kind of spiritual origin."[9] Much earlier he had written, "I believe that Russia will give me the words for those religious depths of my nature that have been *striving to enter into my work* since I was a child."[10] And in 1924 Rilke makes the following striking statements:

> However extensive the external world may be, with all its sidereal distances, it hardly bears comparison with the dimensions, *the depth-dimensions*, of our inner being, which has no need even of the vastnesses of the universe to be itself all but illimitable. . . . It seems to me more and more as though our ordinary consciousness dwelt on the summit of a pyramid, whose base broadens out in us and beneath us so much that the more deeply we see ourselves able to penetrate into it the more boundlessly do we seem implicated in those factors of our earthly, and in the widest sense, *worldly* being which are independent of space and time. . . .
>
> . . . I was always disposed to concede a multiplicity of shapes to the Possible. . . .

. . . Anyone who, within the framework of poetry, is initiated into the unheard-of marvels of his own depths, *or is in any way used by them as a pure and unconscious tool*, must eventually see in his wonder the development of one of the most essential capacities of the spirit. . . .

. . . It belongs to the original tendencies of my nature to accept the Mysterious *as such*, not as something to be exposed, but as the mystery that is mysterious to its very depths and is so everywhere, just as a lump of sugar is sugar in every part.[11]

The *multiplicity of shapes to the Possible* will strike a chord with many readers. It makes Rilke elusive as well as fascinating. The ambiguity itself feels true, spacious and welcoming. Weeks ago, when I was committed to give a talk that I had little energy to prepare, a writer friend said, "Use it to speak about Rilke, think about Rilke—when else would you need and read Rilke other than when you are *in* that place of ambiguity, on the edge or depleted? That's when you need him!"

It is clear from his writings and from other firsthand accounts that Rilke was highly available to the infinitely unfinished nature of a questing life. Yet it doesn't seem to be a contradiction that he was also dependent on intense experiences of inner direction or even "dictations," to be used by them *as a pure and unconscious tool*. His agonies when this kind of experience was absent for extended periods were devastating for him. Those experiences went far beyond the usual notions of "inspiration." Rilke believed some of the poems in *The Book of Hours* were "given" to him, as well as the rush of the *Sonnets* and the final "bounty" of the *Elegies*. It is tempting to suggest that he may have experienced this, whatever his undoubted theistic reservations, as the Invisible "speaking" to and through him.

Sufi teacher and mystic Hazrat Inayat Khan, almost exactly contemporary with Rilke, shares a similar view. "The artist who has arrived at some perfection in his art, whatever his art may be, will come to realize that it is not he who ever achieved anything: it is someone else who came forward every time. And when the artist produces a perfect thing, he finds it difficult to imagine that it has been produced by him. He can do nothing but bow his head in humility before that unseen power and wisdom which takes his body, his heart, his brain and his eyes as its instrument." Then, echoing something central in Rilke's thinking, but now from an entirely devotional perspective, Khan continues, "It is through man that God completes his creation." And finally: "One must not only be an artist; one must become art itself."[12]

This sense of being beauty or poetry's "instrument" echoes Rilke when he wrote: "*The Poet*, here where the great name no longer matters, one can say Dante or Spitteler—it is the same, it is the Poet, for in the last resort there is only one—undying, manifesting himself here and there down the ages, in this or that genius from whom he exacts subjugation."[13]

Only for you do poets hide themselves away
and store up images rustling and rich
and go out again to ripen by comparing,
yet still stay lonely all their lives . . .

And painters paint their images just to give
creation back to you.
Something imperishable
that you made perishable:
Everything will become eternal . . .

. . . Those who create are like you.
They want eternity. They say: Stone,
be everlasting! What they mean is:
Be yours.[14]

These are strongly felt ideas, yet tensions remain between Rilke's exceptional understanding of our need for the holy or sacred *and* his richly imagined explorations of God's mirroring need for human beings' and especially artists' creativity *so that God may come more fully into being*—or completed. This conjoined "growing" is also an "unfolding" or "ripening," words used often by Rilke, and it points to ways in which we human beings create images of God—a version of "creating God"—through the power of our experiences, longings and projections. This theme also emerges in some of Rilke's most self-revealing letters. Here he is in 1915, writing to Lotte Hepner:

Let us agree that since the dawn of time man has fash-ioned gods in whom only the deadly, the threatening, the annihilating and the terrible elements of life were contained . . . all amassed in one dense, malevolent concentration—something alien to us, if you will, yet at the same time permitting us to recognize it, to suffer it, even to acknowledge it for the sake of a certain mysterious kinship and involvement with it: this also was part of us, only we did not know how to cope with this side of our experience. . . . Could not the history of God be treated as a completely unexplored tract of the human soul, one that has always been stored and saved up, only to be neglected in the end, one for which time, will and address had been there but which, relegated to an external plane, gradually charged itself with such a tension that the impulse of the individual heart, continually dissipated by petty usage, was absolutely powerless against it?[15]

Does this leave Rilke and his readers essentially Godless, then? Should we conclude that we tune into atavistic religious needs, human needs so urgent that they generate the God we are seeking? Are we, in truth, *forsaken*? No simple answers will be found in Rilke's work.

In another letter, written exactly five years before his death, Rilke makes what might appear to be a significantly affirmative series of remarks about God's "presence." If this seems reassuring to some readers, however, then I fear that may be misplaced. And if it seems contradictory I would again suggest that a more accurate interpretation might be that it reflects an obsessive yearning that he never loses nor substantially denies, as well as an omnipresent ambivalence within his writing, to which I suspect many readers quite specifically respond. Rilke writes:

Belief!—there is no such thing, I almost said. There is only—love. The forcing of the heart to hold this and that for true, which we commonly call belief, has no sense. First one has to find God somewhere, experience him as so infinitely, so utterly, so enormously present; then *whatever* one feels toward him—be it fear, be it astonishment, be it breathlessness, be it after all *love*—it hardly matters any more. But for belief, that compulsion to God, there is no room where one has begun with the discovery of God, in which there is then no stopping any more, at whatever point one may have begun.—And you, as a Jewess, with so much most spontaneous experience of God, with such ancient fear of God in your blood, should not have to bother about a "belief." But simply *feel* his presence in yours. . . . You have, do not forget, one of the greatest gods of the universe in your descent, a God to whom one cannot just be converted at any time as to that Christian God, but a God to whom one *belongs*. . . .[16]

The desire to *belong* is palpable here; the paradoxes of yearning also remain explicit. Slowly the reader learns that ambivalence and absence demand a certain kind of stubbornness, especially when familiar versions of "faith" or "belief" won't do. Even as one yearns, one experiences frustration and constriction. Even as one experiences constriction, one also experiences the longing for connection. Letting go occurs and must recur; it's part of the surrendered reading that I wrote of in the first part of this book. Letting go of satisfying endings and of absolutes: there is honesty and truthfulness, even liberation in that.

In one of his last poems, written in French as many of his poems were, Rilke writes:

All my farewells are made. So many partings
have slowly formed me since my childhood.
Yet I come back. I start again;
this honest return frees my gaze.

All that remains is that I should fill it
and my joy will be guilt-free always
for having loved the things resembling
those absences that teach us how to act.[17]

All spiritual teachings of any seriousness make it plain that we mature as much through the losses (*farewells*) and absences in our lives that *teach us how to act* as through what is more welcome. "Joy is the ultimate achievement of which human beings are capable," Rilke wrote. Joy is "timeless from the beginning."[18] But in the world of "time" where I am writing and you are reading, there are also sorrows, losses and the need for repeated convalescence. My sense is not that Rilke is "teaching" this perennial lesson in this late poem so much as reflecting it—as well as reflecting upon it.

The piercing quality of much of Rilke's writing far transcends its aesthetic power, as mighty as that is. Thinking about this, you may want to consider what, precisely, is "pierced" as you read. It may be your daily defenses against deep feeling, or perhaps *noticing*—and especially the vulnerability that this emotional disturbance causes, even when we long for it. Such arousal of spirit as well as feeling is difficult to describe abstractly. It may not be that until we surrender or submit to where the poems are taking us, until we are indeed *pierced*, that we will comprehend just how defended we routinely are against deep feeling and perception, and how limited by habit our assumptions and expectations may have become. There is a parallel here, surely, with another kind of inner disturbance: falling in love. That too takes us to the cusp between beauty and loss, joy and fearful desolation. When love "strikes," when we are "swept off our feet," it is in part because that other person—the object of our love—wakes and exposes our longings. But even as we project them outwards, isn't it also that the other person or, rather, something within that other person, is waking our own fragile, innocent innerness? As we *fall*, we come to know ourselves differently and maybe better—yet rarely without an accompanying rush of poignancy. *Pierced*, we grow more vulnerable and more truth-abiding. We inhabit the truth of how love shakes as well as sustains us—and we see with horror how transitory mortal love is, even until death. Our own mortality is freshly etched; the mortality of our loved ones bites even deeper. The very transitoriness of life becomes naked and more precious.

Gaston Bachelard quotes a story taken from an edition of Rilke's letters published in France in 1934. "One very dark night, Rilke and two friends perceive 'the lighted casement of a distant hut, the hut that stands quite alone on the horizon before one comes to fields and marshlands.' This image of solitude symbolized by a single light moves the poet's heart in so personal a way that it isolates him from his companions. Speaking of this group of three friends, Rilke adds: 'Despite the fact that we were very close to one another, we remained three isolated individuals, *seeing night for the first time.*'"[19]

Like a parable, this glimpse literalizes and universalizes the desire for connection that is everywhere in yearning. It also brings to life the heightened self-consciousness and isolation that yearning may simultaneously provoke. And, again like a parable, it points to the gifts that come with darkness, as well as the losses.

WAYS OF KNOWING

In the Mundaka Upanishad, a little older than Moses's tablets, levels of knowledge are defined: "There are two kinds of knowledge, a lower and a higher. The lower is the knowledge of the four Vedas and such things as pronunciation, ceremonial, grammar, etymology, poetry, astronomy. The higher knowledge is the knowledge of the Everlasting . . . that which the wise name the Source."[1]

"Lower knowledge" is, for most readers, safe ground, although many who are expert in some corner of its illimitable territories may feel insulted that "lower" is used to describe what was so hard won. For all that, it is "higher knowledge," with its inherent lack of distinct signposts and its inclusion of the Absolute while deliberately avoiding absolutism, that is far more easily dismissed by contemporary well-fed minds. But this is to miss the adventure that "higher knowledge" may sometimes offer: its perils, uncertainties and thinned air. Earlier I offered examples from Dom Bede Griffiths and Plotinus writing about exactly this, and it remains relevant not only to a more surrendered, "inward" way of reading Rilke but also to understanding better the yearning that might underpin such reading, with its roots somewhere far deeper than "culture" or even instinct.

Yeats was writing in the pre–Second World War world of the 1930s when he noted, "It pleases me to fancy that when we turn toward the east, in or out of church, we are turning not less to the ancient west and north . . . our genuflections discover in that East something ancestral in ourselves, something we must bring into the light before we can appease a religious instinct that for the first time in our civilization demands the satisfaction of the whole man."[2]

These lines from Goethe's *West-östlicher Divan* express something similar:

> *God, He is the East!*
> *God, He is the West!*
> *North—and Southern lands,*
> *Rest in the peace of His hands.*

Two distinct levels of "knowing" also emerge in this widely loved poem from Rilke.

> *Sometimes a man stands up during supper*
> *and walks outdoors, and keeps on walking,*
> *because of a church that stands somewhere in the East.*
> *And his children say blessings on him as if he were dead.*
>
> *And another man, who remains inside his own house,*
> *stays there, inside the dishes and in the glasses,*
> *so that his children have to go far out into the world*
> *toward that same church, which he forgot.*[3]

Do any of us *not* know how tempting it is to remain inside the tidy familiarity of house, dishes, glasses, and to leave exploring beyond the world of "things" to later generations? Or how lonely it can be to "keep on walking" and to have one's children "say blessings" in our absence, or to sit shiva? *Keeping on walking*—opening to visionary and potentially transformative moments—can be confronting as well as sought for. It is easy to understand why some of Rilke's readers may want to turn away from all that's unconsoling. What will fit onto a fridge magnet or greeting card is enough for some, even when it means they miss that drive to wholeness which must, as Joseph Campbell famously wrote, "say yes to everything," and accept the tides of darkness with those of light.

It anyway seems fair to acknowledge that relatively few people are likely to be concerned with the more elusive levels of knowledge and that even those who do will sometimes actively yearn "in reverse"; looking also for what is more familiar, concrete and self-evident. Perhaps it is surprising to know that this was occasionally true of Rilke. Despite regarding his writing as "self treatment," in 1912 he was writing, "Never have I looked more passionately than in the last year toward those who pursue some good, regular occupation which they can always do, which depends more on intellect, brain-power, understanding, skill—whatever it is—than on those mighty tensions of one's inner life over which one has no control. . . . Only by . . . some great aberration, probably, can art proceed from nature."[4]

> To glorify the world: *love makes no claim less*
> *than this on hearts: loved, lover—who is who?*
> *A nameless something praises here the Nameless,*
> *as birds the season they're vibrating to . . .*[5]

High and deep may be the same direction. Both can make one dizzy.

~

Theologian R. C. Zaehner places the distinction between differing levels of knowledge within a religious framework. "It should be remembered that the Hindus and Buddhists . . . base the claim for the truth of their doctrines on experience. In mystical experience, they would say, the human soul reaches certainty that it is immortal since it is merged in the universal spirit or Brahman in which all sense of individuality is lost. . . . The experience cannot adequately be put into words, for it is an experience of eternity, and words [concepts, arguments, theories] can only describe what is limited by time and space. In the mystical experience of *samadhi*, however, subject and object are done away with; knower, knowledge, and known are all one. The experience cannot be seized or fastened down by rational thought, for it is a form of 'knowledge' to which the mere discursive intellect cannot attain."[6]

Words quoted earlier from *The Book of Hours* return forcefully.

> *God speaks to each of us as he makes us,*
> *then walks with us silently out of the night.*
>
> *These are words we dimly hear:*
> *You, sent out beyond your recall,*
> *go to the limits of your longing.*
>
> *Embody me . . .*

As familiar as those lines have become over countless readings, as I type that ardent call, *Embody me*, it catches me by the throat. For a moment I have no more need to breathe. *Yes*, I feel myself responding. But to whom? And to what?

Rilke offers something marvelous in this early work which is also timely. With a characteristic absence of preliminaries, he writes of a divine being who is both unknowable and intimately present, both freeing and in urgent need of freedom. What's more, he does so with his signature intensity. The intensity of our own yearnings is *met*. Perhaps we did not know that we yearned. Perhaps we even now have no idea what we are yearning for—or if "yearning" is the word to fit and describe the experience. Nonetheless, with quicksand strength, Rilke draws us to a place that may be as familiar as it is nameless. For the "no time" of this poem, absence recedes. The reader is not just "in" a poem but "in" an awesome presence, a presence that has, Rilke assures us, cared about us as "he makes us" (as we come into being, in this familiar bodily, incarnate form), and who continues to care as he walks with us "silently out of the night" of our prenatal self.

Do we have a prenatal self? What does "self" mean now, away from the familiar contexts of personality and being? Is this "self" in the Upanashadic sense not *der Geist* (mind or spirit) but *die Seele* (soul)? This silence is less than total. It seems there are words we have "dimly hear[d]." A passionate divinity is imploring us to live passionately. The bodiless One pleads:

> *. . . Embody me.*

Rilke offers us a poem that itself offers a promise, encompassing the range of human experience without artifice or pretense.

Flare up like flame
and make giant shadows that I can move in.
Let everything happen to you: beauty and terror.
Just keep going. No feeling is final.

Let everything happen to you. . . . Find God *where he is*: not in the light only, also in the darkness—those *giant shadows that [the divine] can move in.* Find God or the divine dimension of existence where *we* are: not in the light only, also in the darkness. Trust the chaos; it is essential to the All.

"The chaos is in God. Creation is chaos," writes Dom Bede Griffiths. "That is why discovering the darkness is so important . . . enlightenment is the union of this divine reality with the chaos of life, of nature, of matter, of the world. . . ."[7] And elsewhere: "When the mind . . . goes beyond images and concepts, beyond reason and will to the ultimate Ground of its consciousness, it experiences itself in this timeless and spaceless unity of Being."[8]

Rilke's poem sings the divine promise of union, and the longed-for promise of unconditionality. Sheep *and* goats are called, not separated. Shadowed by ignorance and fear, we can nevertheless find the eternal in the now. We have only to *flare up like a flame*, risking brightness bright enough to cast a shadow; risking living a flawed completeness; risking a brave surrender.

Let everything happen to you: beauty and terror.

Echoes resound here of familiar teachings, including the First of the historical Buddha's Four Noble Truths. In life there is suffering (*dukkha*). Worse is ignorance and terror *about* suffering, and most especially about the suffering we experience in the face of our own fragility. Then comes a reminder of the teaching that's at the heart of Christianity:

that we will have our sorrows, our losses, regrets and humiliations. *And* we have the capacity and chance to rise up again: the promise of resurrection. Life triumphs over death. *Just keep going. No feeling is final.* In other words, and back to Buddhism again, everything in life is transitory except the eternal that is eternally present.

"Good" is what we most desire. That will pass, as sorrow will. So how consoling it is to know that there is no final feeling and there is no "final."

The mysterious but profoundly reassuring sense of unity that Rilke lures us with is an echo of what's to be found in countless sacred texts, like this verse in the *Bhagavad Gita*: "I am the ritual and the worship/the medicine and the mantra/the butter burned in the fire/ and the flames that consume it."[9] The song of Oneness sings exultantly. In the Psalmist's voice now: *See that I follow not the wrong path and lead me in the path of the eternal.*[10]

What will help us to see that we already are on *the path of the eternal*; that however blind to it we may be, there is no other path? What courage would it take to live as unreservedly as we are being invited to do? And what will help us to subdue the greatest terror of all: *that our lives don't matter*? The poem continues, its promises accumulating with each rereading.

Flare up like flame
and make giant shadows that I can move in.
Let everything happen to you: beauty and terror.
Just keep going. No feeling is final.

Don't let yourself lose me.

The "voice" is urgent here as well as profound: *Don't let yourself lose me.* (Stay mindful. Stay aware.) In fact, it urges, remember not the mystery only, but also *who and what you are.*

> *Nearby is the country they call life.*
> *You will know it by its seriousness.*

> *Give me your hand.*

Throughout, the poem remains personal and builds in intensity. Remember where you have come from, it implores (and to where you will return), as you enter *the country they call life.* And how will you know "life" when you get there?

> *You will know it by its seriousness.*

Like so many of Rilke's explicitly spiritual poems, this one relies for its power on an affirmation that human life is, itself, an unparalleled gift, as serious as "serious" can get; gratitude floods in. This gift is also daunting. Relying only upon our limited cleverness ("lower knowledge") we can feel too small. We are right to feel small. How should we manage? How will we survive? As the poem ends, intimacy prevails along with hope. The poet of solitude assures us: you are not alone. God speaks.

> *Give me your hand.*

Within this mesmeric and deceptively simple poem, many of the greatest consolations of spiritual life reach the reader. Years after the Russian trip with Rilke that inspired the writing of *Hours*, Lou Andreas-Salomé described the God of those poems as "Russian." She continues, "This Russian

God does not reign as a strange abstract authority. . . . He
cannot prevent or improve all things; he can only represent
closeness and intimacy for all time. . . ."[11]

Andreas-Salomé's view is one possibility among many.
Regardless, in those few lines key themes emerge almost
like presences—not to be "thought about" or worried
over, but realized.

They include the genesis of our being and of being
human; awareness of "soul" taking human form; the
"forgetting" of the soul as it becomes preoccupied in the
physical world; a promise that the divine is to be found in
the shadows as well as the light; the certainty that divine
qualities can only be lived out through our human efforts,
and especially through our kindness and consideration
of one another; the risks of living in and through an
awareness of the eternal presence of love.

These are the treasures of a spiritual response. In that
context, the poem seems almost to confirm: "You know
this. All the mind needs to do is remember." Those lines,
and Rilke gives us many at least somewhat like them, speak
freely to the religious impulse common to humankind,
however varied its forms. Yet what is so striking is the
spaciousness of the poem. How can it be simultaneously
intense and spacious, personal and universal, immediate
and timeless? It can be. It is. And in being what it is, it
"speaks" in a way that effortlessly engages those readers
more used to and drawn to the spaciousness of Eastern
spiritual and some Western mystical poetic experiences
than the constrictions of Western rationalism.

It is a powerful example of the intensity of yearning,
free of even a whiff of dogma or religious piety. What's
more, the depth of spiritual assurance it conveys gives
few clues about Rilke's own far less assured belief system,

and certainly goes little toward clarifying one of the most fascinating paradoxes in Rilke's life: that he could feel so deeply about spiritual matters and yearn so nakedly, yet remain in some essential way unmet.

In Rilke's hands even an elusive or absent God can be described with great tenderness. ("I rustle like a bush in which a great wind is stirring and I must let it happen to me."[12]) Or this:

> *I love you, you softest of laws*
> *which ripened us in the wrestling;*
> *you great homesickness which we could not overcome,*
> *you forest from which we never emerged,*
> *you song which we sang with every silence,*
> *you dark net*
> *which seize, fleeing, our feelings.*
>
> *You began yourself with an infinite immensity*
> *on that day when you made us,—*
> *and we are so ripened in your suns,*
> *so widened and so deeply planted,*
> *that now you can complete yourself*
> *within people, angels, and madonnas in a quieting way.*
> *Let your hand rest on heaven's edges,*
>   *and endure mutely what we do darkly to you.*[13]

Rilke yearns for God off and on the page; he also turns his back. He turns his back on a presence and toward an absence. He praises. He excites through the directness of what he writes. And still ambivalence must be accepted.

Pray: to whom? I cannot tell you. Prayer is a radiation of our being suddenly set afire; it is an infinite and purposeless direction, a brutal accompaniment of our hopes, which travel the universe without reaching any destination. Oh, but I knew this morning how far I am from those greedy ones who, before praying, ask whether God exists. If He no longer or does not yet exist, what difference does it make? My prayer will bring Him into being, for it is entirely a creative thing as it lifts toward the heavens. And if the God that it projects out of itself does not persist at all, so much the better; we will do it over, and it will be less shabby in eternity.[14]

For the moment it may be better to refrain from using the word *belief*, deformed as it is within us, in order not to upset right away the innocent proximity to god.[15]

And here is Rilke again, in related mood, speaking to the divine in its Orphic shape now:

Silent friend of such great distances, feel
your breath and how it expands the room.
Let yourself ring out among rafters hidden
inside the dark belfries. What depletes you

will turn to strength through this nourishing.
Go forth in this transforming: entering and leaving.
What is your greatest experience of suffering?
If what you drink is bitter, make wine of it.

On this night, be magical power in great excess
as you go by the way of the cross in your senses;
be the meaning held within this rare encounter.
(Sei in dieser Nacht aus Übermaß
Zauberkraft am Kreuzweg deiner Sinne,
Ihrer seltsamen Begegnung Sinn.)

And when the earthly realm has forgotten you,
to the quiet earth say: I flow.
   To the rushing waters say: I am.[16]

~

In the introduction to her translation of *Das Stunden-Buch,*
American scholar and priest Annemarie Kidder notes that:
"Toward the end of the 'Florentine Diary,' Rilke emerges
not as the self-seeking artist but as one who sees the need
to share his findings so as to help others free themselves
from the dark fetters within. In conversations with other
boarders at his hotel, including with a Russian woman,
he discovers an inner force able to comfort and lend hope
to others. 'I feel,' he says, 'as if I had to convert all those
who hesitate and doubt; for I have more power within
than I can manage to hold in words, and want to use it to
free people from their strange fear, the same fear I escaped
from.'" Extrapolating from this Kidder adds, "The role
of the artist, then, is to free people from their fears, to
prepare the way for the birth of 'some force.'"[17]

There is no questioning the spiritual force in Rilke's
work. Even his doubters rarely doubt that. There is no
questioning, either, that his words, images, imaginative
brilliance and insights may bring hope. (Sometimes they
bring confusion.) However, my understanding of Rilke's
own quite explicit testimony is that there is too much
concrete purposefulness and utility in what Kidder is
proposing. At the time she is pointing to, Rilke was still
in his early twenties and preoccupied with his inflamed
feelings about Lou and Russia, but neither then nor later
did Rilke write to teach or "help." The service he offered
was to poetry itself; what readers take from it is secondary.
When Rilke famously wrote, You *must change your life,*

he was not, I believe, suggesting that we readers should change our thinking. Rather, I suspect that *life* is exactly what he meant. And *life*—with all its messy emotions and entrails—is never, in Rilke's work, an intellectual construct only.

"Life is severe and unyielding like the stepmothers and evil queens of the fairy tale," Rilke wrote in 1906, "but it also harbors those sweet and diligent forces that ultimately will finish the tasks for those who are patient and good but who cannot master them alone."[18] In 1911, when Rilke was barely known to readers limited to English, but appreciated widely in France, Aline Mayrisch wrote a critical essay that included a comment that Rilke ". . . thinks with his heart, which is tormented by a Pascalian thirst for the absolute." This comment appears in H. F. Peters's biography of Rilke, where Peters goes on to say that, "Many years later [French poet] Paul Valéry used an almost identical phrase when he said that, although he could not understand the language of Rilke's poetry, he 'divined' its meaning."[19]

Rilke wrote because writing *was* living for him; he had no choice. But again, this was a reflection of *his* needs, not ours.

"There can be no question, none whatsoever, of making 'helpful' books," he wrote in a letter to Nanny Wunderly-Volkart, late in 1925. "The help must not be located *in* the book but at best in the relation between the reader and the book . . ."[20] And again, in 1925, to Arthur Fischer-Colbrie: "I never read what my works call forth among the critics . . . these voices do not seem to me to belong among those reactions that I would have to take into consideration again . . . Even at twenty-three, at the time of the *Book of Hours*, I ceased bothering about applause or disapproval, and since then individual voices at most have reached me which, whether they applauded or rejected or were undecided, work back into life and (unlike mere criticism) are resolved in it."[21]

When Rilke writes, as in the sonnet quoted above:

Let yourself ring out among rafters hidden
inside the dark belfries

he retrieves more from the experience of suffering than any simple-minded reminder of what suffering is. (Or the dictum attributed to Nietzsche repeated so painfully often: "What does not kill you makes you stronger.") Rilke's words plunge us into the truth of life: life and death, suffering and joy, despair and hope, darkness and light, back to back—always. They echo lines from Rumi: *The cure for pain is in the pain. / Good and bad are mixed.* Rilke's poetry calls to those depths of experience as well as understanding within the reader. It sings to the reader: *Be* the mystery. *Be* the meaning discovered at the crossroads of your senses. Remember the mystery. And even to the supposedly inanimate earth (that "lives in us"): speak. Dare to be. Dare to flow. In the presence of rushing water, testify and say: *I am.*

On this night, be *magical power in great excess . . .*
be *the meaning held within this rare encounter.*

And when the earthly realm has forgotten you,
to the quiet earth say: I flow.
To the rushing waters say: I am.

Easy conclusions cannot be drawn here, nor "knowledge" easily claimed. "A God comprehended is no God" is a famous statement made in the eighteenth century by the great hymn writer Tersteegen, echoing the earlier thirteenth-century German mystic Meister Eckhart: "Whatever we can say God is, God is not." And, again from Eckhart, and with even greater relevance for this reading of Rilke: "Man's last and highest leave-taking is leaving God for God."

In a world surfeited with words about God, Rilke's implicit invitation is not to *comprehend* God; God is not for comprehending. We are returned to the fourth-century Eastern Christian mystic Gregory of Nyssa, who said, "The divine nature . . . transcends every act of comprehensive knowledge, and it cannot be approached or attained by our speculation. Men have never discovered a faculty to comprehend the incomprehensible; nor have we ever been able to devise an intellectual technique for grasping the inconceivable."[22]

Rilke's invitation is not to *grasp* but to *see* and to be transformed by seeing. But if we include here Ramakrishna's remark: "At the break of day [God] disappears into the secret chamber of His House,"[23] then it becomes necessary once more to ask: to see what? And how? Rilke points toward. He suggests. He holds up a light and takes it away again. He may also shine light into his own eyes or in some direction where his light cannot reach.

Halfway through his life, in 1900, Rilke wrote in his diary: "What we experience as spring, god views as a fleeting, tiny smile that passes over the earth . . . Even when taken together, all the springs that you and I have experienced are not enough to fill even one of god's seconds. The spring that god is supposed to notice must not remain in the trees and meadows but somehow has to assume its force within people, for then it takes place, as it were, not in time but in eternity and god's presence."[24]

Notice, he is saying as he writes of spring that it *has to assume its force within people*. *Notice*, he is saying as he steps beyond the familiar and literal to assure us that this force-forming *takes place, as it were, not in time but in eternity.*

Notice. And again: *notice.* In that same year, and once more in his diary, he wrote:

> *And again my deep life rushes louder,*
> *as if it moved now between steeper banks.*
> *Things seemed ever more akin to me,*
> *all images more intensely seen.*
> *I've grown more at ease with the nameless—*
> *with my senses, as with birds, I reach*
> *into the windy heavens from the oak,*
> *and into the small ponds broken-off day*
> *my feeling sinks, as if on heavy fishes.*[25]

A superficial reading of the diary entry or even the poem above—a poem announcing his fidelity to his *deep life*—might condemn them as romantic. And those dangers are present. The end of the nineteenth and early years of the twentieth century was a time when Rilke was more than usually flooded with idealizations, not least about the women in his life and what his feelings for them were revealing to him about life more generally. It was, however, Rilke himself, much later—when writing from Muzot to a friend in 1923 about his *Sonnets*—who pointed out that his work "actually often concerns the most delicate, that which lies *on the borderline of what can barely be expressed.*"[26]

The notion of "borderline," with its mighty undercurrents of trespass and transgression, jumps off the page. But dare one comment? A typically brilliant observation from American writer Annie Dillard is relevant now: "Emotional impact and simplicity are two virtues which traditional fiction may possess but which nevertheless strike textual criticism dumb."

Avoiding the parameters of "textual criticism"—as I am also wishing to do—Dillard then asks: "How can prose be said to penetrate and dazzle? How can it call attention to itself, waving its arms as it were, while performing metaphysics behind its back? But this is what all art does, or at least all art that conceives of the center of things as insubstantial: as mental or spiritual . . . If you scratch an event, you get an idea. Fine writing does not actually penetrate the world of familiar things so much as it penetrates what, for lack of a better term, we might call the universe. . . ."[27]

Rilke himself writes, "Sometimes I myself wrestle for the meaning that *used me as an instrument*, in order to burst through in human form, and the light of some parts I myself own only in unique blessed moments."[28]

And when the great rush of the final stages of the *Duino Elegies* came, after a decade of anxious waiting, Rilke wrote from Muzot to Princess Marie von Thurn und Taxis-Hohenlohe, chatelaine of Duino Castle, where the *Elegies* had begun: "So, this is what I survived for, through everything. Through all of it. And that, after all, was what I needed. *Only* this . . . Finally there is 'something.'"[29]

In a more muted but still significant way it takes confidence for a reader to inhabit and to be inhabited by "something," by words moving from the page and through one's heart as well as mind, sifted through one's own experiences and carried into the most elemental levels of one's consciousness and being. To "welcome" a writer in this Rilkean sense, and to be "used" by what the writer is saying, indicates a deep engagement, an authentic response to the primal command inscribed on the Temple of Apollo at Delphi: "Know thyself."

Literature traditionally had a vital role to play in the discovery of self and "the fullness of its potentialities." *What are poets for?* Exploring the processes of inspiration, allowing oneself to be "used" and transformed by them—as a writer or as a reader—demands humility as well as risk. Its rewards, however, may be of a literally different nature from those emerging out of a more conventionally distanced approach. Those rewards may shift one's boundaries and expectations about what writing can achieve and even the exhilarating prospect of what reading, as much as writing, may be *for*.

SEEKING BEAUTY

Irish scholar Joseph O'Leary sets the scene: "When we think of 'beauty' in connection with modern literature the two names that spring to mind are those of Yeats and Rilke. As the poet Sidney Keyes (1922–43) remarked, these great figures, straddling the nineteenth and twentieth centuries, retrieved arcane lore from a sort of *Ultima Thule* of Romanticism. But they did so in order to present it anew to the world under the problematic conditions of modernity."[1]

There is undeniable beauty in Rilke's writing for all that "beauty" is as dense with paradox in his work as belief is. Beauty arises from the work; what's more, the work directly reflects and expresses the power and meaning that beauty had for Rilke. Yet this word—like *belief, God* and *love*—is in dire need of emancipation. Describing the impact on Rilke of walking into an art gallery and being so affected by an archaic statue that the moment gave birth to his sublime *Sonnets to Orpheus*, another Joseph, Joseph Phelan, editor of Artcyclopedia.com, comments on that miracle of deep noticing and then appropriately mourns that beauty and reflection upon beauty ". . . were always a part of the philosophical enterprise [yet] for the past half-century . . . contemporary analytic philosophy—which is to say, philosophy as practiced in most academic departments in the Anglo-Saxon world—has largely turned its back on this kind of investigation."[2] In considering Rilke, it is impossible to ignore that absence or pretend it doesn't matter.

Joanna Macy is a widely published writer who, late in her career and, I suspect, as a labor of love, teamed up with poet and psychologist Anita Barrows to translate many of Rilke's most-loved poems, some beautiful examples of which are included here. The depth of Macy's interest means that she can't be seen as a typical reader, yet what she describes perfectly captures what I have heard others say as they reflect upon the effects of reading Rilke's poetry. "I felt a sense of release, as if I had been let out of a cage I had not known I was in. Rilke's images lent some pattern, even meaning, to a life I thought had failed in its spiritual vocation."[3]

Macy's experience is a recent example of a timeless phenomenon. In *The Enneads* (1.6,2), Plotinus writes: "When the soul sees anything of its kin [the divine] or trace of that kinship, it thrills with an immediate delight, takes its own to itself, and thus stirs anew to the sense of its nature and of all its infinity."

John Armstrong has written at length about beauty. It is he who made the editorial insertion "[the divine]" above, and he comments: "The less damaged the soul, the less it is corrupted by matter, the more quickly and intently this kinship is recognized, the more ardently the soul cleaves to what it has encountered, and the more adequately it is healed—and so the process of becoming ourselves continues.

"This thrill, this sense of recognition, is what we call the 'experience of beauty.' To find something beautiful is to register the kinship between the object and the most important part of oneself—one's soul. . . . In the encounter with beauty the soul sees more of itself."

Armstrong makes this clearer still by using as contrast the specter of ugliness or noise or "fear for the well-being of a person one loves" as experiences that go "directly against our deepest longings."[4]

Our deepest longings are not readily assuaged by the relentlessly "rational," however brilliant. We need beauty as much as we need meaning: sometimes the two are inseparable. We need to be able to create beauty, even if simply, and we also need images, ideas and symbols that lift our spirits as they engage our minds. We need to live imaginatively in order also to live completely. Such images, ideas and symbols connect us to a greater sense of wholeness within ourselves and possibly beyond ourselves. George Steiner writes of Rilke's *Sonnets* particularly that in them "language mediates with delicate precision on its own limits; the word is poised for the transforming power of music."[5]

The idea of beauty must remain ambiguous in Rilke's writing, but this does not mean that it is not worth circling. Hans-Georg Gadamer takes us back to Plato: "Plato describes the beautiful as that which shines forth most clearly and draws us to itself, as the very visibility of the ideal. In the beautiful presented in nature and art,

we experience this convincing illumination of truth and
harmony, which compels the admission: 'This is true.'"[6]

~

The stillness that communion, as well as beauty—or per-
haps the "gaze"—demands and occasionally enforces, is
exquisitely caught for me in this, one of Rilke's earlier,
little-known poems:

> If only it could all become once completely silent.
> If the accidental and approximate
> were muted, as well as the laughing next door,
> and if the constant noise of my senses
> didn't burden me so greatly in my waking—:
>
> then I could imagine you all the way to
> your edges in a thousand-fold thought and
> claim you—if only in the moment of a smile—
> and thus offer you as a gift to all that lives
> like a word of thanks.[7]

Rilke's poem captures and expresses something of the same
immense thought as this, from Saint Augustine of Hippo,
written in what we now call North Africa as the fourth
century gave way to the fifth:

> Imagine if all the tumult of the body were to quiet down, along
> with all our busy thoughts about earth, sea and air; if the very
> world should stop, and the mind cease thinking about itself, go
> beyond itself, and be quite still;
>
> if all the fantasies that appear in dreams and imagination should
> cease, and there be no speech, no sign:

Imagine if all things that are perishable grew still for if we listen
they are saying, "We did not make ourselves; He made us,
who abides forever." *Imagine, then, that they should say this*
and then fall silent, listening to the very voice of Him who made
them rather than to the voice of his creation;

So that we should hear not his word through the tongues of men,
nor the voices of angels, nor the clouds' thunder, nor any symbol,
but the very Self which in these things we love, and go beyond
ourselves to attain a flash of that eternal wisdom which abides
above all things.

And imagine if that moment were to go on and on, leaving
behind all other sights and sounds but this one vision that
ravishes and absorbs and fixes the beholder in joy; so that the rest
of eternal life were like that moment of illumination which leaves
us breathless:

Would this not be what is bidden in scripture: Enter thou into
the joy of the Lord?[8]

Yet still it needs to be asked: How afraid are we of genuine
beauty and the tenderness and vulnerability it arouses?
How eager are we to tame those feelings by distancing or
trivializing them—or our yearning selves? How defended
(and diminished) are we?

O'Leary notes that "both Yeats and Rilke knew that
they had no successors, that they were the end of the
line."[9] The word *beauty,* so frequently debased in our
postmodern world, has become virtually impossible to
define and difficult to use. Fear of sentimentality drives
this; fear, too, that one might think something beautiful
that others condemn or despise. When it comes to our
need for beauty, we are easily shamed. So perhaps beauty's

greatest "sin" is not that it is easily sentimentalized but that the complex feelings it arouses (envy, desire, sorrow?) are all too real. Either way, could it not be argued that this makes it more and not less urgent to explore beauty's authentic claims?

"Ordinary readers" still seek beauty, I believe, or many do. But they must also know that to see beauty freshly they must once more set aside preconceptions. They must also set aside self-consciousness, not least about what other people think or even what other people may be seeing, and be prepared to take up innocence.

It is a positive discipline within spiritual practice also: returning to the familiar to find the fresh; letting go of what is known; returning faithfully, regardless of whether you "feel like it"; honoring the rhythm of returning through one's simple presence. There is beauty in that kind of rhythmic attentiveness alone: the moment that is allowed its "time," rather than being rushed through, barely tasted. That is, in fact, a radical experience of beauty, dependent not on culturally conditioned notions of aesthetics, but on connection.

Crucially, this diminishes notions of "otherness." In his wholly engaging book on Goethe, John Armstrong writes of Goethe's perception of the state of his soul as "'like a sock that is being turned inside out.'" Armstrong comments: "At first glance it is a disarmingly banal analogy; nevertheless it is a revealing statement of his personal ideal of life. . . . His thoughts and feelings seek external manifestation: the inner is to become outer. And through externalization, his inner states will—hopefully—lose their fleeting, private and capricious character and be made precise, ordered and available to others."

This vivid image of one's soul being turned "inside out" works here, too, thinking about Rilke. This becomes clearer still when Armstrong goes on to describe what distinguishes authentic moments of reception: "It is obvious that we can encounter great objects—like Strasbourg Cathedral—or great individuals—like [Johann Gottfried von] Herder—and yet be untouched by them; they remain 'outside' us. Admiring them, saying that they are great, doesn't automatically enrich your inner world. Goethe is alluding to the most intimate, and elusive, aspect of experience: that in which we take possession of the things we encounter and make them our own."[10]

Deep looking was crucial to Rilke. He perceived this differently from Goethe: not that we make things "our own" only, but that they may make us "their own." Either way, he knew deep looking to be an act of union, or, more precisely, an awareness of preexistent union. Post-Rodin, and freed by the sculptor's example to respond to "things" outside himself and not exclusively to inspiration, emotion or "dictations," Rilke began to write the *Dinggedichte* (thing poems).[11] "The idea that hard, patient, laborious toil could take over the function and hasten the appearance of inspiration was an entirely new notion to Rilke, who had hitherto never dared to write unless the mood was on him," writes Rilke's early biographer E. M. Butler.[12]

This shift was liberating for Rilke in several ways. Through these poems, he is describing from the outside in (moving inwards from surfaces) "things" (including people, places, events) that had meaning for him and that, through his patient observations of their inward effect on him, and to some extent his perceptions of their "inward life," he endowed with meaning.

These processes are not dissimilar to the ideas that transformed late-nineteenth-century European painting, and this is Rilke at his most "painterly." Patricia Pollock Brodsky makes this clear: "He rarely describes a thing straightforwardly, stating color, shape or dimensions. Instead, he uses the methods of a painter . . . [and] hints at parallels in other unrelated realms, until the object stands before us . . . linked with other objects or experiences in the material world, as well as with internal events."[13]

In a letter to Lou Andreas-Salomé, Rilke elucidates the beauty in this actual process: not just in capturing what is seen but *how* it is seen. "The incomparable value of these rediscovered Things lies in the fact that you can look at them as if they were completely unknown . . . no irrelevant voice interrupts the silence of their concentrated reality. . . ."[14]

Space also plays a crucial role in these intimate processes, shown in the lines that follow, written by Rilke in 1914 and dedicated to Hölderlin, the poet who died in 1843 and who had originally asked, "What are poets *for*?"

> *Lingering, even among what's most intimate,*
> *is not our option. From fulfilled images*
> *the spirit abruptly plunges toward ones to be filled;*
> *there are no lakes until eternity. Here falling*
> *is our best. From the mastered emotion*
> *we fall over into the half-sensed, onward and onward . . .*[15]

The invitation intensifies to think about beauty itself as a "body" of ideas that we could look at *as if [it] were completely unknown . . . no irrelevant voice interrupt[ing] the silence of [our] concentrated reality.* Our conditioned entanglements and uncertainty will not then disappear, but they may be subdued. After all, *Lingering . . . is not our option.* Looking with and through Rilke's eyes, it may be possible to see and think about beauty in ways that are freshly truthful. There are two distinct reasons for this. The first is that Rilke was writing at a time—albeit at the end of that time—when to think about beauty was less problematic than it is now.

The second and more powerful reason is that Rilke inspires through beauty without draining it of its shadow, a shadow that is as essential to it as darkness is to light. Rilke's achievement here is to allow us to see clearly that the shadow of beauty is not ugliness. The shadow of beauty is loss—and especially the loss of this transitory human existence. Again: *Lingering . . . is not our option.* Death, and the little everyday "deaths" of grief, loss, guilt and disappointment, shadow our joys yet paradoxically may also intensify them.

There are many poignant reflections on beauty in the series of letters written in 1907 by Rilke to his wife, Clara, about the Post-Impressionist painter Paul Cézanne. The two shared a passion for this great artist who died in 1906, and were eagerly influenced by him. What emerges strongly in these meditative letters is Rilke's awareness of how much stillness and surrender must underpin the activity of seeing if one is to have "the right eyes." He ends one of those letters by writing, "I know a few things from [Cézanne's] last years when he was old and shabby and children followed him every day on his way to his studio, throwing stones at him as if at a stray dog. But inside, way inside, he was marvelously beautiful, and every once in a while he would furiously shout something absolutely glorious at one of his rare visitors. You can imagine how that happened. . . ."[16]

~

Perception and revelation of inner beauty characterize Rilke's work quite exceptionally. It is a direct appreciation of "soul" or spirit that is not limited to people or nature only. In much of Rilke's poetry, but perhaps especially in *New Poems*, there is an almost shocking sense of animation within "things." This evokes the child René who turned early to "things" for comfort when people failed him, or were not there. That the child could successfully project life and feelings into supposedly inanimate objects is not an unfamiliar scenario; many imaginative, needy children do something similar, making emotionally satisfying "love objects" out of blankets, teddies and other toys. For the adult Rilke, the "thingness" (spiritual force) within things was characteristically complex. Things (which may include people and ideas) are both solid and space-filled.

My room and this vastness
wake over a darkening land,—
as One. I am a string,
stretched tight over broad
rustling resonances.

Things are violin-bodies
filled with murmuring darkness:
in it dreams the weeping of women,
in it the resentment of entire
generations stirs in its sleep . . .[17]

The power of Rilke's gaze is explicit: things grow both greater and less than they previously were, simultaneously more of "something" and less of "anything." Critic Helen Sword comments: "[The] Things that make up Rilke's universe alternate between submitting abjectly to the poet's piercing gaze and exercizing a reciprocal control over their observer." Sword quotes Rilke: "'And now I must go on struggling with my Things; some of them are on my side and lie there obediently, behaving like model pupils, but most of them are [untrainable] and are having fun behind my back.'"[18]

These are the transformations in perception and experience that only art can make possible, inextricably linked with transformations of the soul achieved not necessarily in the presence of beauty but in the confidence of it.

From the height of the *Dinggedichte* period comes this exquisite still life, "Das Rosen-Innere." There is nothing explicitly "religious" about this poem and yet, like so many others, it lets us recognize the profound interconnectedness of "forms" that turn us, as well as what we are observing, "inside out."

Where, for this Inside,
does Outside exist? On what pain
is linen placed?
What skies are mirrored
in the inland sea
of these open roses,
these sublimely unworried ones . . . ?
. . . They scarcely can
contain themselves; many let themselves
fill up with inner space
to flowing over and streaming
into the days, which keep on
closing more and more completely,
until the entire summer becomes
a room, a room inside a dream.[19]

To notice, to find words for, *the inland sea/of these open roses* is something more than clever imagery. Rilke is using familiar still-life forms to slow the eye of the observer/reader, to see inside things, to turn insideness itself *out*; to move sky into a lake into a rose; to turn summer into a room and a room into a dream.

~

Neue Gedichte (*New Poems*) was published in two volumes in 1907 and 1908. Part Two of Rilke's monograph on Rodin was also written at the time. That began life as a lecture, and in it we hear Rilke say: "Reflecting on my task . . . it has become clear that I have not come before you to speak of people, but rather of things.

"*Things.* When I say the word (are you listening?), it grows silent; the silence that surrounds things. All motion subsides and becomes contour, and something permanent is formed from the past and the future: space, the great calm of things, liberated from desire."[20]

The centrality of "things" (speaking not of people but things) as well as those twin phrases, *all motion subsides* and *liberated from desire*, let us glimpse that even with and in things there is nothing to be clung to (and, essentially, no "one" to cling). Not from the *Dinggedichte* or the *New Poems* but from the *Sonnets* come examples (and there could have been so many) of how everyday assumptions, like some "things," prove, in Rilke's company, to be no more graspable than a mirage.

SEEKING BEAUTY

You who let yourselves feel: enter the breathing
that is more than your own . . .

. . . The trees you planted in childhood have grown
too heavy. You cannot bring them along.
Give yourselves to the air, to what you cannot hold.

. . . Even as the farmer labors
there where the seed turns into summer,
it is not his work. It is Earth who gives . . .

How far it is between the stars, and how much farther
is what's right here. The distance, for example,
between a child and one who walks by—
oh, how inconceivably far.

. . . Everything is far, nowhere does the circle close . . .[21]

The quote from the Rodin monograph continues, as though speaking directly to a somewhat bemused twenty-first-century reader: "No, you do not feel it [motion] growing silent. The word 'things' means nothing to you—too much and thus too ordinary—and passes right by. And in this sense it is good that I have evoked childhood: perhaps this sense of something precious, something associated with many memories, can help me bring this word home to you. . . . If kindness, trust, and the sense of not being alone could be counted among your earliest experiences, do you not owe it to that thing? Was it not with a thing the first time you shared your little heart like a piece of bread that would suffice for two?"[22]

The emphasis remains inward, but where is that? It is Edward Snow who points out that "Seldom is visual perception an end in itself, and often it is the focus of a poem's deconstructive energies . . ." Snow continues: "'As ifs' proliferate through the poetry [*Neue Gedichte*], keeping the reader's attention fixed not so much on the object world as on the zone where it and the imagination interact . . . This interanimation of object and consciousness is, finally, the great theme of the *New Poems*. . . ."[23]

Rilke's view of "things" is deepened further in this 1909 poem, "Poverty of Words."

I am so afraid of people's words.
They describe so distinctly everything:
And this they call dog and that they call house,
here the start and there the end.

I worry about their mockery with words,
they know everything, what will be, what was;
no mountain is still miraculous;
and their house and yard lead right up to God.

I want to warn and object: Let the things be!
I enjoy listening to the sound they are making.
But you always touch: and they hush and stand still.
That's how you kill.[24]

In translation the rhyme-effort of the final line of this poem jars. (*Ihr bringt mir alle die Dinge um* would more literally read: *You kill all things to me.*) Yet the poem offers a timely warning against domesticating the divine, as well as a thoughtful contrast to the more familiar Rilkean idea that we can praise and take comfort in *naming* things. (One of the best-known examples of that occurs in the Ninth Elegy: *Are we perhaps* here, *then, in order to say house, bridge, fountain, gate, pitcher, fruit tree, window. . . .*) Here, though, the poet warns against another danger, inherent in our power to trivialize and censor. "Knowing everything" is not a virtue for this poet of questions. Noise, invasiveness and certainty may prevent us from *listening to the sound [that things] are making* and from entering their space or becoming spacious in their presence with necessary humility.

Rilke's warning is timely.

⁓

The movements here are among presence, absence and essence. B. D. Barnacle calls this Rilke's "spatial mysticism" and says, "The presence/absence of objects is crucial: the space surrounding an object, the calm silence [the gaze], reveals their presence. Contemplating the presence leads to a revelation of the object's essence. Essence is the soul or spirit or inner reality of a thing: presence is how this inner soul is manifested."[25]

Beauty, then, is not necessarily found where one expects it, or how. Awareness is also needed of the innate contradictions of "holding" something through deep looking while simultaneously recognizing that nothing in fact can be "held"—especially "essence." This letter from Rilke to Clara—itself a poem—lets us see unalloyed beauty in the presence of decay:

> Never have I been so touched and almost gripped by the sight of heather as the other day, when I found these three branches in your dear letter. Since then they are lying in my Book of Images, penetrating it with their strong and serious smell, which is really just the fragrance of autumn earth. But how glorious it is, this fragrance. At no other time, it seems to me, does the earth let itself be inhaled in one smell, the ripe earth; in a smell that is in no way inferior to the smell of the sea, bitter where it borders on taste, and more than honeysweet where you feel it is close to touching the first sounds. Containing depth within

itself, darkness, something of the grave almost, and yet again wind; tar and turpentine and Ceylon tea.[26]

The American poet William Stafford helps us think about this. "Art will, if pursued for itself and not for adventitious reasons or spurious ways, bring into sustained realization the self most centrally yours . . ."

How does art do this? I like Stafford's guess. "Art has its sacramental aspect. The source of art's central effect is one with religion's and those of other soul endeavors: the discovery of the essential self and the cultivation of its felt, positive impulses. . . . You create a good poem [not by tinkering with the poem but] by revising your life . . . by living the kind of life that enables good poems to come about."[27]

Impossible not to think of Rilke's honoring of receptiveness, a "submitting to" (*Unterwerfung*) achieved not through the intellect only but also through the senses. Impossible, too, not to return to Rilke, contemplating the aged Cézanne while writing to Clara: ". . . inside, way inside, he was marvelously beautiful. . . ."

Another contemporary philosopher prepared to *dwell* on and write about beauty is American scholar Robert Baker. He walks the borderlands between literature and philosophy and (of course!) includes Rilke in his thinking. Some of his notes on "Archaic Torso of Apollo," perhaps Rilke's best-known poem from *New Poems*, are relevant here. It seems essential, though, to read that quite extraordinary poem first.

We never knew his legendary head
in which those apple-eyes ripened. But
his torso glows still, like a lamp dimmed
in which his gaze, lit long ago,

holds steady and gleams. Otherwise the surge
of his chest could not blind you, nor could a smile
run through that slight twist of the loins
toward the mid-point where potency once thrived.

Otherwise this stone would stand deformed and shortened
under the shoulders' translucent fall
and would not glisten like wild beasts' fur:

and would not burst forth from all its edges
like a star: for there is no place here
that does not see you. You must change your life.[28]

In this poem's presence—and it is a presence: *there is no place here/that does not see you*—it is effortless to believe that a stone could *burst forth from all its edges/like a star* and, experiencing that, to accept that to change one's life (one's vision of life and therefore one's living of it) is not a choice; it has become inevitable.

Baker comments upon ". . . a power recovered from the mystery of ruins . . . a power to strike the reader like a star, to radiate the reader with an erotic aura, to stare at the reader with the force of a prophetic command or a call to conversion . . . a transformative wandering at once evoked and performed by language."[29]

Is this *power,* or the allurement evoked by this power, just another way of saying *beauty*? Perhaps it is, but not simply. The poem does quite wonderfully "stare at the reader," an awesome achievement given the headlessness of its central image.[30] What is also thrilling is the sense of beauty as a potent evolutionary principle "ripening" within the poem and within the gazer's perception.

The beauty in Rilke's writing is at least sometimes reflective of wisdom, often hard won. The beauty that's inside Cézanne is beauty that *sees*. It sees beyond children's facile cruelty as they throw stones and beyond one's aged "ugliness," even beyond the everywhere-imminence of death. It is beauty that sees itself. Such depth of seeing is not a matter of "wishing," "hard work" or "genius." In Rilke it was all those things—*and* it was an expression of inner development or "evolution."

Writing to his lover "Merline" (Baladine Klossowska) in 1921, Rilke considers the *Duino Elegies* and their long gestation. This period of time (1912–22) dramatically illustrates how dependent Rilke remained not on hard work only, or conscious looking, or even constant writing—throughout that time he *was* writing—but on something far less tangible. Rilke writes:

> The *Elegies* themselves (or whatever it was that was once given me) were only the result of an inner constitution, an inner progress, of a purer and more extensive becoming of my entire interrupted and shaken nature. That is why I was so startled when you recently referred to the *Elegies* as a "work"—and why (oh forgive me!) I nearly reprimanded you.
>
> Understand me: so strongly do I belong to and serve my work—I cannot in any way draw it forth—which is why I was so moved by [German writer Waldemar] Bonsels' words that no extreme state can achieve more than that of "readiness"—it is for readiness that I am constantly struggling.

Here we may appear to be moving far away from the Rodin notion of *Travailler, rien que travailler,* but "readiness," the poise it suggests and the focus it demands, is essential to work that begins from the inside out. And what allows this "readiness" of inspiration and perception? Rilke continues: "The most distant influences that reach us when we stand within the constellation, unperturbed by chance, caprice, desire, or resistance!"[31]

These *most distant influences* return us to images of ripening: to the images themselves and to ideas maturing from within, in ways that cannot be forced but only trusted and anticipated. That's part of readiness. What I am attempting to describe is subtle and far from precise. Some lines from the ancient *Tao Teh Ching* may make it clearer: "Only simple and quiet words will ripen of themselves/ For a whirlwind does not last a whole morning . . . The softest of all things/Overrides the hardest of all things./ Only nothing can enter into no-space."[32]

Rilke himself had written of *what ripens into fruit deep within us, behind all stir and agitation.* Here is an example from the Second Elegy:

> . . . *Like dew from morning grass*
> *we relinquish what is ours as easily as steam from a warm dish.*
> *O smile, where are you going? O upturned glance:*
> *gone in the glitter of a fresh splash, and its little ripple across*
> *the heart . . .*
> *nevertheless, that's what we are. Does the great world we*
> *dissolve in*
> *taste of us, then? Do the Angels really*
> *recapture only the radiance that's streamed out from them,*
> *or sometimes, by mischance, is there a bit of our being*
> *brought back?*[33]

Heat cannot be contained within a steaming dish. It rises because it must. What is most intimately and intrinsically ours must rise—has to rise—similarly. And does the world, then, taste of us?

Another poem follows, written shortly before Rilke left Paris in 1914. It, too, shows what looking can achieve: beauty dependent not on things being "pleasant" or conventionally "beautiful" but on the truthfulness of seeing *what is*. The consolations of beauty even, and sometimes especially, in the presence of ambiguity "ripen" when observed. That is the power of the gaze. It changes what is seen; it changes the viewer also. Steady unguarded looking is itself a practice of stillness. Poetry through Rilke's eyes also creates stillness.

> *Heart, whom will you cry out to? More and more alone,*
> *you make your way through the unknowable*
> *human beings. All the more hopeless perhaps*
> *since it holds to its old course,*
> *the course toward the future,*
> *that's lost.*
>
> *Happened before. Did you mourn? What was it? A fallen*
> *berry of joy, still green.*
> *But now my oak of joy is breaking,*
> *what is breaking in storm is my slowly*
> *grown oak of joy.*
> *The loveliest thing in my invisible*
> *landscape, helping me to be seen*
> *by angels, that are invisible.*[34]

This lament records near-unbearable loss. Again, the emotional power of Rilke's writing dominates, as emotion does in music. We feel (not simply "hear") the darkness in the beauty. So many avoidances in Rilke's life—*but not here.* Wolfgang Leppmann writes that "It is one of the clichés of literature, formulated in Germany by Goethe in the second part of *Faust* and in a famous sonnet by the Romantic poet August von Platen, that beauty is a near neighbor of what is terrible and too powerful for us to bear face-to-face."[35] In this poem, the heart is unheard, echoing the cry of the First Elegy: *Who if I screamed out/would hear me amid the hierarchy of angels?* The "slowly grown" (hard-won) "oak of joy" is breaking. These are dramatic images but what may move the observant reader even more is the berry of joy, still green as it falls. It is the berry that "writes" the mesmeric sorrow of incompletion . . . which itself "carries" the yearning for wholeness.

Rilke wrote the poem just weeks before the outbreak of war. He had recently experienced a personal ending that caused him considerable grief. Almost forty, and in the midst of a crisis about his own abilities and the elusive source of his inner inspiration, he had begun a notably intense love affair with the pianist Magda von Hattingberg, almost instantly renamed by Rilke as "Benvenuta"—the Welcome One. The welcome was not to be long-lived. Their relationship is, predictably, charted in transparently self-revealing letters,[36] and presages the outpouring of letters and similar hothouse feelings about five years later between Rilke and "Merline," the painter Baladine Klossowska.

The personal loss was hard for Rilke and Benvenuta. Far more gravely, the reality was impending that it was not just berries but countless thousands of young men who would fall, still green, never to "ripen" or mature, never to have even a brief reign as an "oak." The image offers a startling reminder of impermanence, yet is itself buried in a relatively minor poem and easily trampled.

To "see" something of genuine beauty, or to see the beauty in the everyday, is to risk being moved: moved on from the person you were to the person you may become. The languages of analysis may not only miss that experience, they may also miss the point. This becomes clearer still when Edward Snow reminds us that Rilke believed "his poetry spoke for itself." Snow continues: "He distrusted commentaries as dilutions and foreclosures of the individual's reading experiences. When a friend wrote to him that she felt the key to one of the *Sonnets to Orpheus* lay in the idea of the transmigration of souls, he responded, "You are thinking too far out beyond the poem itself . . . I believe that no poem in the *Sonnets to Orpheus* means anything that is not fully written out there, often, it is true, with its most secret name. All 'allusion' I am convinced would be contradictory to the indescribable 'being-there' of the poem."[37]

My own remarks about impermanence and young men dying "unripe" may be just as marginal to Rilke appreciation. "Being-there," in the presence of the poem itself, is everything. And that has to be firsthand rather than received. What an exciting paradox emerges: that yearning is not simply a reaching-after but is possibly most fully experienced when surrender is risked in the here and now. This demands not so much the scholarly practice of reading "well" as the spiritual discipline of reading freshly.

In the Seventh Elegy, Rilke writes:

Life *here is magic. Even* you *knew that, you girls*
who seemed deprived of it . . .
. . . For each of you there was an hour, perhaps
not even a full hour, but between two intervals
a space not marked by the measures of time—,
when you had an existence. *Everything.*
        Veins filled with existence.
But we so easily forget what our laughing neighbor
neither covets nor confirms. We want to lift it up
and show it, even though the most visible happiness
only reveals itself when we've transformed it, within.

Veins filled with existence. Beauty is itself an invitation to
engage, to *transform [happiness]*—or perception itself—*within.*
Within is critical here. Beauty causes a pause: shifts the space
between the viewer and the viewed. Rushed by, beauty
loses meaning as well as value. Reception continues to be
as critical as creation. It is the experience of beauty that a
yearning reader seeks; not the abstract idea of beauty, but
that mysterious "something" that inhabits them as they
inhabit it. The Seventh Elegy continues:

. . . Nowhere, Love, will World exist but within. Our lives
pass in transformation. And all the while the outside realm
diminishes. Where once a solid house endured,
some abstraction shoves itself into view, completely at ease
among concepts, as if it still stood in the brain . . .

Reading those lines, we do more than witness. We *live* the
tension between transformation and abstraction; we live in
the space of true feeling.

Our lives pass in transformation. And all the while the outside
realm diminishes.

The Elegy reflects now on the world in which Rilke was writing and, presciently, on the world in which we read. Again we are in the presence of a lament, this time on a grand scale:

> *The Zeitgeist is building vast reservoirs of power, formless*
> *as the thrusting energy it wrests from everything.*
> *It no longer recognizes temples. Furtively we hoard*
> *what the heart once lavished. Where one of them still survives,*
> *an object once prayed to, revered, knelt before—*
> *it's already reaching, secretly, into the invisible world.*
> *Many no longer see it, yet without the gain*
> *of rebuilding it greater now, with pillars and statues,* within![38]

These paradoxes are brave. This makes it more and not less interesting when novelist and critic J. M. Coetzee comments on the passage immediately above, and the lines from the same *Elegy* given a little earlier:

> As a critique of the capitalist-industrial dynamic and the mental habits that go with it, this is, by the time of the 1920s [when Rilke was writing], neither novel nor particularly interesting. It comes out of the reading of Carlyle, Nietzsche, Ruskin, Pater and Jacob Burckhardt that Rilke did when, as a young man, he was most deeply under the influence of Lou Andreas-Salomé; it is of a piece with his youthful enthusiasms for Russia as the home of true spirituality and for *quattrocento* Florence. . . . It is only when the Rilkean project of rescuing the world by the act of absorbing and transforming it (*Verwandlung*) . . . is dramatized in the speaking voice that it begins to come alive.[39]

Coetzee is writing about Rilke in the context of reviewing Gass's *Reading Rilke*. Context is important to Coetzee, as it should be. His lengthy response to the book is largely enthusiastic although he regrets that Gass did not write more fully about "the back-to-nature movement that was so strong in German-speaking countries at the turn of the century, divorced from which Rilke's nude sunbathing, vegetarianism, etc., look like mere personal fads."[40]

There is anyway never a shortage of "personal fads" when it comes to Rilke. Yet when it comes to reading Rilke and writing about his work, Coetzee seems to overlook that Rilke himself is an inescapable "context." Of course he did not write in a bubble. He is a product of his time and the intellectual and social influences of that time and place. He could be nothing but European, hovering on the cusp between Romanticism and Modernity, strikingly influenced by Christianity even when he has turned his back on it. That's self-evident. What is just as evident is that Rilke is living from and certainly writing from a state of "passionate inwardness" that is at least somewhat resistant to the usual "time and place" logarithms. It is difficult even to imagine Rilke offering a refreshed "critique of the capitalist-industrial dynamic and the mental habits that go with it," as fascinating and as necessary as that might be. And perhaps not so necessary, given Coetzee's list.

Elsewhere in the same essay Coetzee puts the *Elegies* and "the story or myth of their composition" together and calls this package "surely the great poem of our age about being called as a poet."[41] *Called*, with its explicit sense of destined vocation, is powerful here.

Judith Ryan throws a different light on Rilke's inner lineage. "Upon first reading, Rilke's *Duineser Elegien* [*Duino*

Elegies] seem new and strange; the imagery they develop is astonishing and almost surrealistic . . . In Rudolf Kassner's *Die Mystik, die Künstler und das Leben* [*Mysticism, Artists and Life*] there is a characterization of Blake's prophetic books that could almost pass for a description of Rilke's *Duino Elegies.* . . ."[42]

An earlier note from Yeats gives an even more exciting glimpse of inward context: "Between 1922 and 1925 English literature, wherever most intense, cast off its preoccupations with social problems and began to create myths like those of antiquity, and to ask the most profound questions. I recall poems . . . which have displayed in myths, not as might some writer of my youth for the sake of romantic suggestion, but urged by the most recent thought, *the world emerging from the human mind.*"[43]

Coetzee, too, questions whether they (the poems, and the "myth" of their creation) are "imaginable in the absence of the notion of an artistic destiny." However, in his own quotation from the Seventh Elegy, Coetzee omits these final two lines:

Many no longer see [the Temple], yet without the gain
of rebuilding it greater now, with pillars and statues, within![44]

Those lines offer an understanding of what Rilke was simultaneously mourning and offering. *Life here is magic.* I see them honoring hard-won inner knowing, however tentative that may be, over received opinions. I see them standing up for something admirable and true, even when the powerful world "outside" diminishes or ignores that. I see them honoring inwardness itself, without displaying the least contempt for "outwardness." And I see beauty in that.

Nowhere, Love, will world exist but within.

Is there an echo here from the first lines of the Buddhist scripture, the Dhammapada?

We are as we think.
All that we are arises with our thoughts.
With our thoughts we make the world.

This does not diminish or deny *visible happiness*, or make the outer world illusory. Rather, it points to the force of perceptions arising within us, often unconsciously, projected into and onto the "outside" and lived out through countless choices.

I also see that whatever is "novel" or "interesting" in Rilke will arise from virtually any direction but a social analytic one. Starved of their meaningful intention, starved of passion (this *is* poetry), the lines become ridiculous or turn to dust. Quite apart from those questions of inspiration and inner knowing, Rilke is mourning aloud the hardening of some structures, "vast reservoirs of power," and more ambivalently mourning the loss of others. *It no longer recognizes temples. Furtively we hoard/what the heart once lavished.*

Could Rilke have more accurately described our own time, and the desolations as well as hopes of today's yearning readers? The *vast reservoirs of power* that Rilke identifies are intellectual and religious as much as they are ideological. This doesn't delegitimize them or our interest in them. Rilke's own gaze, however, is elsewhere.

Affirming that is the poet's task.

MYSTICISM AND THE HOLY

Perhaps one of the questions that most engage Rilke's readers is whether he can be read, thought about or "claimed" as a mystical poet or as a mystic. But would this change the way in which they/we read him? His biographer J. F. Hendry writes, "Everything for Rilke was enclosed in the unity of life, even the forces that lead us out of it: love and death. Our fear is created by what we see as the finality and singleness of death. But in love and death we must, he thought, surrender ourselves completely and become a twin being, or all beings. In love and in death we enter the general life, are given the power of decision and called upon to use it."[1]

This describes a mystical vision, and yet my own sense is that *mystic* is not a word we have any right to apply to Rilke. He had his own impatience with early twentieth-century ideas of mysticism, saying, "Mysticism I read as little as philosophy."[2]

This may be only half true. Rilke "read avidly about religious, mystical and occult traditions," according to Judith Ryan.[3] Yet perhaps he associated mysticism with excessively pious forms of Christian thinking and practice, of which he had a visceral loathing, although that would do mysticism a poor service. The term can be maddeningly imprecise and yet the "yearning" within Rilke's work—sometimes genuinely mystical in flavor—as well as the response it awakens in readers, demands at least some understanding of mysticism's historical and cultural resonances. The real problem with calling Rilke a mystic is, perhaps, that it claims too much. Mark Burrows sees in Rilke's work a "mystical aesthetic . . . but without any hint of sentimentality."[4] This is the context, I believe, within which much of his current popularity has developed.

Wittgenstein's famous comments on mysticism are helpful generally and are particularly apposite in thinking about Rilke: "It is not *how* things are in the world that is mystical, but that it exists. (6.44) . . . We feel that when all possible scientific questions have been answered, the problems of life remain completely untouched. Of course there are then no questions left, and this itself is the answer. (6.52) . . . What we cannot speak about we must consign to silence. (7)"[5]

As I look around the edges of silence, one of the clearest definitions of mysticism that I have found comes from Evelyn Underhill. Her classic work, *Mysticism*, was published in 1911, a time when theosophy and anthroposophy were introducing Eastern wisdom and mystical thinking and experience to a small though enthusiastic audience in Europe, the United States and beyond. But this quote is from one of her minor works, *Concerning the*

Inner Life, where, quite casually, she refers to mysticism as a "sense of the Eternal as a vivid fact."[6] Yet it must also be said, "fact" is rather less than vivid in contemporary mainstream thinking.

"It is a commonplace of twentieth-century thought that we live in a world that is demystified by the force of technology and the rationalized thinking that grounds such technology," writes Thomas A. Carlson.[7] He seems to be echoing the statement I shared much earlier in this book from Max Weber, Rilke's contemporary: "The world is disenchanted."

A "demystified" or "disenchanted" world increasingly worshipful of and dependent upon technology, feeding a mechanized view of life and people, was genuinely a place of horror for Rilke. He felt the losses that implied deeply. So without rewriting Rilke, or posthumously telling him what he *really* thought, it is tempting to suggest that his apparent disregard for mysticism, or for writings about mysticism, may genuinely be a problem of cultural context and definition, as well as an example of his marked preference for experience over theory and engagement over detachment. To define too closely may be to miss the experience, the unfolding, illimitable understanding that:

> . . . *truly being here is so much; because everything here*
> *apparently needs us, this fleeting world, which in some*
>   *strange way*
> *keeps calling to us. Us, the most fleeting of all.*
> *Once for each thing. Just once; no more. And we too,*
> *just once. And never again. But to have been*
> *this once, completely, even if only once:*
> *to have been at one with the earth, seems beyond undoing.*

And so we keep pressing on, trying to achieve it,
trying to hold it firmly in our simple hands,
in our overcrowded gaze, in our speechless heart,
Trying to become it. Whom can we give it to? We would
hold on to it all forever . . . Ah, but what can we take along
into that other realm? Not the art of looking,
which is learned so slowly, and nothing that happened here.
Nothing.
The sufferings, then. And, above all, the heaviness,
and the long experience of love,—just what is wholly
unsayable . . .[8]

We know Rilke through words. Words are the medium through which we discover and live alongside him, through which we *press on.* James Rolleston makes a relevant point in his study of Rilke's early poetry: "Words belong to the public as well as the private realm, and a poem is an intersection between the two worlds, a summation in public terms of feelings that are in origin private. We can never know the feelings themselves, only their public expression."[9]

Throughout Rilke's writings are countless examples of an exceptionally *public expression* of a *sense of the Eternal as a vivid fact.* In a letter written from Munich in 1915, reflecting on the Spanish landscape and specifically Toledo, Rilke says: ". . . there the external thing itself—tower, hill, bridge—already possessed the incredible, unsurpassable intensity of the inner equivalents through which one might have been able to represent it. External world and vision everywhere coincided as it were in the object; in each a whole inner world was displayed, as though an angel who embraces space were blind and gazing into himself. This world, seen no longer with the eyes of men, but in the angel, is perhaps my real task. . . ."[10]

This world, seen no longer with the eyes of men, but in the angel, is perhaps my real task. That is an immense statement. It is tempting to take Rilke completely seriously. Eight years later, in 1923, he is writing: "I do not like the Christian conceptions of a Beyond, I am getting farther and farther away from them . . . to me they contain . . . the danger not only of making those who have vanished more imprecise to us and above all more inaccessible—; but we too, drawing ourselves yonder in our longing and *away* from here, we ourselves become thereby less definite, less earthly . . . so *deep* is death implanted in the nature of love that . . . it nowhere contradicts love . . . where would this always secret influence be held more secure than *in* us?"[11]

Then in 1925, the year before his death, comes this to Witold von Hulewicz: "We of the here and now are not for a moment hedged in the time-world, nor confined within it; we are incessantly flowing over and over to those who preceded us, to our origins and to those who seemingly come after us. In that greatest *open* world all are, one cannot say 'simultaneous,' for the very falling away of time determines that they all *are*. Transiency everywhere plunges into a deep being. . . ."[12]

These are profound revelations of Rilke's *public expression* that grow through rereading. The limitations they implicitly reveal of more conventional ideas about belief, knowledge and truth—or mysticism—seem aptly illustrated by this dream from a six-year-old boy, retold in Roberto Gambini's *Soul & Culture.*

Gambini quotes the boy: "'I was alone in the desert, and I saw a light. I followed it. I came to a tent, which was lit from inside, and there I was to meet God. But can you imagine? He did not shake hands with me. So, in the end, I could not see his face. Maybe it was not God at all.'"

The context of this "knowing" or experience becomes clearer when Gambini shares with readers that the boy is at a school that provides no religious teaching of any kind. He then adds: "But this boy is dreaming the fundamental question of Western theology: Can man see God?" Gambini continues: "How do we know if we have been in God's tent in the desert? Maybe it is an invention. Maybe it is true. How do we know? Must we believe in something we do not know? Or can we know? When the BBC reporter asked [Carl] Jung, 'Do you believe in God?' Jung answered, 'Believe? I don't need to believe. I know.'"[13]

~

The difficulty of using limiting means to describe the unlimited is captured in these lines from Plato's Seventh Letter: "Concerning these things there is not, nor will there be any treatise written by me. For they do not at all admit of being expounded in writing as do objects of other [scientific] studies . . . Only after long, arduous conversance with the matter itself . . . a light suddenly breaks upon the soul as from a kindled flame, and once born keeps alive of itself."[14]

As one reads Rilke, a light may indeed *break upon the soul*. That this is not true *always* does not make it less true *sometimes*. Listening to how people speak of Rilke, and the value they give to lines they have learned by heart, I am convinced that this experience is central to his continuing attraction. Rilke offers the reader something rare and truly beautiful—while being ever mindful of the shadow of death. Exactly this *breaking upon the soul* is what can keep readers simultaneously sated and hungry: ravenous for more of what may not actually be on the page or, indeed, on any page.

My eyes already touch the sunny hill,
going far ahead of the road I have begun.
So we are grasped by what we cannot grasp;
it has its inner light, even from a distance—

and changes us, even if we do not reach it,
into something else, which, hardly sensing it, we already are;
a gesture waves us on, answering our own wave . . .
but what we feel is the wind in our faces.[15]

The obvious needs to be stated: reading Rilke will always achieve what reading (or writing) *about* Rilke never can. Poetry—authentic poetry—will always achieve what theory can't. Poetry provides a dwelling place big enough for hearts and souls as well as minds. It invites in. It connects and reconnects. It allures. "For Rilke [the] transformation of matter into language is the very function of poetry itself," writes Jungian analyst Robert Romanyshyn. "Before the word is spoken, we pause, take a breath, and draw into ourselves the open world that lies there in front of our gaze. And then, inspired by the world we speak. But who is speaking in this moment? Is it us or the world? For Rilke there is no doubt—or is it no separation? Is this a defiance of space between 'world' and 'word'? 'Earth,' he asks, 'isn't this what you want: an invisible/re-arising in us?'"[16]

Extending our idea of what the "word" is or may be, and, indeed, what the "world" is or may be, Romanyshyn adds more when he writes: "In the Ninth Elegy Rilke offers us the image of the wanderer who brings back from the mountain slope not some handful of earth [that is *unsayable*] 'but only some word he has won, a pure word, the yellow and blue gentian.'"[17]

The physical and sensual are essential music in the song of the spiritual: they sing of the inseparable. Abstractions are not enough. We live in bodies; our insights need embodiment. The daring dialectic that Rilke proposes between the human and the divine is never more outrageously demonstrated than in the last lines below.

Just as the winged energy of delight
carried you over many chasms early on,
now raise the daringly imagined arch
holding up the astounding bridges . . .

. . . Take your well-disciplined strengths
and stretch them between two
opposing poles. Because inside human beings
is where God learns.[18]

Denn im Manne/will der Gott beraten sein. Inside human beings/ is where God learns. "It is through the language of the heart that the world of nature is transformed," writes Romanyshyn. One could add: the world of nature also transforms heart— and soul. A mystical invitation, Rilke shows, is not to cease attending to this world, this life; it is to *attend* more fully. It is, in fact, to be ever present, even to yield.

A god can do it. But tell me, how does
a human follow him through that narrow lyre?
The mind divides. Where two heart-ways
cross, there can be no temple for Apollo.[19]

In 1916, Rilke wrote a letter to a friend that is especially relevant to the yearning reader: "The question whether art is to be experienced as a great forgetting or as a greater insight is perhaps only apparently to be answered in one sense or the other; one could imagine both might be correct, in that a certain abandonment reaching to the point of forgetfulness could constitute the first step to new insights, as though the shift were to a higher place of life, where a riper, larger awareness, a seeing with rested, fresh eyes, then begins. To *remain* in forgetfulness would of course be entirely wrong. . . ."[20]

To live fully on this earth, to allow earth to live fully in us, Rilke is surely saying, we have to move with the elemental forces in our lives, rather than defending ourselves against them or living as though abstractions were enough. Through Rilke's eyes, we see that they are not enough. This most sensual of writers calls us through the internal sounds and rhythms of his writing as well as his imagistic gifts and deep feeling to know more of the world that "arises in us": to be one with its troubled and troubling beauty. He calls us to observe the rhythms of nature also—tides in and out; moon waning, moon waxing—and to move with, not observe only, the rhythms of our own existence. This gives us essential permission to face the truths of transience. It invites us to risk the terrors as well as the bliss of love, in its most divine and inclusive sense.

Withholding ourselves from knowledge about the nature of life is not possible in an existence where we are called to "know thyself." Poetry is unafraid of love, or ought to be—even in the hands of a poet who seemed to retreat from the human demands of love, often. It is impossible, in fact, to think about poetry or mysticism, or the imaginal worlds, without also thinking about love.

Similar assertions were made in Rudolf Otto's classic text, *The Idea of the Holy.* Otto was born in Hanover in 1869, a few years earlier than Rilke, and died in 1937. His book is formal, yet a plainly yearning writer shines through. It's a book I find difficult and ceaselessly rewarding. In it, too, "deep calls to deep." The book's depth meets the depth of the reader's own dilemmas and questions as Otto urges the reader to disentangle the functional from the sublime, and obligation and duty from the authentically holy.

The title of his book borrows from and responds to Plato's idea of the good. In *The Idea of the Holy*, Otto reminds his readers of Plato's argument that the deity had to become identical with (or *is* identical with) the "Idea of the Good" and thus "rational and conceivable."

"Godness" seems harnessed to goodness. But Otto goes on: ". . . the most remarkable characteristic of Plato's thought is that he himself finds science and philosophy too narrow to comprise the whole of man's mental life. . . . No one has enunciated more definitively than this master-thinker that *God transcends all reason,* in the sense that He is beyond the powers of our conceiving, not merely beyond our powers of comprehension. 'Therefore is it'"—and now Otto is quoting Plato directly—"'an *impossible* task both to discover the creator and father of this whole universe and to publish the discovery of him in words for all to understand.'"[21]

Annie Dillard expresses this with the force of poetry: "Every day is a god, each day is a god, and holiness holds forth in time. I worship each god, I praise each day splintered down, splintered down and wrapped in time like a husk, a husk of many colors spreading, at dawn fast over the mountains split.

"I wake in a god."[22]

What Rilke also shows is that holiness has no other way to "hold forth" in our physical universe but in time. Our time. The mere fact that we face an "impossible task"—to get back to Plato—does not make it worthless. It makes it holy: restoring worth. Rilke says: *it is not too late/to dive into your increasing depths/where life calmly gives out its own secret*. The secret of life, he repeatedly says and shows, is within life: your life, and mine.

THE SOUL'S SEARCH FOR GOD

Rilke was never conventionally religious, nor was he ever a "religious" poet. He loathed institutionalized religion and especially Christian religiosity, condemning what he perceived as its suffocating dogmatic certainties and obsession with sin. He could be fierce, too, about the God in whom he never easily believed.

> *His caring is a nightmare to us*
> *and his voice a stone.*
>
> *We would like to heed his words,*
> *but we only half hear them . . .*
>
> *. . . We feel endlessly distant,*
> *though we are endlessly bound by love . . .*

Rudolf Otto, taking a Christian perspective, suggests that "unity" (with God) is "the very signature of the mystical."[1] A yearning for unity plays its part in Rilke's writing, but no more so than distinctness and distance, and love remains difficult. In the poem above, distance, disappointment and love play a mournful game, the worst kind of peekaboo. The poem continues with this startling paradox:

> . . . *That is Father to us, And I—*
> *I should call you Father?*
> *That would open a gulf between us.*
> *You are my son.*[2]

Rilke turns the doctrine of the Trinitarian "father" on its head. Nevertheless, he also had strong feelings about the "son," and particularly disliked the idea of Christ as divine sacrifice or the intercessionary coming "between" human beings and a God who was for Rilke, if "anything," always more holy spirit, more "wind," than father.

> . . . *Listen to the wind's breathing,*
> *that uninterrupted news that forms from silence . . .*[3]

In his diary of 1900, Rilke wrote: "For young people . . . Christ is a great danger, the all-too-near, the coverer of God. They grow accustomed to seeking the divine with human means and measures. They pamper themselves with the human and later freeze to death in the bleak summit-air of eternity . . . They become disillusioned with the half-akin that does not astonish them, does not cause them terror, does not rip them out of their daily lives. They learn to content themselves, when to know God they would have to grow immodest."[4]

This is a provocative statement, less for its outburst about Christ than for its suggestion that young *people* should *not* seek the divine *with human means and measures* but instead look to the *bleak summit-air of eternity* and a God who can *rip them out of their daily lives.* The transcendent was, for Rilke, within life. This statement does not necessarily confound that view so much as again point to an unlimited view of what "life" is.

Half a lifetime later, in 1923, Rilke wrote to Ilse Jahr: "The Christian experience enters less and less into consideration; the ancient God outweighs it infinitely. The view that one is sinful and needs ransom as premise for God is more and more repugnant to a heart that has comprehended the earth. Not sinfulness and error in the earthly, on the contrary, its pure nature becomes essential consciousness, sin is surely the most wonderfully roundabout way to God,—but why should *they* go on pilgrimage who have never left him?"

And then: "The strong, inwardly quivering bridge of the Mediator has sense only where the abyss is granted between God and us—, but *this very abyss is full of the darkness of God*, and where one experiences it, let him climb down and howl in it . . . all the angels decide, singing praises, in favor of earth."[5]

To understand these ideas more comprehensively, and their effect on our own reading, it is helpful to return to Rilke's earliest days and years in Prague.

At the time of his birth, Phia, his feverishly religious mother, was still mourning his dead infant sister. Rilke himself was born almost two months prematurely and his mother describes this event in a letter written on 17 December 1922.[6] First Phia recalls the icy weather in Prague that December of 1875, with snow "mountains high," and then, despite the cold, how she and "Papa" went to visit her own mother and after that, in high spirits, how they bought a little golden cross for their expected child. She goes on, remembering her unexpected labor, the midwife arriving and then: "At midnight—the same time that Our Savior was born—and it was almost Saturday—you at once became one of Mary's children! Consecrated to the gracious Madonna . . . Small and delicate was our sweet little boy, but splendidly developed—and as he lay in bed in the forenoon, he received the little cross—so Jesus was his first present."[7]

Jesus was not a present that Rilke could accept gratefully. The mother who alternately gushes and withdraws, the piety that forms sugar crystals on whatever remnants of authentic spirituality might have been sustaining, the romanticized rear-vision view of family life, the feelings of intrusiveness that such a letter might arouse in an adult man: all this highlights what would cause Rilke to recoil from his mother repeatedly, to the end of his life. And not only to recoil from Phia but also from the religion that, in Rilke's perception, similarly sought to clutch, possess, limit and disfigure.

In a 1921 letter written from Spain to Princess Marie von Thurn und Taxis-Hohenlohe, Rilke writes: "Since my visit to Cordoba I am of an almost violent anti-Christianity. I am reading the Koran, which in certain passages assumes a voice within me that I inhabit with as much force as the wind in a pipe organ. Here [in Spain] you think you are in a Christian country, but this is long over . . . Now boundless indifference reigns here."

Then, in case the princess had not quite got his drift, or perhaps because the force of this outburst was so delightful to express, Rilke went on: "The fruit has been sucked dry; now it's time, to put it bluntly [and he does], to spit out the skins. And yet Protestants and American Christians[8] always create a new brew with this tea that has been steeping for two millennia. Mohammed was certainly the closest alternative, bursting like a river through prehistoric mountains toward the one god with whom one can converse so magnificently every morning without the telephone 'Christ' into which people continually call, 'Hello, who's there?' and there's no answer."[9]

This is the same Rilke who drew lavishly upon multiple aspects of Christian iconography and wrote a large number of poems about Christ and the Virgin Mary. It is also the same Rilke who, in his post-1906 poem "Elegy of a Nun," could write, in his "nun" persona, these silken lines of longing:

> *My life went—Lord Jesus.*
> *Tell me, Lord Jesus, where did it go?*
> *Have you seen it coming?*
> *Am I within you?*
> *Am I in you, Lord Jesus?* [10]

And, again, it is the same Rilke who wrote these lines in the poem "Before the Passion," published in his 1912 collection *The Life of the Virgin Mary*, a collection that significantly opened the way to the longed-for completion of the *Elegies*, a decade after they had begun. The "voice" is that of Christ's mother, Mary (whom we can assume to have been a teenage girl at the time of her mysterious conception):

> *Oh had you wanted this, you should not*
> *have sprung from a woman's womb.*
> *Holy ones must be quarried from mountains*
> *where hardness can be born from hardness.* [11]

The "softness" implicit in a human birth, from an ordinary woman's womb, makes for an uncomfortable and uncomforting contrast with the mythical "hardness" of a mountain birth, the birth a sculptor but not a woman can achieve. It is easy to imagine that Rilke is suggesting that softness has served Christ badly—and himself.

There are other themes here, too. The "Passion" of Christ that the poem anticipates takes the reader to Christ's agonizing moment of realization that his mission on earth was apparently to be incomplete; that he was about to die in the most terrifying way; and that neither his inner divinity nor his love for his heavenly father could save him. Jesus' "human, limited self" could not know that this event was a precursor to his overcoming death, on the third day "rising again" from death to life: in spiritual terms, from limited consciousness to unlimited consciousness.

Another fiercely dramatic poem, "Christ's Descent into Hell," moves the story on.

When it was too much, he passed out
of the body's unspeakable suffering. Rose. Stepped
*   away.*
Left alone, the darkness grew afraid . . .
. . . Nocturnal life struck him as gentle,
and like a mourning space he reached out beyond
*   it.*
But the earth, parched from the thirst of his
*   wounds,*
ripped open below him unleashing its shrieks.
He, knower of tortures, heard all hell
scream out and demand to know
if it was over yet . . .
. . . Suddenly (higher,
*   higher)*

suspended right over the middle of the boiling
    screams,
he stepped forth from the tall
tower of his perseverance: without breathing,
stood there, without a railing, landlord of agony.
    Silent.[12]

This is an exceptionally detailed, emotive account growing out of the most unrestricted feelings. Snow captures the strangeness as well as the horror in his English translation: *"suffered-out, his being exited the terrible/body of pain."* That is exactly what we call the release of death, when the pain of living is greater and more intolerable still than the pain of "exiting." Snow's startling word choices are perfect.

And yet, none of these poems or extracts should be read as theological commentary. They say most about Rilke himself. Years earlier, in April 1904, he had written to Lou:

> My mother came to Rome and is still here. I see her only rarely, but—as you know—every meeting with her is a kind of relapse. When I have to see this lost, unreal woman unconnected to anything and unable to grow old [Phia was in her fifties, hard to blame her for a reluctance to grow old—unless you were her son longing for a little maturity], I feel how even as a child I struggled to escape her. . . . I feel a horror of her mindless piety, of her obstinate religiosity, of all those distorted and deformed things to which she had clung, herself an empty dress, ghostly and terrible. And that still I am her child; that some scarcely discernible concealed door in this faded wall that is not part of any structure was my entrance into the world—(if indeed such an entrance can lead into the world at all . . .)![13]

Remembering that Phia left her husband, Josef, and in many ways also her son, René, when the boy was only nine, the "empty dress, ghostly and terrible" hangs as a reminder of reaching out for . . . and not finding. Echoes resound here again of the power of "things," of the animism that William Gass alerts us to: ". . . that all things, as well as the parts of things, are filled with life"[14]—or, in this case, emptied of it. The *scarcely discernible concealed door in this faded wall that is not part of any structure* but was Rilke's *entrance into the world* summons up a horrifying picture. Small wonder then that a mythic birth, straight from the mountain, fully formed like Athena from the head of Zeus, no mess then or later, could seem so desirable, even noble.

In some heart-attic, wrote Rilke of his mother, *she is tucked away and Christ comes there to wash her every day.* And yet the mountain does not consistently prevail. *Sometimes it happens that an earnest traveler arrives,/penetrating our hundred spirits like a brilliant flash,/showing us, trembling, a new hold . . .* Rilke was also able to assert. Fleeing fast from the god of might and power, hearing whispering that enhances and does not end an inward silence—but *reaches out* from it—a reader may lean forward, eagerly, to hear, from the praising poet of the *Sonnets* now:

> *To praise is everything! The one chosen to praise*
> *reaches out to us like ore from the silences*
> *of stones. His mortal heart presses out*
> *for us an immortal wine.*
>
> *When the god's guidance seizes him,*
> *his is the eternal voice, not dust to dust.*
> *All is vineyard. All is grape*
> *ripe for picking in the sunshine lands of being.*

No mortal decaying even in the tombs of kings
can make these songs untrue.
Not even shadows cast by gods.

This messenger is constant,
venturing far through the doors of the dead,
bowls piled high with praise-packed fruit.[15]

For all the hesitations, withdrawals and plunges into darkness and confusion, there is in Rilke's work a genuine covenant with the yearning reader. *Here* meaning is honored; *here* is consolation—*To praise is everything*; *here* are actual and immediate experiences of immanence and transcendent beauty—[reaching] *out to us like ore from the silence/of stones*; *here* "things" grow in depth and dimensionality; *here* space between things is transformed through self-understanding (and understanding what limits our conceptions of the self). And yet, the more one observes this and experiences it, the less possibility there is of "grasping" it, or of attempting successfully to colonize it through one's own analytic or critical claims.

What is also quite clear, however, is that for some readers it is precisely the love-rich, mystical or simply "yearning" qualities that are the greatest obstacles to appreciation. Introducing Walter Arndt's translations of *The Best of Rilke* (a dangerously assertive title in a volume empty of *Elegies*), critic Cyrus Hamlin, for example, praises Rilke highly. "His mature poems," says Hamlin, "are unsurpassed in the sense of mastery and consummate craftsmanship which they convey." So, technical brilliance gets a big tick. The "poet's poet," as Rilke is often called, can stand center stage. But Hamlin also warns of "a sensibility almost too painful in its intellectual and emotional subtleties" and of refinements "almost too extreme for the drawing rooms of [Rilke's] various wealthy patrons and friends."[16]

Then, just pages into the collection, Arndt himself pins the tail firmly on the donkey. Commenting on a poem called "Der Knabe" ("The Boy") from *Das Buch der Bilder* (*The Book of Pictures/Images*), Arndt also refers to *Das Stunden-Buch* (*The Book of Hours*), describing it as "a sad throwback to the mannered piety of Rilke's beginnings as a poet." There is worse to come.

"*Stundenbuch* is embarrassingly intimate with the Almighty, seriously features a persona called 'the pallid boy of blood,' and presents its three cycles under a subtitle of archaic and pretentious solemnity. . . . This retardation of Rilke's imagination and poetic practice lasted till 1905 [when he was thirty] and worried his friends. It is mentioned here because echoes and whispers of it recur in the mature Rilke."[17]

Not all of Rilke's friends were worried, then or later. Karl von der Heydt, reviewing *Das Stunden-Buch* in the *Preußisches Jahrbuch* in 1906 just two weeks after its December 1905 publication, had this to say (and how difficult it is to imagine any contemporary mainstream critic daring to be so flamboyantly inspired): ". . . the content, in its great and deep unity, raises *Das Stunden-Buch* far above that of its predecessor [*The Book of Pictures/Images*, 1902], for the theme it develops is the most powerful theme for which ever a singer's harp may sound, the most elevated theme the lyric can attain: the theme of the Soul's search for God."[18]

It is precisely this theme, *the Soul's search for God*, as well as Rilke's highly subjective response to the theme, that draws yearning readers while simultaneously arousing the kind of ire and distaste Arndt's outburst typifies. This makes it especially relevant when Otto, introducing "elements in the 'numinous,'" invites readers to direct their minds to "a moment of deeply-felt religious experience, as little as possible qualified by other forms of consciousness." The person who cannot do this, however:

> . . . is requested to read no farther; for it is not easy to discuss questions of religious psychology with one who can recollect the emotions of his adolescence, the discomforts of indigestion, or, say, social feelings, but cannot recall any intrinsically religious feelings. We do not blame such an one, when he tries for himself to advance as far as he can with the help of such principles of explanation as he knows, interpreting "aesthetics" in terms of sensuous pleasure, and "religion" as a function of the gregarious instinct and social standards, or as something more primitive still. But the artist, who for his part has an intimate personal knowledge of the distinctive element in the aesthetic experience, will decline his theories with thanks, and the religious man will reject them even more uncompromisingly.[19]

Otto's acceptance of the futility of attempting to engage someone in discussions about the transcendent when their powers of recollection are limited to *the discomforts of indigestion,* or their mind is made up in a different direction, is neither resigned nor defensive. It is admirably detached. Describing William James's attitudes of mind as evidenced in *Varieties of Religious Experience* (1904) Otto writes: "James is debarred by his empiricist and pragmatist standpoint from coming to a recognition of faculties of knowledge and potentialities of thought *in the spirit itself.* . . ."[20]

This mirrors the thinking of Thomas Aquinas: "The thing known is in the knower, *according to the mode of the knower.*" Or these memorable lines from an ancient Hindu song, reprised by Hazrat Inayat Khan:

Ah! how desirous I was to see the divine Beloved!
It is not the fault of the Beloved that you do not see;

He is before you!
It is the fault of you who recognize Him not.
Everything, whatever you see, is nothing else but
the Presence of God![21]

What is *before us*? Again, we return to the permeable issue of "kinds of knowledge." The standpoint that Otto recognizes in James is now so common as to be considered self-evidently "natural." Indeed, in a book that celebrates the centenary of *Varieties*, Jerome Bruner claims that: "James's pragmatic outlook has become so implicit in and so endemic to American thought [and Western thought more generally] that it is like the water in the famous proverb about the fish who will be the last to discover what he's been swimming in all along. James made pragmatism so self-evident that succeeding generations took it as their implicit starting point, and were lured thereafter into its less obvious implications [including] 'constructivism' or the 'social construction of reality.'"[22]

It is in this context, while steadfastly looking toward the ineffable and numinous, that Otto is urging us, his readers, to *use our minds more flexibly*. I would say that implicit in Otto's urging is a broader understanding of what "mind" is.

> *. . . You have not grown old, and it is not too late*
> *to dive into your increasing depths*
> *where life calmly gives out its own secret.*[23]

How else can we approach, much less experience, *the Soul's search for God* or the *idea of the Holy* other than through *diving* into our *increasing depths?* Spiritual insight, Otto is suggesting, cannot arise from intellect alone. In applauding that severing of limitations, I am not claiming a crude hierarchy of insight, with those who are *debarred by [their] empiricist and pragmatist standpoint* at the bottom. What I am tentatively speaking for is the idea that "knowledge" is variously acquired and that any writing of depth will be experienced just as variously. The Keatsian "negative capability" I wrote of earlier returns at one end of the continuum; a quiet "knowing" of the numinous is at its facing end; each has neither "beginning" nor "end."

"The deity of one's worship is a function of one's own state of mind," writes the mythologist Joseph Campbell. He also quotes a Hindu tantric saying that "by none but a god shall a god be worshipped." He further points out that the deity of one's worship (as distinct from "the deity," the mystery) "also is a product of one's culture . . . a metaphor, therefore, and thus to be recognized as transparent to transcendence. Remaining fixed to its name and form, whether with simple faith or in saintly vision, is therefore to remain in mind historically bound and attached to an appearance."[24]

~

It seems safe to suggest that in twenty-first-century culture, outside circles of fundamentalist thinking, there is increasing ease in speaking up for an uncertain and continuously evolving vision of the sacred, the mysterious, God, that finds its way with singular meaning into the heart of people's lives. The ways in which this mirrors Rilke's own ambivalent vision accounts for some of his contemporary popularity at least. It may even be central. I don't want to go too far here; nonetheless, there is a timeliness in Rilke's uncertainty *about* God that coexists with his persistent leaning toward and yearning *for* God, as well as the transformative beauty with which he writes about life, earth and inwardness that brings exceptional gifts to contemporary readers ready to accept them. To return to Heidegger: *To be a poet in a destitute time means: to attend, singing, to the trace of the fugitive gods. This is why the poet in the time of the world's night utters the holy.*

"[Rilke] expresses in song that which would otherwise remain unknown to us . . . and sometimes he answers to secret aspirations which were sleeping in the depths of our minds," Federico Olivero wrote just a few years after Rilke's death.[25] His words ring true, now.

"THE OPEN"

In a talk given in 1964 to activist poets, mainly from South and Central America, Trappist monk and poet Thomas Merton had this to say:

Poetry is the flowering of ordinary possibilities . . . This is its innocence and dignity.

Let us not be like those who wish to make the tree bear its fruit first and the flower afterward—a conjuring trick and an advertisement.

Let us obey life, and the Spirit of Life that calls us to be poets, and we shall harvest many new fruits for which the world hungers—fruits of hope that have never been seen before . . .

When the poet puts his foot in that ever-moving [Heraklitean] river, poetry itself is born out of the flashing water. . . .

No one can enter the river wearing the garments of public and collective ideas. He must feel the water

on his skin. He must know that immediacy is for
naked minds only, and for the innocent.

Come, dervishes: here is the water of life. Dance
in it.[1]

Poets may, indeed, sometimes be dervishes. B. D. Barnacle
calls Rilke a "shamanic poet . . . the one who can travel to
other worlds and bring back news of what goes on there."[2]
We are back to Heidegger's "traces." Some poets—Merton
and Rilke among them—are naked and innocent enough
indeed to sow and harvest "fruits of hope that have never
been seen before" (and fruits of darkness and of sorrow).[3]
What's more, it would seem that some readers, like some
poets, hunger for those fruits—and perhaps through their
hunger, call them into being.

And yet so much *gets in the way*. So much we put in
the way—and no obstacle is greater in seeing life and
being inside life than our fears of death and perhaps our
misunderstandings of what death means. The Eighth
Elegy mourns those clumsy "misses" in its great howling
call of regret.

With all its eyes the natural world looks out
into the Open. Only our eyes are turned
backward, and surround plant, animal, child
like traps, as they emerge into their freedom.
We know what is really out there only from
the animal's gaze; for we take the very young
child and force it around, so that it sees
objects—not the Open, which is so
deep in animals' faces. Free from death.

. . . Never, not for a single day, do we have
before us that pure space into which flowers

endlessly open. Always there is World
and never Nowhere without the No: that pure
unseparated element which one breathes
without desire and endlessly knows . . .⁴

"*Das Offene*" could be translated as *vacancy* or *empty space*, although in all the English-language translations I have, from Leishman (1948) onward, "open" is used. Translating may be the least of our difficulties with this dense and elusive phrase—and where it points—but Siegfried Mandel offers more depth to our understanding when he explains that "Rilke makes a distinction between two kinds of openness: '*Offen*' as the open vistas of the landscape for instance, and '*das Offene*' as a mystical concept of pure space (*reiner Raum*) or the inner-world space (*Weltinnenraum*), a silent communal space that courses through all beings."

"The Open" is a profound concept, perhaps one of the most exceptional of Rilke's gifts to his questing, yearning readers, exploding as it does conventional notions of separation between living forms within the world, and between the worlds of the living and the dead. It is extraordinarily difficult to write about, literally unavailable as it is to our usual ideas of duality. We are returned to the humility of Keats's call for "negative capability," a contentment with not-knowing, or at least "not knowing" with a certainty that might satisfy the rational mind.

We are also returned to Rilke's own call to "live into the answers," rather than grabbing onto them or creating them (out of "thin air"). Of all the forces within Rilke's writing—and the idea of the Open *is* a "force"—it is the most ineffable, and rich. Mandel continues: "Just as all beings are surrounded by an outer space that gives them a visible contour, so for Rilke there is an inner space continuum, *the other side of nature*, that forms a realm jointly for all beings." Mandel points out that this makes it possible for Rilke "to say poetically and graphically, 'I look outward and the tree grows within me,' 'Birds fly silently through us,' a maiden 'made herself a bed in my ear': the outer-viewed object (*Ding*) is metamorphosed into an inner image and the inner side of nature becomes the magic mirror into which outer representations swim dimensionless."

Referring specifically to the Eighth Elegy, some of which is given just above, Mandel comments that "Rilke's mystical open space is seen and inhabited directly by the animals while man, living in his circumscribed material world (*Welt*) of illusory reality, can only surmise from the face of the animal what the space-outside-the-world is like. . . . The animal is not aware of death; only man sees death. . . .

   "Man's destiny (*Schicksal*), Rilke laments, is always to be opposite to the inner world."[5]

> *With all its eyes the natural world looks out*
> *into the Open. Only our eyes are turned*
> *backward . . .*
>
> *. . . Never, not for a single day, do we have*
> *before us* [never are we truly awake to] *that pure space into*
>   *which flowers*
> *endlessly open . . .*

It is also Mandel who points out that Rilke's idea of the poet, or poetry, enriching "the life beyond and the inner space," reflects Plato's idea of the good: "that all things here [on earth, in the material realm] are but reflections of absolute prototypes."[6] Mandel does not relate this to Rilke's canvassing of the possibility that people—and especially artists—are "creating" God (a God "waiting to be born of the artist's alert and sensitive consciousness," as Babette Deutsch describes it)[7] but it seems possible to do so.

Mandel is not uncritical of Rilke's thinking, describing his "mythology of the realms of being" as "primitive, if not atavistic."[8] That is not the only interpretation possible, but nor is there any reason to be wholeheartedly accepting of what Rilke is suggesting. It is what it is. This is Rilke's attempt imaginatively to unify the visible and invisible worlds, the sayable and the unsayable; to hold and *witness* their existent unity poetically. The subject matter itself implicitly warns against the need for conclusions. Possibilities themselves must remain "open."

"Am I the one who might provide a correct interpretation of the elegies?" Rilke asked. "They extend infinitely beyond me."[9]

The mystical union of the soul with the divine rests without conclusion in Rilke's writing. Yearning is not the same as union; it hints at and may drive union but does not need to achieve it. What there is in Rilke is consciousness of spirit transcending form, of the temporal as coexistent with the eternal. It is this that transforms the meaning of death, as of life. *Death is a state/Of weariness and ceaseless repetition, until we begin/To grasp a fragment of eternity . . .*[10] This returns us to Underhill's definition of mysticism as a *sense of the Eternal as a vivid fact*. The same interweaving of the worlds brings angels into the perceived realm—and allows for "dictations."

～

A vivid account exists from Princess Marie von Thurn und Taxis-Hohenlohe of Rilke's experience of "receiving" the first of the *Elegies*. She writes, "A violent north wind was blowing, but the sun shone and the blue water had a silvery gleam. Rilke climbed down to the bastions [of her Duino Castle] which, jutting to the east and west, were connected to the foot of the castle by a narrow path along the cliffs. These cliffs fall steeply, for about two hundred feet, into the sea. Rilke paced back and forth, deep in thought . . . Then, all at once, in the midst of his brooding, he halted suddenly, for it seemed to him that in the raging of the storm a voice had called to him: 'Who, if I cried out, would hear me among the angelic orders?' He stood still, listening. 'What is that?' he half whispered. 'What is it, what is coming?'"

This is a moment of exceptional creative drama. She continues, "[Rilke] took out his notebook . . . wrote down these words, together with a few lines that formed themselves without his intervention. Who had come? And then he knew the answer: the god.

". . . By that evening the entire elegy had been written down . . ."[11]

Who if I cried out would hear me amid the hierarchy
of angels? And even if one of them were to take
me suddenly to heart, I'd waste away because of
that stronger presence. Because beauty is nothing
but the beginning of terror which we can just endure,
and we are amazed by it precisely in its calm spurning,
and for the way it threatens to destroy us. Each and every angel
is fearsome.[12]

The philosopher R. C. Zaehner calls the "truth" that "all is one"—so crucial in Rilke's work and particularly to an understanding of the Open—pantheistic, another way to describe nondualism. Zaehner quotes Heraclitus: "'Conjunctions: wholes and not wholes, the convergent and the divergent, the consonant and the dissonant, from all things one and from one all things.'" For readers steeped in Christian literature, a more striking parallel may come in this prayer from Christ on behalf of his disciples, also quoted by Zaehner: "Father, may they be one in us, as you are in me and I am in you."[13]

Heidegger writes of the term as meaning "something that does not block off because it does not set bounds. The Open is the great whole of all that is unbounded . . . what Rilke experiences as the Open is precisely what is closed up, unlightened, which draws on in boundlessness. . . ." Heidegger then quotes Rilke, from a letter written ten months before his death:

> You must understand the concept of the "Open," which I have tried to propose in the elegy [the Eighth], in *such* a way that the animal's degree of consciousness sets it into the world without the animal's placing the world over against itself at every moment (as we do); the animal is *in* the world; we stand *before it* by virtue of what peculiar turn and intensification which our consciousness has taken. . . . By the "Open," therefore, I do not mean sky, air, and space; *they* too are "object" and thus "opaque" and closed to the man who observes and judges. The animal, the flower, presumably *is* all that, without accounting to itself, and therefore has before itself and above itself that indescribably open freedom which perhaps has its (extremely fleeting) equivalents among us only in those first moments of love when one human being sees his own vastness in another, his beloved, and in man's elevation toward God.[14]

This is a "mighty" passage, concluding as it does with so much feeling, and such testament, "when all has been said and done," to the vastness illuminated by love. Yet however the term *das Offene* is considered, one thing is certain: Rilke was not aiming to convince. He was describing something that he was himself seeking to understand and by which he was moved. This idea inhabited him; he inhabited it. It was central to his desire to understand the forces of the Invisible and express or manifest them and to face death within life (and life within death?).

> The true pattern of life extends through both domains [death and life] . . . there is neither a This-side nor a That-side, but a single great unity in which the beings who transcend us, the angels, have their habitation . . .
>
> . . . The earth has no alternative but to become invisible—in us, who with a portion of our being have a share in the Invisible, or at least the appearance of sharing; we who can multiply our possessions of the Invisible during our earthly existence, in us alone can there be accomplished this intimate and continual transmutation of the Visible into the Invisible . . . just as our own destiny becomes unceasingly more present, and at the same time invisible, in us.[15]

An exceptional commentary on this complex notion of "the Open" comes in the French philosopher (and Roman Catholic convert) Gabriel Marcel's *Homo Viator*. His book includes two talks he gave on Rilke in 1944, two years earlier than Heidegger was asking, "What are poets for?" Marcel explains the Open as "that which surrounds created things—not however in the manner of empty space or a fluid in which they are bathed; it is the fact that the creature is finite, that it has limit, or, more exactly, it is the alternative aspect, complementary to the aspect of its limitation."

Marcel continues in a way that may at first seem oblique, but it is worth persisting. "We are not, then, concerned with the relative limit of a being . . . but with its absolute limit, with the Other, purely and simply, with the Other in its utter otherness, that is to say with God, with the creative power of God. . . . This absolutely is in the one case the mystery of inwardness, in the other that of transcendence, and of absolute space (*absolute Weite*). In either case man leaves himself behind, insofar as he is a particular being who observes, judges, covets, etc. And in so doing he fulfills his being as a pure creature. The being swells, begins to flower and thus becomes itself. The open is the direction in which this comes about."[16]

The "Open" as direction or "way" of "becoming" and perceiving, especially perceiving, may help us to see further into this dense but exciting idea. What he is describing is being more "inside" than "outside" while also conflating inside and outside! This is emphasized by Mark Burrows when he writes that Rilke's poems "lure us through his vulnerability to what he calls 'the Open,' beckoning us to live in this world with what he [Rilke] calls an essential 'defenselessness' (*Schutzlossein*)."

What's more, the poems "entice us to be addressed by the world we inhabit with often numbing indifference, invite us to confide in the word as a source of genuine communing with the 'other,' and embrace *unknowing* as a meandering path leading toward insight."[17] The emphasis on *this* world remains crucial.

Ah! What would it mean to a seeking reader to be *addressed by the world we inhabit with often numbing indifference*? Letting "the world" speak is, like letting God speak, an essential Rilkean promise but easily skirted. Does this mean taking the world seriously (and our place in it); living intimately with the world around us, as well as intimately with the world within us? I believe so.

Similar calls may be heard in a poem that Rilke wrote in Paris in 1914, two years after writing the first of what would eventually become the *Duino Elegies*.[18] This poem alerts us to a literal version of the desired psychological "openness" by contrasting the well-being of trusting animals with the horrors of the containment of a "cage" or even a "hotel room."

Rilke had, at that pre-war point, spent more time in dingy hotel rooms than in the more luxurious rooms that were to be his lot in the post-war years. At a less banal level, what the poem evokes is the gulf between unlimited consciousness (*unthinkable freedom*) and everyday limited awareness. This demonstration is stark and affecting. What is also affecting is the notion that even a partial understanding of the "Open" brings an increase of "life" to life, a chance to live more wondrously.

> . . . *Animals stepped trustingly*
> *into his open gaze as they pastured,*
> *and the caged lions*
> *stared in, as into unthinkable freedom.*
> *Birds flew straight through it,*
> *feeling its welcome; flowers*
> *gazed back into it*
> *hugely, as they do with children . . .*

. . . When he, forever waiting, sat far from home; the hotel's
disinterested, turned-aside room
sullenly around him, and in the avoided mirror
again the room
and later from the tormenting bed
again:
there was argument in the air . . .

. . . For gazing, you see, has its limits.
And the more gazed-upon world
wants to prosper in love.

Work of the eyes is done,
begin heartwork now
on those images in you, those captive ones;
for you conquered them: but you still don't know them . . .[19]

To do *heartwork* on *those images* has primary significance: it is
the making of oneself. "In a manuscript note to the poem,"
we discover, "Rilke expressed the wish to free himself
from an interior-based gazing outward and substituting
'a loving preoccupation with inner fullness'; perhaps this
would transform him into a being capable of love and a
poet capable of deeper perception. . . ."[20] *For gazing, you*
see, has its limits.

~

Das Offene and all that this elusive idea carries with it relate
in a profound way to those central notions of "inwardness."
Where does inwardness end, after all?

Burrows writes of the possibility not only of transcen-
dence "*beyond* us . . . but also *within* us," and of the Open,
as a "posture of vulnerability [steering] us beyond the
known toward the depths we yearn for." This aligns with

what John Hick calls "the fifth dimension of our nature, the transcendent within us," which, in turn, "answers to the fifth dimension of the universe, the transcendent without."[21] This idea of a mirroring "within" and "without" seems essential to even the most primitive understanding of the Open.

Poetics, Burrows also suggests, using the term as much to describe a state of mind or consciousness as what arrives and is received on the page, "honors this margin of the inarticulate not as the *limit* but as the *lure* of language . . . a longing that arises in the places of absence, in the consciousness of what is not and cannot be spoken. . . ."[22]

Is the Open, then, a vision of life in its ungraspable vastness, shedding ideas that close us in or down with false certainty, and especially shedding ideas that direct our attention away from this world rather than more courageously into it in all its mysterious depth and dimensions? This was an idea with real significance to Rilke and my sense is strong that it is essential in our thinking about him.

The sacred, even the supernatural, in Rilke's vision of it, "and therefore the poetic also," is not *elsewhere*.[23] It is not an abstraction. One need not withdraw from this world to glimpse its infinite dimensionality; one must be *in* the world, although genuinely open to it, dancing like dervishes in Merton's *water of life*, not skating on surfaces.

Wasn't it a miracle? O be amazed, angel, because we are
  the ones,
we ourselves; O you immense one, give witness to our capacities,
because my breath
doesn't suffice to render such praise. And yet we didn't squander
these spaces, so generous and ours. (How frighteningly immense
they were
that even after thousands of years gathering our feelings they
weren't yet overfilled.)

But one tower was marvelous, wasn't it? O angel, that was the
  one—
immense it was, even in your presence. It was Chartres—, and
the music
carried on further and rose above us. But not even
a lover—, oh, even if in the nearest window . . .
didn't she reach at least up to your knee—?[24]

In a letter to Elisabeth and Karl von der Heydt, written late
in 1906 during a time of rather more waiting than writing in
Capri, Rilke observed, "Not for me a monk's life in the close
association and isolation of a cloister, but rather I must see
to it that little by little I myself shall grow into a cloister
and stand there in the world, with walls about me, but
with God and the saints within me, with very beautiful
pictures and furnishings within me, with courts around
which moves a dance of pillars. . . ."[25]

"Growing into a cloister," and refusing the cloisters
created by others, is something more than a charming
or "poetic" idea. Literalizing the union between oneself
and the outer environment—or countering conventional

notions of separation between oneself and the outer world—while at the same time inviting God and the saints inward *and* expanding inner space even into infinity, is immensely expressive of an inclusive vision that is, for all that, difficult to envision.

Two examples of what could arguably be called an experience of the Open may help to make these ideas clearer, or at least demonstrate that in thinking about the Open we are meeting Rilke at his most explicitly mystical, even while this may not simplify or unify our own levels of comprehension. The first description comes from Thomas Merton. The date was 18 March 1958.

> In Louisville, on a corner of Fourth and Walnut, in the center of the shopping district, I was suddenly overwhelmed with the realization that I loved all these people, that they were mine and I was theirs, that we could not be alien to one another even though we were total strangers. It was like waking from a dream of separateness, of spurious self-isolation in a special world, the world of renunciation and supposed holiness. The whole illusion of a separate holy existence is a dream. . . . I have the immense joy of being *man*, a member of a race in which God Himself became incarnate. As if the sorrows and stupidities of the human condition could overwhelm me, now that I realize what we all are. And if only everybody could realize this! But it cannot be explained. There is no way of telling people that they are all walking around shining like the sun.[26]

The second example comes from Rilke's own life, described by him in the third person. The time was spring, 1912.

Walking up and down with a book in his hand . . . he
had the idea to seek support against the shoulder-high
fork of a shrub-like tree, and immediately he felt
pleasantly at ease and completely at rest in this posi-
tion, so that, without reading his book, he remained
totally immersed in nature, in almost unconscious
contemplation. Gradually his attention was drawn to
a sensation he had never yet experienced: it seemed
as though hardly perceptible vibrations were being
transmitted to him from the interior of the tree. . . .
He became increasingly astounded and moved by
the effect this incessant communication was having
on him: he thought that he had never felt a more
tenuous movement . . . Moreover, during the first
few seconds he had not even been able to ascertain
which of his senses was transmitting this tenuous and
universal communication to him: the state it brought
about in him was total and non-intermittent. . . .
Nevertheless, striving to define the subtlest things, he
asked himself urgently what was happening to him,
and almost immediately he found a formula which
satisfied him, saying to himself that *he had arrived on
the other side of Nature.* . . .

Nora Wydenbruck, who includes the above account in her
memoir of Rilke, comments briefly: "The spiritual value of
Rilke's experience . . . [lies] . . . in his final liberation from
the fear of death."[27]

Language, for Rilke, was primarily a tool of experi-
ence and inquiry, a "probe" sent to the outer reaches

of human imagination and experience and then beyond them. His own essential "inwardness," his engagement with esoteric ideas, his instinct for mystical inquiry and his confidence in art as the primary means through which life will be more truthfully "unfolded" or "seen," take his achievements further than the realms of the merely poetic or narrowly aesthetic, where they nevertheless also shine. Perhaps this is nowhere truer than in his dense but translucent discussions and poetic enactions of the Open.

Rilke writes, "No one has ever made beauty. One can only create kindly or sublime conditions for that which sometimes dwells amongst us, an altar and fruits and a flame. The other is not in our power. And the thing itself which goes forth indestructible from human hands is like Socrates' Eros, is a daemon, is something between god and man, not in itself beautiful, but expressing pure love of and pure longing for beauty."[28]

This is the same Rilke who, as a young man, had written religion off as "the art of the non-creative." He made this rather startling statement in his "Florence Journal," written in 1898 when he had been sent by Lou to absorb at least some of what the cultural life of Florence had to teach. He was then barely at the beginning of his accomplished writing life yet describing the unfortunately "non-creative" he said, "They become productive in prayer: they shape their love and their thankfulness and their longing and liberate themselves that way. . . . The non-artist must possess a religion—in the deepest sense of the word—even if it is only one that rests on communal and historical agreements. To be an atheist in this context is to be a barbarian."[29]

An uninhibited contempt for conventional religion and sometimes for the conventionally religious was encouraged and applauded by Lou as well as other less influential friends. And their views fell on fertile ground. Rilke needed no persuading to turn his back on conventional piety and religion. He abandoned the demands and some of the constraints (and rewards) of "ordinary life" and certainly of conventional religious thinking (and conventional thinking!) perhaps in order to liberate within his poetry that immense, alluring pull *into* rather than *away from* life that is intensely, exhilaratingly spiritually focused. His is a radical vision of what life may be and *is*, a vision that includes this perplexing view and embracing of the Open.

What Rilke also made explicit was the idea of creating God being the responsibility of artists. (Non-artists need religion; "God" needs artists.) As the artist develops, and as his or her work becomes more mature, so does "God." Here an extraordinary paradox arises: even while holding in mind those glimpses of the infinite spaciousness—and interconnectedness—of the Open, we experience in Rilke's work the severe constrictions and limitations of a vulnerable divine being.

A literal glimpse of the artist "creating" God is to be found in Rilke's *Stories of God*, a book written over a few days in 1899, a time of astonishing productivity in the life of the mid-twenties Rilke.[30] In one of the stories, "The Man Who Listens to Stones," Rilke describes God feeling so much anxiety about Michelangelo's strength and power that God, in some confusion, asks him, "Who is in that stone?"

Rilke's story continues: "Michelangelo listened: his hands were trembling. Then he answered in a muffled voice: 'Thou, my God, who else? But I cannot reach Thee.' And then God sensed that he was indeed in the stone, and he felt fearful and confined. The whole sky was but a stone, and he locked in its midst, *hoping for the hands of Michelangelo to deliver him. . . .*"[31]

The image of the *whole sky [as] a stone* is already sur-real, with its literalized heaviness and opaqueness, and its echoes of the pre-Enlightenment "home" of the traditional Judeo-Christian "God" in the sky/heaven far from where "the eye can reach." Many of Rilke's readers may agree that this God did indeed need liberating, not least from our own confining perceptions. A number of parallels with this story occur in *The Book of Hours*. In the poem that follows we can feel how intensely the poet yearns to release God from his enmeshment in matter.

In deep nights I dig for you, you treasure,
because all the superfluous things which
I saw were poverty and a poor substitute
for the beauty that hadn't yet occurred.

But the way to you is so incredibly long and
obscured, since none has lately come this way.
O, you are lonely. You are loneliness,
you heart, which wanders to distant valleys.

And I lift my bloodied hands up
from the grave into the wind,
so that they spread out like a tree.
With them I cleanse you from the room
as if you'd once wrecked yourself
with the force of an impatient gesture,
and were felled now, a scattered world,
out of distant stars as these fell softly
again upon the earth like a spring shower. [32]

There are many who would believe it blasphemous to suggest that "God" needs liberating, never mind from the "stone" of the most dense or unyielding of our beliefs. Yet others may find this initially startling proposition quietly convincing, not the liberation of "God" perhaps, but of some of humankind's impacted, "stony" ideas about God.

~

In seeking to understand this complex vision, it may be tempting to put the idea of the Open and the Buddhist notion of "emptiness" side by side to see what one might reveal about the other. But it would be unwise to run too fast toward any conclusion. Each phrase describes *a perception* of experience. Each may even describe experience itself. But are these "ways" similar? Each offers hope for a far less limited understanding of who we are and who we are becoming. Each resists absolute definition.

Perhaps Buddhism offers something less predictable but more relevant here with its traditional story of Shakyamuni (Siddhartha Gautama), the historical Buddha who lived 2500 years ago and was spiritually formed within Hinduism, that ancient and most devotional of religions. The Buddha is said not to have denied the existence of God, but rather to have regarded the "question" of God as unanswerable.

The "unanswerable"—with its own specific openness—is vivid also in Rilke's work and especially in relation to the Open. It is the most "Buddhist" of Rilke's English-language translators, the distinguished teacher Joanna Macy, who brings something particularly fresh to this discussion. In the preface to her beautiful *Rilke's Book of Hours: Love Poems to God*, Macy writes:

When I undertook meditative practice, I did not feel the divine presence, the encompassing Other to be held and supported by, that was there for the young Rilke.

Don't you sense me, ready to break
into being at your touch? (1,19)

But gradually over time, as the mind relaxed, capacities bred by my earlier Christian experience resurfaced and infused my understanding of Buddhism. The presence that I became aware of, around and within me, is apprehended through an act of rapt, silent attention, both passive and probing, like sonar. And what the presence seems to be is the web itself, the thrumming relationality of all things. [Could we see *this* as "the Open"?]

Rilke's recognition of the reciprocal nature of our relationship to God and to life itself is a poetic and profoundly personal complement to the Buddha's central doctrine of dependent co-arising, which asserts the radical interdependence at the core of existence.[33]

~

There is nothing original about the idea of the Open. Readers of the mystics will know it well. What is original and sometimes startling is how Rilke names it and, more crucially, his manner of allowing the reader to glimpse, if not momentarily experience it. This is again, however, neither philosophy nor theology. It is poetry.

It is also a version of "dreaming," meaning experiencing and listening to the so-far unconscious, or to the unfolding "conscious." If we take ancient stories, including those in the Hebrew Bible, one bit seriously, that is one of the ways through which God speaks. It is also, gloriously and paradoxically, one of the ways in which we are most likely to "come awake." This echoes

Gaston Bachelard's ideas in *Poetics of Space* about writing and reading demanding the space or surrender of reverie in order to "awaken daydreams in each other." This "space" is, nevertheless, quickly stuffed with words. It is J. R. von Salis who warns: "It was not Rilke's way to fit his experiences and insights into a philosophical system and then to deduce theories from them. He had read no philosophy. Conceptual thinking was alien to him, and he was without scientific education. *He needed complete freedom for the full flow of his powers.* . . . No ideology can lay claim to him. He was too transparently sincere to put up with any of the compromises, half measures and conventions called for in adapting oneself to programs and orthodoxies. His humility did not extend to obeying the laws of earthly authorities, among which he counted the churches."[34]

Reflecting what they yearn for, it is understandable that some readers will seek to turn Rilke into a God-lover. Others will bypass God and turn Rilke into a self-lover. Or admire his brilliance, aesthetics and imagistic skills without asking: what are these for? Such ambiguities are unlikely to be resolved. Here is a poem, written in 1898 when Rilke was twenty-three, before the *Gebete* (prayers) that were the first stage of *Das Stunden-Buch*. The poem (the poet?) here seems both to grieve and affirm an ambivalence that is not without hope. The poem moves between mourning for a God who has been "hymned" almost out of existence and yearning for "some trace." (How would we live, God, if you were entirely gone . . . ?)

Out of that spacious, proud resplendence
they pried God and forced
him into their time . . .
And they surrounded him and hymned him
and now he's all but vanished
into their darkness.

And they light candle after candle
in that darkness and pray
that the flames won't all flicker out
before they see some trace
of God's heart . . .[35]

The poem feels as personal to me as a lullaby, although not as soothing. I experience its melancholy and see myself in it and others too: lighting candle after candle, faithfully seeking that infinitely desired trace of God's heart—or the trace of ourselves within God's heart. Rilke was also faithful in his seeking, driven by his twin desires: to be available to the sacred, the holy, the numinous and to discover what poetry could achieve through his mediumship. To achieve this he was willing to offer his life to his art and above everything to make himself "available" to inspiration. In 1921 he wrote:

> As soon as an artist has located the vital center of his activities, nothing will be more important for him than to remain within this center and never move further away from it (which is, of course, also the center of his nature, of his world) than to the interior walls of his quietly and steadily expanding achievement. His place is not, *never*, not even for a moment, next to the beholder and critic . . . one basically needs to be an acrobat to leap back safely and unharmed from this

point of view into one's inner center. . . . Most artists today use up their strength in this back-and-forth, and in addition to wasting their energy they get terribly confused and lose a part of their essential innocence to the sin of having taken their work from the outside by surprise, to have tasted it, to have joined others in enjoying it![36]

The contradictions in Rilke's life and between his life and work are self-evident. And yet there are ways in which his mature life is also strikingly consistent. William Gass describes Rilke's profession as "Waiting." Rilke's was a remarkably vital and active form of waiting: itself witness to what heightened receptivity can achieve. Gass writes, "He had begun his career as a poet of effusion, then trained himself to be a poet of reception." But that was not all. From 1914 onward ". . . he needed to become a poet of internal intensity . . . work[ing] on himself and all the material he has stored like compost for a garden."[37]

The results of that "composting" are far richer than any single critic could convey yet they remain appropriately inconclusive. This core idea of the "Open," for example, is not in Rilke's hands an invitation to make easy assumptions about life after death. Von Salis writes, "[Rilke] refused to relate the soul's experience to a 'beyond' . . . what is external to man and the things of the earth has no part in Rilke's conception of God. He always spoke disparagingly of all 'oppositeness' . . . the division into heaven and earth was displeasing to him. . . . God, he believed, was somehow contained in creation and created beings."[38]

The leaves are falling, falling as though from a great distance,
as if in the heavens far-away gardens are withering:
they fall with gestures that tell us "no."

And in the nights too the heavy earth falls
from all the stars into loneliness.

We are all falling. This hand is falling.
And look at the others: it is in them all.

And still there is One who holds this falling
with ceaseless softness in his hands.[39]

Und doch ist Einer (And still there is One) . . . Did Rilke believe this view of God as contained in creation and created beings? *Believe* is too strong. In his discussions of Rilke, Gabriel Marcel asks us to ". . . remember that there is one side of the world that is not turned toward us . . . where metamorphosis is carried out."[40]

This takes us close to Rilke himself, writing in 1923. "I am certain that the sole purpose of the [ancient ceremonies of] 'initiation' was the transmission of a 'key' to the understanding of 'death' that had no negative aspect. Like the moon, life surely has a side constantly averted from us, which is not the opposite of the side we see but, rather, the complement of it, rendering it complete, full—the true whole and complete sphere and globe of existence."[41]

Setting "belief" as well as convention aside, a more instinctive knowing, even "higher knowing," seems both truer and more supple. Poetry is itself an "initiation" when the spaces of reception/creativity/reception yield and allow that. Another poem about Mary, Christ's mother, suggests that ideas about transformation and initiation may move the reader in the same direction. Rilke evokes Mary's imagined death as an expression of the most dramatic initiation of all.

> *The identical angel, the great one who*
> *brought down the news of her conception*
> *stood there, waiting for her to notice him*
> *and said: It is now time for you to appear . . .*
> *. . . Then he grew radiant and stepped so near*
> *he disappeared into her face . . . she lay*
> *there in the narrow bed, weirdly immersed*
> *in her election and in her dying,*
> *completely intact, like one unused*
> *in life, tuned to angelic song . . .*
>
> *. . . the moment she stepped into heaven,*
> *as much as she longed to, she didn't approach him:*
> *there was no room, only he was there, giving*
> *a radiance that hurt her eyes . . .*
> *. . . Then they all saw*
> *how God the Father eclipsed our Lord*
> *so that surrounded by a gentle dusk*
> *the empty place grew visible, like*
> *some small sadness . . . a residue*
> *of earthly time, a partially healed wound . . .*
> *. . . And suddenly she pitched forward.*
> *But the angels lifted her up, supported her*
> *and singing carried her that last few feet in the air.*[42]

Rilke's own last days were not filled with singing. He died of leukemia on 29 December 1926 after weeks of unrelieved agony. At the age of fifty-one, he was unreconciled to dying, only days earlier denying the imminence of death, forbidding any overt discussion of it even and especially from his doctor, although saying to Nanny Wunderly-Volkart, "'Help me to my own death—I don't want the doctor's death—I want my freedom.'"[43] Given the place of death in his thinking and his work, the suffering and avoidances of those final days seem especially poignant.

What he wished most to avoid, other than death itself, was the presence of priests. "'Bad enough,' he noted, 'that in my physical needs I must admit mediators and negotiators in the form of doctors; in my soul's move toward the "Open," any spiritual middlemen would be insulting and revolting.'"[44]

It would seem that last desire was fulfilled. When it came to the moment of Rilke's physical dying, for his soul to *move toward the "Open,"* as he described it, ". . . the doctor and the nurse who were in the room said that Rilke took three deep breaths, opened his eyes wide and looked out into space with a shining gaze."[45]

At his simple, priestless burial, these lines were read, from the First Elegy:

> *Finally, those torn from us early no longer need us;*
> *losing their attachments to earthly things as naturally as*
> *one outgrows a mother's breasts. But we who need*
> *such great mysteries, for whom so often blessed progress*
> *grows from grief—could we be without them?*[46]
> *. . . könnten wir sein ohne sie?*

IRRATIONAL TRUTHS

Almost two years before finishing this book, I sat in a hotel room in Nice, in the south of France, with my friend Susanne Kahn-Ackermann. She had traveled to Nice from her home in Munich via a spiritual retreat nearby. I had traveled from my home in Sydney, via days in Paris. We met at the hotel we had chosen on the Internet from opposite sides of the world: a twenty-first-century moment. As we sat together, renewing a precious friendship that looks back through much of our adult lives, Susanne took from her handbag a small pile of letters. The striking handwriting was already familiar to me, although only from books. The letters had been written by Rilke to Susanne's grandmother, one of many cultured, artistic women with whom he had corresponded. But this was different. This wasn't just another cultured woman. It was my own dear friend Susanne's grandmother. Ink, pen, paper, envelopes, stamps; the handwriting that Rilke had changed for Lou's sake: I held the letters in both hands and gazed.

The emotion I experienced was not awe. I have come to understand and appreciate Rilke's gifts as quite exceptional. The highest praise is merited, at least for much of his work. But the emotions I experienced were gratitude and tenderness. Gratitude for the insight, pleasure and sacred unfolding that the poetry and some of his prose and letters have given so many readers, and me, and tenderness because whatever else Rilke was or was not, he was without doubt the most persistent of seekers. In the Christian scriptures "seeking" is not just acknowledged; it is wholly rewarded. "Seek, and you will find. Knock, and the door will be opened to you" (Luke 11:9). Seeking is not simply "reading" (or writing). It is an activity of intellect, soul and spirit that *uses* reading (and writing). There is energy to it and an essential trust within it. It is, intrinsically, counterpoint to complacency or despair.

~

The year 1914 was a time of social devastation as Europe plunged into the obscenity of war, and a time of personal and professional desolation for Rilke (though not without some wonderful poems; Rilke was never "not writing"). Yet in a letter he wrote at that time, he once more makes seeking and yearning seem as necessary as breathing. "When I saw others straining toward God, I did not understand it, for though I may have had him less than they did, there was no one blocking the way between him and me, and I could reach his heart easily. It is up to him, after all, to have us, *our* part consists almost solely in letting him grasp us. In its essential soundness, the soul knows no effort toward God; *the love of God is the quietly predominant bent of our nature."*[1]

Rilke's words are beautiful—and ambiguous. Read in isolation they could seem like a testament of faith; they are not. But they do show seeking to be both movement and surrender, a subtle, vital dance that is itself reflective of the primary gestures of nature.

> *I find you in all these things of the world*
> *that I love calmly, like a brother;*
> *in things no one cares for you brood like a seed;*
> *and to powerful things you give an immense power.*
>
> *Strength plays such a marvelous game—*
> *it moves through the things of the world like a servant,*
> *groping out in roots, tapering in trunks,*
> *and in the treetops like a rising from the dead.*[2]

That translation is one of Robert Bly's and I find it perfect. This time, though, I want also to include the German that Rilke wrote and heard.

> *Ich finde dich in allen diesen Dingen,*
> *denen ich gut und wie ein Bruder bin;*
> *als Samen sonnst du dich in den geringen*
> *und in den großen giebst du groß dich hin.*
>
> *Das ist das wundersame Spiel der Kräfte,*
> *daß sie so dienend durch die Dinge gehn:*
> *in Wurzeln wachsend, schwindend in die Schäfte*
> *und in den Wipfeln wie ein Auferstehn.*[3]

Throughout this time of writing, I have harbored the desire to remember that I am reading and writing about a "poet" who was a real person. Abstractions and theories can be manipulated more easily than people; in every sense they are more "knowable." And yet the *divine radiance of things* that Heidegger declared lost in these *destitute times* is not glimpsed through abstractions alone. If it is to be seen at all it will be found through complex, conscious experience, and often in the uneasy darkness of "not knowing."

English literature professor Richard Cross brings to life a moment from an academic conference in Chicago in 1985, still charged with meaning as he is writing more than twenty years later: "Everyone here keeps using the word *discourse*," observed the young man from Johannesburg. "Back home we're chary about reducing literature to abstractions. We talk about books as though our lives depended on them."[4]

Is it possible also to talk about and to *read* poetry in that same way: as though our lives depended on it? This "destitute time" that we live in is marked by a widespread spiritual poverty that takes no regard of material plenty other than to show its satisfactions to be painfully incomplete. According to Heidegger, the time is "destitute not only because God is dead, but because mortals are hardly aware and capable even of their own mortality. Mortals have not yet come into ownership of their own nature. . . . The mystery of pain remains veiled. Love has not been learned. But the mortals *are*."

The nature of human nature—"what mortals *are*" and, arguably, its divine dimension—can become central to our reading of Rilke. Heidegger lets us somewhat off the hook when we return to his thought that we are not ". . . experienced travelers in the land of the saying of Being . . . the realm in which the dialogue between poetry and thinking goes on can be discovered, reached, and explored in thought only slowly. Who today would presume to claim that he is at home with the nature of poetry as well as with the nature of thinking . . . ?"[5]

Who indeed? What we struggle with here are not paradoxes only, but an urgent search for meaning at a time of considerable distraction. "Oh how I long just once to feel the hand within me that throws the larks so high into sky," wrote Rilke to Lou, commenting on the impulses that had inspired and allowed the writing of *The Book of Hours*.[6] What is Rilke describing? There was no "hand." Some would argue there is no "within." Larks fly; they are not thrown. Does this tell us anything?

> *But still for us existence is enchanted: from a*
> *hundred places*
> *it is still origin. A play of pure forces*
> *that no one touches unless he kneels and admires.*
>
> *The Unutterable, words fragilely slip by . . .*
> *and from the most vibrant stones music anew*
> *aspires*
> *building her deified house in the useless space*
> *of the sky.*[7]

Here and now, and in the here and now, people are read-ing and writing. They are also singing, locking their houses, hurrying to work, getting on and off trams or planes, comforting a momentarily brokenhearted child or dancing a tango with an ancient aunt. They are eating food they love or will regret, marrying the wrong person or the right one, breaking or keeping promises, praying, chanting, cursing, laughing or crying when possibly they shouldn't. The contradictions within life *are* life: Rilke lived that. The limitations of language wrestle with what language makes possible. That tension, too, lives in Rilke, and passes like a gift into our reading of him. Leishman speaks for me: "Again and again I feel, in reading [Rilke], that we have come round the spiral to another 'dawn of consciousness,' where language is in the making, and where myth and symbol must often supply the place of *not yet thinkable thoughts.*"[8]

Rilke's biographer H. F. Peters comments: "It is well to remember, as C. G. Jung has pointed out, that 'rational truths are not the last word, there are also irrational truths. In human affairs what appears impossible upon the way of the intellect has very often become true upon the way of the irrational. . . .' Rilke often insisted that the key to an understanding of these poems is to become 'like-minded.'"

This level of reading empathy is more easily described than achieved because, as Peters explains, the average reader ". . . cannot rid himself of the suspicion that what is not intelligible *is not true* and inclines to dismiss such artists as visionaries, mystics or madmen."[9]

Yet if irrational—or differently "rational"—truths are to be found anywhere, they will be found in poetry. It is precisely this that occasionally makes poetry the most subversive of arts. Sometimes no more effort is needed to find those truths than making oneself available through alert surrendering. At other times what one is yearning for, seeking or even finding is more elusive. It is also Leishman who points to Rilke's acute awareness of the limitations of language, even in the hands of someone who, as Leishman expresses it, ". . . did so much to extend them." He quotes Rilke: "One often finds one-self at variance with the external behavior of language . . . a language of word-kernels, a language that's not gath-ered, up above, on stalks, but grasped in the speech-seed. Would it not be in this language that the perfect Hymn to the Sun would have to be composed, and isn't the pure silence of love like heart-soil around such speech-seeds? Oh how often one longs to speak a few degrees more deeply! . . . One's left with a mere intimation of the kind of speech that may be possible there, where silence reigns."[10]

Where silence reigns . . . This is an astonishing quote, pow-ered by Rilke's own desire for the capacity to *speak a few degrees more deeply*. What would it mean also to read or yearn a few degrees more deeply? To "be" where silence reigns with greater surrender? To "go" with willingness where poetry can take you?

Kathleen Raine was both a poet and a Blake scholar. She tells of a conversation with the Russian Metropolitan Archbishop during the height of the power of the Soviet Union, when she suggested to the Archbishop that atheism could have no poetry. His response was disarming. "Poetry," he said, "is the language of longing." And, we might ask, when does longing cease? Raine responds: ". . . only when the soul is dead can there no longer be poetry."[11]

~

Perhaps, then, it is not so much a question of "What is poetry for?" as "What does poetry *allow*?" To gather (pluck? harvest? no verb does it) those Rilkean word-kernels is already much. To "grasp" speech-seeds is already more. Poet David Whyte writes of the value of reading Rilke and asks us to imagine "a man looking out of his window at summer's end, having been busy with everything except the one harvest that mattered. . . ."[12]

Silence's reign is awesome—and brief. We may need to be increasingly trusting to experience it—trusting not the poet so much as ourselves. As Kathleen Raine expresses it: "Certain experiences are not otherwise attainable than by exploring regions of experience whose very existence is destroyed by the materialist philosophy which denies access to them . . . Poetry, God knows, does not deal in certainties so much as in the glimpses of that country seen at certain moments by that eternal exile Psyche."[13]

This means genuinely valuing what is gleaned through the senses and imagination as well as what is gathered by the intellect, while knowing that what is learned thus cannot be reduced to the "imaginary."

Raine captures something crucial to Rilke's quest as a writer and perhaps to our reading quest also when she writes, "A work of art is precisely an expression in words of some intuition of imaginative reality. Poets may or may not have been religious men (who knows if Shakespeare was?) but all poetry of the imagination is the language of spiritual intuition and spiritual knowledge."[14] Psyche has, sometimes, a means of approaching home.

～

In twenty-first-century life our reading—those countless small acts of attention and reception—is shaped within a cultural context that critic Ellman Crasnow calls ". . . a pessimistic worldview in which, amid worsening conditions, regret passes through despair into crisis and apocalypse."[15] Is this another way of naming "destitute times?" And yet:

> *Even when we don't want this*
> God is growing.
>
> *Auch wenn wir nicht wollen:*
> Gott reift.[16]

~

The significant themes within Rilke's work are challenging to define and powerful to experience. To write about Rilke openheartedly, to remain in the presence of the memory of that flawed human being whose letters to Susanne's grandmother I held in my hands, is to live with insufficiency as well as curiosity. His own friend, Rudolf Kassner, said that Rilke was the most fascinating human being he ever met, that he remained a poet even when he was washing his hands.[17]

Perhaps, paraphrasing Joseph Campbell's quote that only a god can worship a god, perhaps only a poet *like* Rilke could fully appreciate the poet who *is* Rilke. And yet, what is perhaps just as remarkable is how freely Rilke gives permission to honor what is inward and uncertain, to grow in spaciousness, to live in the world of senses, beauty and nature, to remain open to the signs of the numinous and sacred, to wonder at life in a more conscious awareness of death, and to believe in the value of life while one is fully living it.

A poem not from Rilke but from Goethe expresses the joy in this.

Tell a wise person, or else keep silent,
Because the massman will mock it right away.
I praise what is truly alive,
what longs to be burned to death.

In the calm water of the love-nights,
Where you were begotten, where you have begotten,
A strange feeling comes over you
When you see the silent candle burning.

Now you are no longer caught
In the obsession with darkness,
And a desire for higher love-making
Sweeps you upward.

Distance does not make you falter,
Now, arriving in magic, flying,
And, finally, insane for the light,
You are the butterfly and you are gone.

And so long as you haven't experienced
This: to die and so to grow,
You are only a troubled guest
On the dark earth.[18]

The "desire for higher love-making"—Platonic yearning—
and a willingness to "praise what is truly alive" remain
potent for many readers. For some, those longings are
central. The times we live in may be destitute but they
are our own times and are as dear and as precious as any
other. Thomas Merton writes, wonderfully in my view,
about grasping the truth of the times we live in—whenever
they are: "If I had no choice about the age in which I was
to live, I nevertheless have a choice about the attitude I
take and about the way and the extent of my participation
in its living ongoing events. To choose the world is not

then merely a pious admission that the world is acceptable because it comes from the hand of God. It is first of all an acceptance of a task and a vocation in the world, in history and in time. In my time, which is the present."[19]

Poetry cannot change these "times." It may not transform a life. But it can help restore meaning. It is an absence of meaning (of care, connection, engagement and beauty) that makes life dangerous as well as "destitute"; it is the presence of meaning that restores "divine radiance": the infinite light of epiphany.

"If your everyday life seems poor," Rilke wrote to Franz Kappus and perhaps to us, "don't blame *it*; blame yourself; admit to yourself that you are not enough of a poet to call forth its riches; because for the creator there is no poverty and no poor, indifferent place."[20]

~

Choice arises. The ambiguities, hyperboles, despairs, abstractions and complexities make it difficult sometimes to read Rilke or even to think about him. Yet in the yearning for "riches"—for unfolding inner space, illumination, connection and perhaps divine transformation—we make crucial choices. And perhaps it is those characteristics of ambivalence and contradiction precisely that make the "irrational truths" that Rilke's poetry offers still more compelling and the "divine radiance" within the poetry still more familiarly human.

A spiritually focused reading of Rilke can take its primary cue from Rilke: using such reading not to create distance from earthly things, but to allow them to arise, more freely, within us. *Earth! Invisible!*

~

. . . Erde, du liebe, ich will . . .
. . . Siehe, ich lebe. Woraus? Weder Kindheit noch Zukunft
werden weniger . . . Überzähliges Dasein
entspringt mir im Herzen.

Earth, beloved: I want this . . .
. . . Look: I am alive. But how?
Neither childhood nor future
recedes . . . Infinite existence
wells forth in my heart.[21]

LIST OF POEMS

Poems are listed within their original books and by the first line or phrase that appears in this text. The title is added where this has particular significance or is noted within the text. Poems are detailed further in the Endnotes.

In Celebration of Me (1897–8; 1909)
    I am so afraid of people's words (Kidder) 220

From *Diaries of a Young Poet,* written 1898–1900
    O nights, nights (Wydenbruck) 82
    I named You (prayer) (Snow & Winkler) 87
    Whoever walks now (Snow & Winkler) 180
    And again my deep life rushes louder (Snow & Winkler) 204
    Out of that spacious, proud resplendence (Snow & Winkler)
        280

The Book of Hours (1905)

Book of Monastic Life (1899)

Book of Pilgrimage (1901)

ACKNOWLEDGMENTS

It has been my privilege and joy to live closely in the company of Rainer Maria Rilke's writing for a number of years. During those years I completed this book and also a doctoral thesis on Rilke (*Rainer Maria Rilke: Bearing Witness*) with the Writing & Society Research Group at the University of Western Sydney. I was immensely fortunate to have as my thesis supervisor Professor Jane Goodall, and my first thanks must go to her. She had a long-standing interest in Rilke as well as in the fine arts of reading and writing and she brought all of that to our unfailingly rewarding discussions. It is a rare privilege in a professional writer's life to share so much concentrated time around mutual intellectual interests. Jane's engagement and generosity were transformative, and I thank her wholeheartedly. At different stages of my research I also benefited from the interest of Dr. David Phillips, now at the University of East London, and Dr. Christopher Fleming and Dr. Kathleen Olive of the University of Western

Sydney. It was invaluable also to discuss key aspects of Rilke's work and the translations with my dear friend Susanne Kahn-Ackermann of Munich. She and I have shared insights for three decades on writing, publishing and, most crucially, spirituality. It was a gift to share this.

Heartfelt—heart-*filled*—thanks are also due to Professor Mark S. Burrows of Andover Newton Theological School in Massachusetts. Both Professor Burrows and Emeritus Professor Don Evans of the University of Toronto, whom I also wish most sincerely to thank, engaged so positively and fruitfully with my doctoral thesis that a frequently harrowing process became yet something else on the Rilke journey that was richly rewarding. I remain immensely grateful. Post-thesis, Professor Burrows and I took up the mutual love and interest we have in reading Rilke through a spiritually focused lens and began a lively correspondence and continuing discussion, the countless benefits of which percolate through this book. What's more, in his role as fine poet and gifted Rilke translator, Mark S. Burrows has most generously allowed me to use many of his newly translated Rilke poems in this book, some rendered into English for the first time. Whatever faults remain here are mine only but this would be a different and far poorer book without the informed, passionate insights he was willing to share about Rilke and—especially—without his dazzling, tender, "true" translations of some of the most affecting of Rilke's poetry. I am confident readers will share my delight as well as gratitude.

Writing both the thesis and then this book, I was reminded often how many people are quiet Rilke "fans." Among those who took time to share their views, or to bring my attention to pertinent critical writings, are Susan Maley, Ursula Groll, Professor Joe Bessler, Amanda Lohrey, Sally Gillespie, Subhana Barzarghi and Dr. Caroline

Josephs. All my work, but particularly this work on Rilke, has benefited from the myriad ways in which Klaus Endler positively influenced my writing life. My first intellectual mentor, he allowed me an understanding of European thinking and writing that I could never have achieved without him.

I wish also to express my continuing wholehearted appreciation to my Australian publishers, Allen & Unwin, and especially to Sue Hines and Elizabeth Weiss, and to my North American publishers, Tarcher/Penguin, with special thanks to Joel Fotinos. I would also like to note with gratitude the careful work of the copy editors, Ali Lavau (Australia) and Jacky Fernandez (USA), and the book's designer, Emily O'Neill.

Finally, but not least, I want to thank for their love, personal support or generous hospitality during the "Rilke years," my beloved children, Gabriel and Kezia Dowrick, and their partners, Aokie and Sean; as well as Geraldine Killalea, Dr. Kim Cunio, Paul Wilson, Hanan al-Shaykh, Caroline Ward, Donna Idol and all our "Mana" family—especially the Easter retreatants: Judith Ackroyd, Rev. Hilary Star and Rev. Helen Palmer; Rev. Ian Pearson, dear Jolyon Bromley and our treasured Pitt Street Interfaith congregation—and, in ways beyond "numbering," Jane Moore. Jane's kindness and constancy gave backbone to this project. I hope that my dedication to her expresses my gratitude, along with the thanks I wish to express to both my late parents for the lifelong passion for writing and reading they so eagerly nourished in their daughters, expressed here in part through the shared dedication to my mother. Since she was an artist and teacher, this is a book that I believe would have brought her particular pleasure, as it has for me.

ENDNOTES

PREFACE

1. Merton, Thomas, *The Intimate Merton*, ed. Patrick Hart & Jonathan Montaldo, HarperSanFrancisco, San Francisco, 1999, p. 267.
2. Peters, H. F., *Rainer Maria Rilke: Masks and the Man*, McGraw-Hill, New York, 1963, p. 191.
3. Metzger, E. A. & Metzger, M. M., eds., *A Companion to the Works of Rainer Maria Rilke*, Camden House, Rochester, NY, 2001, p. 15.
4. Lines from the Ninth Elegy, *Duino Elegies*, in Rilke, Rainer Maria, *The Selected Poetry of Rainer Maria Rilke*, ed. & trans. Stephen Mitchell, intro. Robert Hass, Picador, London, 1987, p. 201.
5. Gass, William H., in Rilke, Rainer Maria, *The Notebooks of Malte Laurids Brigge*, trans. Stephen Mitchell, intro. William H. Gass, Vintage, New York, 1985, p. xii.
6. Hirshfield, Jane, *Hiddenness, Uncertainty, Surprise: Three Generative Energies of Poetry*, University of Newcastle/Bloodaxe Books, Newcastle upon Tyne, 2008, p. 52.
7. Hofstadter, Albert, in Heidegger, Martin, *Poetry, Language, Thought*, trans. & intro. Albert Hofstadter, Harper Perennial, New York, 2001 (1975), p. xv.
8. Quoted by Peters, H. F., in *Rainer Maria Rilke: Masks and the Man*, 1963, p. 165.
9. Quoted by Bly, Robert, in *The Winged Energy of Delight: Poems from Europe, Asia and the Americas*, ed. Robert Bly, Harper Perennial, New York, 2005. Bly continues: "[Rilke's] emphasis on great art offends many critics so much, they don't even mention it. What's more Rilke doesn't say art is born out of life; he says art gives birth to art," p. 156.
10. In Rilke, Rainer Maria, *The Book of Hours*, trans. Annemarie S. Kidder, Northwestern University Press, Evanston, IL, 2001, pp. xi, xii.
11. From "Der Einsame" ("The Solitary One"), in Rilke, Rainer Maria, *Selected Poems of Rainer Maria Rilke*, intro., trans. & commentary Robert Bly, Harper & Row, New York, 1981, p. 149.

ENDNOTES

12. Bloom, Harold, *Omens of Millennium*, Fourth Estate, London, 1996, pp. 15–17.
13. Final lines from the Seventh Elegy (from *Duineser Elegien*): Rilke, Rainer Maria, *Die Gedichte*, Insel Verlag, Frankfurt a. M., 2006, p. 708. (My translation.)

"GOD IS STILL SPEAKING"

1. Eliot, T. S., in Frank Kermode, ed., *Selected Prose of T. S. Eliot*, Harvest/Harcourt Brace, San Diego, 1975 (1935), p. 105.
2. Burrell, David B., "Religion and the University," *Crosscurrents*, Summer 2006, p. 156.
3. Rilke, Rainer Maria, *Letters of Rainer Maria Rilke 1910–1926*, trans. Jane Bannard Greene & M. D. Herter Norton, W. W. Norton & Co., New York, 1969 (1947), p. 376.
4. McFague, Sallie, *Metaphorical Theology: Models of God in Religious Language*, Fortress Press, Philadelphia, 1982, pp. 1–2.
5. Weil, Simone, *Waiting for God*, Harper & Row, New York, 1973, p. 32.
6. Poem written in Paris, April 1913, in Rilke, Rainer Maria, *Uncollected Poems*, trans. Edward Snow, North Point Press, New York, 1996, p. 57. This is one of a large number of poems written during the period that is often regarded as one of anxiety and disappointment for Rilke as he waited (for ten years) to complete the cycle *Duino Elegies*. In his introduction, Snow calls part of this time, 1912–15, correctly in my view, "one of [Rilke's career's] great florescences" (p. xii).
7. "Herbsttag" (in *Das Buch der Bilder*): Rilke, Rainer Maria, *Die Gedichte*, Insel Verlag, Frankfurt a. M., 2006, p. 304. (Trans. Mark S. Burrows, 2009.)
8. Barnacle, B. D., *Rilke: Space, Essence and Angels in the Poetry of Rainer Maria Rilke*, Crescent Moon, Kidderminster, 1993, pp. 3, 44–5.
9. Final lines from the Ninth Elegy (*Duineser Elegien*): Rilke, *Die Gedichte*, 2006, pp. 712–3. (Trans. Mark S. Burrows, 2009.)
10. Rilke, *Letters of Rainer Maria Rilke 1910–1926*, trans. Greene & Herter Norton, 1969 (1947), p. 309.
11. Rilke, *Rilke: Selected Letters*, ed. Harry T. Moore, Anchor, New York, 1960, p. 325.
12. Brodsky, "Life with Rilke," in Metzger, E. A., & Metzger, M. M., eds., *A Companion to the Works of Rainer Maria Rilke*, Camden House, Rochester, NY, 2001, p. 21.
13. Stearns, Mary Nurrie, "The Presence of Compassion: An Interview with John O'Donohue," personaltransformation.com, undated.
14. Snow, Edward, in Rilke, Rainer Maria, *Duino Elegies: Bilingual Edition*, trans. Edward Snow, North Point Press/Farrar, Straus and Giroux, New York, 2000, p. xii.
15. Rilke, Rainer Maria, *The Poet's Guide to Life: The Wisdom of Rilke*, ed. & trans. Ulrich Baer, Modern Library/Random House, New York, 2005, p. 136.
16. Many appear in Rilke, Rainer Maria, *Poems 1906–26*, trans. J. B. Leishman, The Hogarth Press, London, 1976 (1957).
17. Burrows, Mark S., personal correspondence, 2009.
18. Griffiths, Bede, in Judson B. Trapnell, *Bede Griffiths: A Life in Dialogue*, State University of New York Press, New York, 2001, p. 62.
19. Quoted in Ferrucci, Piero, *Inevitable Grace*, trans. David Kennard, Crucible, Wellingborough, 1990, p. 124.
20. Romanyshyn, Robert D., *Ways of the Heart: Essays Toward an Imaginal Psychology*, Trivium, Pittsburgh, 2002, p. 129.
21. *"Dich wundert nicht des Sturmes Wucht"* in Rilke, Rainer Maria, *Rilke's Book of Hours: Love Poems to God*, trans., preface & intro. Anita Barrows & Joanna Macy, Riverhead Books, New York, 1996, p. 96.
22. "Sonnets to Orpheus," Part II, I, in Rilke, Rainer Maria, *In Praise of Mortality: Selections*

ENDNOTES

from Rainer Maria Rilke's Duino Elegies and Sonnets to Orpheus, trans. Anita Barrows & Joanna Macy, Riverhead Books, New York, 2005, p. 107. This is a moving, if very free, translation. A more literal translation follows, with thanks to Susanne Kahn-Ackermann: *Breathing, you invisible poem/own being continuously purely/exchanged for worldspace./ Counterpoise, in which/I rhythmically occur./Single wave, whose gradually/becoming sea I am/ Space achieved/Of all possible oceans-/gained space/How many of these spaces already/were once within me? Some winds/Are like my son./Do you know me, air,/still replete with places once my own?/You, once smooth bark,/curve and leaf of my words.* Kahn-Ackermann, Susanne, personal correspondence, 2008.

23. Rilke, *The Poet's Guide to Life*, 2005, p. 45.

24. "Sonet an Orpheus, I, XXII" (in *Sonette an Orpheus*): Rilke, Rainer Maria, *Die Gedichte*, 2006, p. 731. (Trans. Mark S. Burrows, 2009.)

25. Quoted in Hendry, J. F., *The Sacred Threshold: A Life of Rilke*, Carcanet, Manchester, 1983, p. 153.

26. Peters, H. F., in *Rainer Maria Rilke: Masks and the Man*, McGraw-Hill, New York, 1963, p. 165.

27. Rilke, Rainer Maria & Andreas-Salomé, Lou, *Rainer Maria Rilke and Lou Andreas-Salomé: The Correspondence*, trans. & intro. Edward Snow & Michael Winkler, W. W. Norton & Co., New York, 2006, p. 332.

28. Weber, Max, "Science as a Vocation" (1918), in Carlson, Thomas A., "Locating the Mystical Subject," in Kessler, M. & Sheppard, C., *Mystics: Presence and Aporia*, University of Chicago Press, Chicago, 2003, pp. 207–8. See also my earlier reference to David Burrell's view of "Weberian 'neutrality.'" It is worth noting Rilke's excited report to Clara Rilke, written 7 November 1918, of hearing Weber speak in Munich. Rilke, Rainer Maria, *Rilke: Selected Letters*, ed. Harry T. Moore, 1960, p. 209.

29. Carlson, "Locating the Mystical Subject," in Kessler & Sheppard, *Mystics*, 2003, pp. 207, 208.

30. "Sonnet II, X," in Rilke, Rainer Maria, *Sonnets to Orpheus*, trans. Edward Snow, North Point Press, New York, 2004, p. 79.

31. Letter to Clara Westhoff-Rilke, 4 November 1917, quoted in Wydenbruck, Nora, *Rilke: Man and Poet*, Appleton, New York, 1949, p. 282.

32. Quoted by Leishman, J. B., in Rilke, Rainer Maria, *Duino Elegies*, trans. J. B. Leishman & Stephen Spender, The Hogarth Press, London, 1948, pp. 15–16.

33. Bachelard, Gaston, *The Poetics of Space: The Classic Look at How We Experience Intimate Places*, trans. Maria Jolas, Beacon, Boston, 1994 (1958), p. 43.

34. Paglia, Camille, *Break, Blow, Burn*, Vintage, New York, 2005, pp. xiv, xvi.

35. Quoted by Peters, H. F., in *Rainer Maria Rilke*, 1963, p. 134.

TRANSLATION AND RECEPTION

1. Bly, Robert, in Rilke, Rainer Maria, *Selected Poems of Rainer Maria Rilke*, trans., intro. & commentary Robert Bly, Harper & Row, New York, 1981, p. 185.

2. Contogenis, Constantine, "Rilke in English" (a review of William H. Gass, *Reading Rilke*), *Essays in Criticism*, Oxford, Vol. 52, No. 2, April 2002, pp. 181–2, (my itals).

3. Prater, Donald, *A Ringing Glass: The Life of Rainer Maria Rilke*, Clarendon/Oxford University Press, Oxford, 1986, pp. 361–2.

4. Rilke, *Poems 1906–26*, trans. J. B. Leishman, The Hogarth Press, London, 1976 (1957), p. 298.

5. Prater, *A Ringing Glass*, 1986, p. 362.

6. Rilke, Rainer Maria, *Rilke: Selected Poems*, trans. C. F. MacIntyre, University of California Press, Berkeley, 1974 (1940), p. 1.

7. Brodsky, in Metzger, E. A. & Metzger, M. M., eds., *A Companion to the Works of Rainer Maria Rilke*, Camden House, Rochester, NY, 2001, p. 20.

ENDNOTES

8. Steiner, George, *Errata: An Examined Life*, Phoenix/Orion, London, 1997, pp. 98–9.
9. Steiner, *Errata*, 1997, p. 99.
10. Perloff, Marjorie, "Reading Gass Reading Rilke," *Parnassus: Poetry in Review*, Vol. 25, No. 1–2, 2001.
11. Rilke, Rainer Maria, *Letters to a Young Poet*, trans. M. D. Herter Norton, W. W. Norton & Co., New York, 1993 (1934), p. 53.
12. Steiner, *Errata*, 1997, pp. 100–1.
13. Gass, William H., *Reading Rilke: Reflections on the Problems of Translation*, Basic Books, New York, 1999, p. 69.
14. Hass, Robert, in Rilke, Rainer Maria, *The Selected Poetry of Rainer Maria Rilke*, ed. & trans. Stephen Mitchell, intro. Robert Hass, Picador, London, 1987, p. xviii.
15. Ryan, Judith, *Rilke, Modernism and Poetic Tradition*, Cambridge University Press, Cambridge, 1999, p. 4. Mark S. Burrows also notes, at least in the *Elegies*, Rilke's "carefully crafted obfuscation, a deliberate entangling of syntax, delight in making new words, new images, new ways of (de)forming rhetorical conventions" in ways he [Burrows] says are often "tamed or ignored by English translators." Private correspondence, 2009.
16. Leishman's translation of *Requiem and Other Poems* appeared in 1935; in 1939 W. H. Auden wrote a critical article, "Rilke in English," published in *New Republic*.
17. Rilke, Rainer Maria, *The Best of Rilke*, trans. Walter Arndt, Dartmouth/University Press of New England, Hanover, 1989, p. 162.
18. Rilke, *The Best of Rilke* (Arndt), 1983, p. 73.
19. Rilke, *Selected Poems of Rainer Maria Rilke* (Bly), 1981, p. 141.
20. "Der Schwan" (in *Neue Gedichte*): Rilke, Rainer Maria, *Die Gedichte*, Insel Verlag, Frankfurt a. M., 2006, p. 450.
21. For a fascinating discussion of the paradoxical extremes of the German language, including the "zones of darkness," see "The Hollow Miracle" in Steiner, George, *Language and Silence: Essays on Language, Literature and the Inhuman*, Atheneum, New York, 1967, p. 99.
22. Hargreaves, Raymond, in *Notes and Queries*, Vol. 42, No. 1, March 1995, p. 128.
23. From *Von der Armut und vom Tode* (*The Book of Poverty and Death*): Rilke, Rainer Maria, *Die Gedichte*, Insel Verlag, Frankfurt a. M., 2006, pp. 265-6. (My translation.)
24. Letter to Countess Margot Sizzo, 6 January 1923, in Rilke, Rainer Maria, *Letters of Rainer Maria Rilke 1910–1926*, trans. Jane Bannard Greene & M. D. Herter Norton, W. W. Norton & Co., New York, 1969 (1947), pp. 316–17.
25. ("Der Tod," November 1915) in Rilke, Rainer Maria, *The Unknown Rilke*, trans. Franz Wright, Oberlin College Press, Oberlin, 1990, p. 140. This is the poem recited by the prodigiously brilliant child in the movie *Little Man Tate*.
26. Hartman, Geoffrey H., *The Unmediated Vision: An Interpretation of Wordsworth, Hopkins, Rilke and Valéry*, Yale University Press, New Haven, 1954, p. 71.
27. "Eingang" in Rilke, Rainer Maria, *The Book of Images*, trans. Edward Snow, North Point Press, New York, 1991, p. 5.
28. Rilke, Rainer Maria, *Rilke: Selected Letters*, ed. Harry T. Moore, Anchor, New York, 1960, p. 389.
29. *"Ich glaube an Alles noch nie Gesagte"* (in *Das Buch vom mönchischen Leben/ Das Stunden-Buch*): Rilke, *Die Gedichte,* 2006, p. 205. (Trans. Mark S. Burrows, 2009.)
30. Bly, Robert, in Rilke, *Selected Poems of Rainer Maria Rilke* (Bly), 1981, p. 6.
31. In Rilke, Rainer Maria, *Selected Letters 1902–1926*, trans. R. F. C. Hull, intro. John Bayley, Quartet Encounters, London, 1988 (1946), p. 187.
32. Bernstein, Michael André, *Five Portraits: Modernity and the Imagination in Twentieth-Century Writing*, Northwestern University Press, Evanston, IL, 2000, p. 31.

ENDNOTES

33. "An die Musik," in Rilke, *Uncollected Poems*, trans. Edward Snow, North Point Press, New York, 1996, pp. 128–9, quoted in Bernstein, *Five Portraits*, 2000, p. 31.

34. "Rilke's experiments with imagery are the most innovative elements in his work . . . In his most daring poetry he aims to develop poetic correlatives for the realm of the imaginary . . . something that lies beyond the realm of empirical experience." Ryan, *Rilke, Modernism and Poetic Tradition*, 1999, p. 224.

35. Bernstein, *Five Portraits*, 2000, p. 31.

36. Hendry, *The Sacred Threshold*, 1983, p. 133.

37. Rilke, *Letters to a Young Poet* (Herter Norton), 1993 (1934), pp. 34–5.

38. "Fortschritt" (in *Das Buch der Bilder*): Rilke, *Selected Poems of Rainer Maria Rilke* (Bly), 1981, p. 101.

39. Leppmann, Wolfgang, *Rilke: A Life*, trans. Russell M. Stockman, Fromm International, New York, 1984, p. 286.

"THE NATURE OF POETRY"

1. Gass, William H., *A Temple of Texts: Essays*, Knopf, New York, 2006, pp. 49–50, 57.

2. Hattingberg, Magda von, ed., *Rilke and Benvenuta: An Intimate Correspondence*, trans. Joel Agee, Fromm International, New York, 1987, p. 23.

3. *"Ich habe viele Brüder in Sutanen"* (in *Das Buch vom mönchischen Leben/Das Stunden-Buch*): Rilke, Rainer Maria, *Die Gedichte,* Insel Verlag, Frankfurt a. M., 2006, p. 201. (Trans. Mark S. Burrows, 2009.)

4. Rilke, Rainer Maria, *Where Silence Reigns: Selected Prose by Rainer Maria Rilke*, trans. G. Craig Houston, foreword Denise Levertov, New Directions, New York, 1978, pp. 68–9.

5. Quoted in Raine, Kathleen, *The Inner Journey of the Poet*, George Allen & Unwin, London, 1982, p. 56.

6. Gadamer, Hans-Georg, *The Relevance of the Beautiful and Other Essays*, ed. & intro. Robert Bernasconi, trans. Nicholas Walker, Cambridge University Press, Cambridge, 1986, p. 140.

7. Rilke, Rainer Maria, *The Poet's Guide to Life: The Wisdom of Rilke*, ed. & trans. Ulrich Baer, Modern Library/Random House, New York, 2005, pp. 127, 128.

8. Randall, J. H., Jr., in *The Role of Knowledge in Western Religion* (Beacon, Boston, 1958), reprinted in Hick, John, ed., *Classical and Contemporary Readings in the Philosophy of Religion,* Prentice Hall, Englewood Cliffs, NJ, 1990 (1964), p. 318.

9. Armstrong, John, *Love, Life, Goethe: How to Be Happy in an Imperfect World*, Allan Lane/Penguin, London, 2006, pp. 151–2.

10. Muzot, despite appearances, is pronounced "Muzotte."

11. "Poetry and Religion" in Murray, Les, *Learning Human*, Duffy & Snellgrove, Sydney, 2003, p. 77.

12. *"Mein Leben ist nicht diese steile Stunde"* (in *Das Buch vom mönchischen Leben/Das Stunden-Buch*): Rilke, *Die Gedichte*, 2006, p. 209. (My translation.)

13. Andreas-Salomé, Lou, *You Alone Are Real to Me: Remembering Rainer Maria Rilke*, trans. & intro. Angela von der Lippe, BOA Editions, Rochester, NY, 2003 (in German, 1927), p. 29.

14. Peters, H. F., *Rainer Maria Rilke: Masks and the Man*, McGraw-Hill, New York, 1963, p. 50.

15. Andreas-Salomé, *You Alone Are Real to Me*, 2003, p. 118.

16. Wilmers, Mary-Kay, in Andreas-Salomé, Lou, *The Freud Journal*, trans. Stanley A. Leavy, intro. Mary-Kay Wilmers, Quartet Books, London, 1987, p. 9.

ENDNOTES

17. In Rilke, Rainer Maria, *Selected Letters 1902–1926*, trans. R. F. C. Hull, intro. John Bayley, Quartet Encounters, London, 1988 (1946), p. 187.

18. Quoted in Hendry, J. F., *The Sacred Threshold: A Life of Rilke*, Carcanet, Manchester, 1983, p. 30. Brodsky notes: "The fact that the pious, melancholy, traditional Russia [Rilke and Lou] chose to focus on was not the whole story, was indeed a dying world, did not disturb them; both found there essentially what they were looking for." Brodsky, Patricia Pollock, *Rainer Maria Rilke*, Twayne, Boston, 1988, p. 8.

19. Letter to Ilse Jahr, 22 February 1923, in Rilke, Rainer Maria, *Selected Letters 1902–1926* (Hull), 1988 (1946), p. 373.

20. Letter to R. J. Sorge, 4 June 1914, in Rilke, Rainer Maria, *Letters of Rainer Maria Rilke 1910–1926*, trans. Jane Bannard Greene & M. D. Herter Norton, W. W. Norton & Co., New York, 1969 (1947), p. 112.

21. From 1,44 and 1,45 in Rilke, Rainer Maria, *Rilke's Book of Hours: Love Poems to God*, trans., preface & intro. Anita Barrows & Joanna Macy, Riverhead Books, New York, pp. 80, 81.

22. Quoted in Prater, Donald, *A Ringing Glass: The Life of Rainer Maria Rilke*, Clarendon/ Oxford University Press, Oxford, 1986, p. 54.

23. Quoted in Prater, *A Ringing Glass*, 1986, p. 54.

24. *"Wir dürfen dich nicht"* (in *Das Buch vom mönchischen Leben/ Das Stunden-Buch*): Rilke, in *Die Gedichte*, 2006, p. 202. (Trans. Mark S. Burrows, 2009.)

25. Brodsky, *Rainer Maria Rilke*, 1988, p. 60. Brodsky also usefully notes that the poems were published "more or less in the order of their composition," pp. 70–1.

26. I have chosen to use the spelling *Das Stunden-Buch*; within quotes the alternate spelling, *Das Stundenbuch*, is sometimes given.

27. Hass, Robert, in Rilke, Rainer Maria, *The Selected Poetry of Rainer Maria Rilke*, ed. & trans. Stephen Mitchell, intro. Robert Hass, Picador, London, 1987, p. xvii.

28. In Andreas-Salomé, Lou, *Looking Back: Memoirs*, trans. Breon Mitchell, Marlowe & Co., New York, 1995, p. 73. (Originally published as *Lebensrückblick*, 1951.)

29. *"Was wirst du tun, Gott"* (in *Das Buch vom mönchischen Leben/ Das Stunden-Buch*): Rilke, *Die Gedichte*, 2006, pp. 216–7. (Trans. Mark S. Burrows, 2009.)

30. Ryan, Judith, *Rilke, Modernism and Poetic Tradition*, Cambridge University Press, Cambridge, 1999, p. 32.

"A DIRECTION OF THE HEART"

1. Andreas-Salomé, Lou, *You Alone Are Real to Me: Remembering Rainer Maria Rilke*, trans. & intro. Angela von der Lippe, BOA Editions, Rochester, NY, 2003 (in German, 1927), p. 38.

2. Merton, Thomas, *The Literary Essays of Thomas Merton*, ed. Patrick Hart, New Directions, New York, 1981, pp. 346, 347, 348.

3. Andreas-Salomé, Lou, *Looking Back: Memoirs*, trans. Breon Mitchell, Marlowe & Co., New York, 1995, p. 88.

4. Hattingberg, Magda von, ed., *Rilke and Benvenuta: An Intimate Correspondence*, trans. Joel Agee, Fromm International, New York, 1987, pp. 125–6 (my itals).

5. In a letter to Franz Xaver Kappus, Rilke spoke of the Bible as one of the few books "indispensable to me." Rilke, Rainer Maria, *Letters to a Young Poet*, trans. M. D. Herter Norton, W. W. Norton & Co., New York, 1993 (1934), p. 25.

6. *"So viele Engel suchen dich im Lichte"* (in *Das Buch vom mönchischen Leben/ Das Stunden-Buch*): Rilke, *Die Gedichte*, Insel Verlag, Frankfurt a. M., 2006, p. 213. (Trans. Mark S. Burrows, 2009.)

7. *"Was irren meine Hände in den Pinseln?"* (in *Das Buch vom mönchischen Leben/ Das Stunden-Buch*): Rilke, *Die Gedichte*, 2006, p. 208. (Trans. Mark S. Burrows, 2009.)

ENDNOTES

8. Peters, H. F., *My Sister, My Spouse*, Gollancz, London, 1963, pp. 210, 211.
9. Marcel, Gabriel, *Homo Viator: Introduction to a Metaphysic of Hope*, trans. Emma Craufurd, Henry Regnery Company, Chicago, 1951, p. 222.
10. Rilke, Rainer Maria, *The Notebooks of Malte Laurids Brigge*, trans. M. D. Herter Norton, W. W. Norton & Co., New York, 1964 (1949), pp. 208–9.
11. Ryan, Judith, *Rilke, Modernism and Poetic Tradition*, Cambridge University Press, Cambridge, 1999, p. 28.
12. Ryan, *Rilke, Modernism and Poetic Tradition*, 1999, p. 28.
13. Cupitt's and Geering's arguments are extensive but relate almost exclusively to the Judeo-Christian "God," the "superhuman referent" in which they no longer believe. A useful summary is provided in Leaves, Nigel, *The God Problem: Alternatives to Fundamentalism*, Polebridge Press, Santa Rosa, CA, 2006.
14. Rilke, Rainer Maria, *Selected Letters 1902–1926*, trans. R. F. C. Hull, intro. John Bayley, Quartet Encounters, London, 1988 (1946), p. 373.
15. "For Hans Carossa" (Muzot, 1924), in Rilke, Rainer Maria, *Poems 1906–26*, trans. J. B. Leishman, The Hogarth Press, London, 1976 (1957), p. 291.
16. Rilke, Rainer Maria, *Diaries of a Young Poet*, trans. & intro. Edward Snow & Michael Winkler, W. W. Norton & Co., New York, 1998, p. 278. (Originally published as *Tagebücher aus der Frühzeit*, 1942.)
17. Hendry, J. F., *The Sacred Threshold: A Life of Rilke*, Carcanet, Manchester, 1983, p. 57. Ellen Key's "Rilke" disappointed her when he wrote *Malte Laurids Brigge*, a book she regarded as "godless."
18. Rilke, *Selected Letters 1902–1926* (Hull), 1988 (1946), p. 373.
19. Peters, H. F., *Rainer Maria Rilke: Masks and the Man*, McGraw-Hill, New York, 1963, p. 95.
20. Hendry, *The Sacred Threshold*, 1983, p. 57.
21. Letter to "L. H.," 8 November 1915, in Rilke, Rainer Maria, *Letters of Rainer Maria Rilke 1910–1926* (Greene & Herter Norton), W. W. Norton & Co., New York, 1969 (1947), p. 146.
22. Letter to "L. H.," 8 November 1915, in Rilke, *Letters of Rainer Maria Rilke 1910–1926* (Greene & Herter Norton), W. W. Norton & Co., New York, 1969 (1947), pp. 147–8 (my itals).
23. Levertov, Denise, in Rilke, Rainer Maria, *Where Silence Reigns: Selected Prose by Rainer Maria Rilke*, trans. G. Craig Houston, foreword Denise Levertov, New Directions, New York, 1978 (foreword unpaginated).
24. *"Ich lebe mein Leben"* (in *Das Buch vom mönchischen Leben/ Das Stunden-Buch*): Rilke, *Die Gedichte*, 2006, p. 201. (Trans. Mark S. Burrows, 2009.)
25. Salis, J. R. von, *Rainer Maria Rilke: The Years in Switzerland*, trans. N. K. Cruickshank, University of California Press, Berkeley, 1964 (1936), pp. 232–3.
26. Salis, *Rainer Maria Rilke*, 1964 (1936), pp. 25, 33, 270, 271.
27. From First Elegy, *Duino Elegies*, in Gass, William H., *Reading Rilke: Reflections on the Problems of Translation*, Basic Books, New York, 1999, p. 191.
28. Olivero, Federico, *Rainer Maria Rilke: A Study in Poetry and Mysticism*, W. Heffer & Sons, Cambridge, 1931, p. 133.
29. "[These poems] presented a superfluous Jesus defeated and shamed by his arrogant attempt to interpose himself between humanity and God. [They] were not published until after his death." Barrows, Anita & Macy, Joanna, in Rilke, *Rilke's Book of Hours: Love Poems to God*, trans., preface & intro. Anita Barrows & Joanna Macy, Riverhead Books, New York, 1996, p. 21.
30. Salomé, *Looking Back*, 1995, p. 88.
31. Lou's exceptional intelligence and empathy are demonstrated by the fact that Freud also felt "understood" by her: "Even during their first meeting Freud felt that Lou understood him perfectly." Peters, *My Sister, My Spouse*, 1963, p. 273.

ENDNOTES

32. Freedman, Ralph, *Life of a Poet: Rainer Maria Rilke*, Farrar, Straus and Giroux, New York, 1996, p. 549. See also: "On December 13 [1926, Nanny Wunderly-Volkart] forwarded his last letter to Lou, together with her own message on his behalf: "You know everything about him, from the beginning until this day. You are aware of his unlimited belief in you—he said: Lou must know everything—perhaps she knows a consolation . . ." in Rilke, Rainer Maria & Andreas-Salomé, Lou, *Rainer Maria Rilke and Lou Andreas-Salomé: The Correspondence*, trans. & intro. Edward Snow & Michael Winkler, W. W. Norton & Co., New York, 2006, p. xvii; Peters, *My Sister, My Spouse*, 1963, p. 251.
33. Salomé, *Looking Back*, 1995, p. 91.
34. Rilke, Rainer Maria, *Uncollected Poems*, trans. Edward Snow, North Point Press, New York, 1996, p. 219.
35. Bachelard, Gaston, *The Poetics of Space: The Classic Look at How We Experience Intimate Places*, trans. Maria Jolas, Beacon, Boston, 1994 (1958), p. 183.
36. Rilke, *Letters of Rainer Maria Rilke 1910–1926* (Greene & Herter Norton), 1969 (1947), pp. 25–6.
37. Quoted in Wydenbruck, Nora, *Rilke: Man and Poet*, Appleton, New York, 1949, p. 65.
38. Letter undated, postmarked 29 July 1920, in Gass, *Reading Rilke*, 1999, p. 183. A slightly different version is quoted in Salis, *Rainer Maria Rilke,* 1964 (1936), p. 242. I refer to this in Section Two.

HUSBAND, FATHER, LOVER—POET

1. Rilke, Rainer Maria, *Diaries of a Young Poet*, trans. & intro. Edward Snow & Michael Winkler, W. W. Norton & Co., New York, 1998, p. 89.
2. Rilke: "Well, if you insist on it, I suppose I am a German poet, but only on my own terms." Quoted in Mason, E. C., *Rilke, Europe, and the English-Speaking World*, Cambridge University Press, Cambridge, 1961, p. 25.
3. Mason, *Rilke, Europe, and the English-Speaking World*, 1961, p. 9. Also, "He feels himself less a native of Austria than of Russia, France, Italy or Spain," p. 11.
4. Mason, *Rilke, Europe, and the English-Speaking World*, 1961, p. 9.
5. The name *Rainer* has the same sound as *reine* (pure), and rhymes with Mari‾a and with Rilk‾e. (In sound we hear "pure Mary.") His name itself became a poem and is also shaped by the feminine (Maria) abutting the more masculine Rainer.
6. Quoted in Mandel, Siegfried, *Rainer Maria Rilke: The Poetic Instinct*, preface Henry T. Moore, Southern Illinois University Press, Carbondale, 1965, p. 4.
7. Mason, *Rilke, Europe, and the English-Speaking World*, 1961, p. 11.
8. Freedman, Ralph, *Life of a Poet: Rainer Maria Rilke*, Farrar, Straus and Giroux, New York, 1996, p. 117.
9. Freedman, *Life of a Poet*, 1996, p. 127.
10. *"Du, Nachbar Gott"* (in *Das Buch vom mönchischen Leben/Das Stunden-Buch*): Rilke, Rainer Maria, *Die Gedichte*, Insel Verlag, Frankfurt a. M., 2006, p. 202. (My translation.)
11. "Prayer" (1900), in Rilke, *Diaries of a Young Poet* (Snow & Winkler), 1998, p. 219.
12. Klee, Paul, *On Modern Art*, Faber & Faber, London, 1989 (1924), pp. 49–50. Reviewing Klee's deeply intuitive writing, Eric Newton in *The Listener* admired it, with some absence of congruity, as ". . . a solid, efficient piece of logical analysis" (quoted on book flap).
13. Untitled poem written about August 1914, in Rilke, Rainer Maria, *Poems 1906–26*, trans. J. B. Leishman, The Hogarth Press, London, 1976 (1957), p. 193.
14. Bachelard, Gaston, *The Poetics of Space: The Classic Look at How We Experience Intimate Places*, trans. Maria Jolas, Beacon, Boston, 1994 (1958), pp. 201, 202.

ENDNOTES

15. Baer, Ulrich, in Rilke, Rainer Maria, *The Poet's Guide to Life: The Wisdom of Rilke*, ed. & trans. Ulrich Baer, Modern Library/Random House, New York, 2005, p. xi.

16. Bly, Robert, in Rilke, Rainer Maria, *Selected Poems of Rainer Maria Rilke*, trans., intro. & commentary Robert Bly, Harper & Row, New York, 1981, p. 157. Although it is unlikely that Rilke was aware of this, it is notable that Cézanne, whom Rilke so admired, believed he could not afford to give up painting time to attend his mother's funeral.

17. Peters, H. F., *My Sister, My Spouse*, Gollancz, London, 1963, p. 213.

18. "Requiem for a friend," in Rilke, Rainer Maria, *The Selected Poetry of Rainer Maria Rilke*, ed. & trans. Stephen Mitchell, intro. Robert Hass, Picador, London, 1987, p. 73.

19. Mandel, *Rainer Maria Rilke*, 1965, p. 45.

20. In Torgersen, Eric, *Dear Friend: Rainer Maria Rilke and Paula Modersohn-Becker*, Northwestern University Press, Evanston, IL, 1998, p. 43.

21. Wydenbruck, Nora, *Rilke: Man and Poet*, Appleton, New York, 1949, p. 112.

22. Rilke, Rainer Maria, *Letters of Rainer Maria Rilke 1910–1926*, trans. Jane Bannard Greene & M. D. Herter Norton, W. W. Norton & Co., New York, 1969 (1947), pp. 262, 263.

23. Pasternak, Boris, Tsvetayeva, Marina & Rilke, Rainer Maria, *Letters Summer 1926*, trans. Margaret Wettling & Walter Arndt, Oxford University Press, Oxford, 1988, p. 14 (my itals).

24. Leishman, J. B., in Rilke, *Poems 1906–26* (Leishman), 1976 (1957), p. 11.

25. Quoted in Leppmann, Wolfgang, *Rilke: A Life*, trans. Russell M. Stockman, Fromm International, New York, 1984, p. 169.

26. Quoted in Kleinbard, David, *The Beginning of Terror: A Psychological Study of Rainer Maria Rilke's Life and Work*, foreword Jeffrey Berman, New York University Press, New York, 1993, p. 122. Kleinbard seems to contradict this, however, when he adds: "Reading Rilke's letters to Clara from 1900 to 1911, one realizes that his respect for his wife grew during this time, although in no way could he see her as his equal in artistic achievement and genius. His respect depended upon her willingness to protect his freedom and distance . . ." p. 122.

27. Freedman, *Life of a Poet*, pp. 547, 550.

28. Torgersen, *Dear Friend*, 1998, p. 90.

29. Letter 1901, quoted in Rilke, *The Poet's Guide to Life*, 2005, p. 36.

30. The complete letter from which this passage is taken can be found in Rilke, Rainer Maria, *Letters to a Young Poet*, trans. & foreword Stephen Mitchell, Vintage, New York, 1986, pp. 65–79. Rilke's use of *distances* is striking here, resonant also of some of his descriptions of God and "new distances" and of the passionate invocation that opens "Sonnet to Orpheus, II, 29": *Stiller Freund der vielen Fernen . . .* (Silent friend of many distances . . .).

31. Hirshfield, Jane, *Nine Gates: Entering the Mind of Poetry*, Harper Perennial, New York, 1998, p.166.

32. Hirshfield, *Nine Gates*, 1998, p. 166.

33. Rilke, Rainer Maria, *Selected Letters 1902–1926*, trans. R. F. C. Hull, intro. John Bayley, Quartet Encounters, London, 1988 (1946), pp. 14–15.

34. Rilke, *Selected Letters 1902–1926* (Hull), 1988 (1946), pp. 14–15 (my itals).

35. Rilke, Rainer Maria, *Uncollected Poems*, trans. Edward Snow, North Point Press, New York, 1996, p. 55. (Written in Paris, early 1913.)

36. "The language barrier is too great. Today I took him my poems—if only he [Rodin] could read them," in Leppmann, *Rilke*, 1984, p. 169. Rilke later fully mastered French and wrote many of his later poems in that language.

37. Rilke, Rainer Maria, *Auguste Rodin*, trans. Daniel Slager, intro. William Gass, Archipelago Books, New York, 2004 (1903). It opens with the unforgettable autobiographically

ENDNOTES

prescient lines: "Rodin was solitary before he was famous. And fame, when it arrived, made him perhaps even more solitary." p. 31.

38. Bly in Rilke, *Selected Poems of Rainer Maria Rilke* (Bly), 1981, p. 63.

39. Quoted in Dirda, Michael, *Book by Book: Notes on Reading and Life*, Henry Holt, New York, 2005, pp. 27–8.

40. Snow, Edward, in Rilke, Rainer Maria, *New Poems*, trans. & intro. Edward Snow, North Point Press, New York, 2001, p. 3.

41. McClatchy, J. D., "Rainer Maria Rilke," *Poetry*, Vol. 185, No. 1, October 2004.

42. Bayley, John, intro., in Rilke, *Selected Letters 1902–1926* (Hull), 1988 (1946), p. xvi.

43. Kirsch, Arthur C., *Auden and Christianity*, Yale University Press, New Haven, 2005, pp. 168–9.

44. Auden, W. H., in Metzger, E. A. & Metzger, M. M., eds., *A Companion to the Works of Rainer Maria Rilke*, Camden House, Rochester, NY, 2001, p. 15. In addition to the story quoted above, Auden evoked "Rilkean" angels in his 1939 collection, *In Times of War*. Auden's image of stroking "that tower" comes from a letter from Rilke to Lou, 11 February 1922: "I went out and stroked, as if it were a great old beast, the little Muzot that had sheltered all this for me [waiting for the *Elegies*] . . ." Rilke, Rainer Maria, *Rilke: Selected Letters*, ed. Harry T. Moore, Anchor, New York, 1960, p. 319.

45. "'Death,'" [Rilke's physician] Dr. Hammerli wrote, "'was among the problems of his *oeuvre*, and yet the idea of having to pass away so young was unacceptable to him; he did not believe it possible, perhaps up to the last day of his illness.'" In Mandel, *Rainer Maria Rilke*, 1965, p. 200.

46. Kinnell, Galway, in Rilke, Rainer Maria, *The Essential Rilke*, trans. Galway Kinnell & Hannah Liebmann, intro. Galway Kinnell, Ecco Press/HarperCollins, New York, 1999, p. xii.

47. Bennett, Alan, "The Wrong Blond," in Spice, Nicholas, ed., *London Reviews*, Chatto & Windus, London, 1985, pp. 85–6.

48. Mendelsohn, Daniel, "A Line-by-Line Safari," *New York Times Book Review*, New York, 30 January 2000.

49. Lines from First Elegy (in *Duineser Elegien*): Rilke, *Die Gedichte*, 2006, p. 689. (Trans. Mark S. Burrows, 2009.)

50. Rilke, *Letters of Rainer Maria Rilke 1910–1926* (Greene & Herter Norton), 1969 (1947), p. 262.

51. Bayley, John, in Rilke, *Selected Letters 1902–1926* (Hull), 1988 (1946), p. xvi.

52. Murdoch, Iris, *Metaphysics as a Guide to Morals*, Penguin, London, 1993, p. 428.

53. Murdoch, *Metaphysics as a Guide to Morals*, 1993, pp. 428–30.

54. *"Ich lese es heraus aus deinem Wort"* (in *Das Buch vom mönchischen Leben/Das Stunden-Buch*): Rilke, *Die Gedichte*, 2006, pp. 203–4. (Trans. Mark S. Burrows, 2009.)

55. Murdoch, *Metaphysics as a Guide to Morals*, 1993, p. 430.

56. In *In Praise of Mortality: Selections from Rainer Maria Rilke's Duino Elegies and Sonnets to Orpheus*, trans. Anita Barrows & Joanna Macy, Riverhead Books, New York, 2005, p. 4.

57. Rilke, *The Selected Poetry of Rainer Maria Rilke* (Mitchell), 1987, p. 289. This is a particularly thrilling translation.

58. Rilke in Pasternak, Tsvetayeva & Rilke, *Letters Summer 1926* (Wettling & Arndt), 1988, p. 129.

59. Norton, M. D. Herter, in Rilke, Rainer Maria, *The Notebooks of Malte Laurids Brigge*, trans. M. D. Herter Norton, W. W. Norton & Co., New York, 1964 (1949), p. 8.

60. Auden, W. H., from "In Memory of W. B. Yeats," *Collected Poems*, ed. Edward Mendelson, Vintage, New York, 1991, p. 247.

61. From a letter to Franz Xaver Kappus (the "Young Poet"), quoted in Wydenbruck, *Rilke*, 1949, pp. 97–8. Wydenbruck uses *parturition* where I have used *birth*.

ENDNOTES

THE MAKING OF A POET

1. Kappus, Franz Xaver, in Rilke, Rainer Maria, *Letters to a Young Poet*, trans. M. D. Herter Norton, W. W. Norton & Co., New York, 1993 (1934), pp. 12–13.
2. Leppmann, Wolfgang, *Rilke: A Life*, trans. Russell M. Stockman, Fromm International, New York, 1984, p. 179.
3. Quoted in Rilke, *Letters to a Young Poet* (Herter Norton), 1993 (1934), pp. 118–9.
4. Hendry, J. F., *The Sacred Threshold: A Life of Rilke*, Carcanet, Manchester, 1983, p. 11.
5. He did occasionally fantasize about studying for other professions, variously: natural sciences, medicine and law. However, he was also self-aware enough to know (at least in 1904) that "Universities have so far afforded me little; there is so much resistance in my nature to their ways . . . Inexperienced in books, I roam about in them in perpetual dumb peasant-wonderment awe." Rilke, Rainer Maria & Andreas-Salomé, Lou, *Rainer Maria Rilke and Lou Andreas-Salomé: The Correspondence*, trans. & intro. Edward Snow & Michael Winkler, W. W. Norton & Co., New York, 2006, pp. 118, 77.
6. "Theresia Mayerhof, Phia's great-grandmother on her mother's side, appears to have been Jewish." In Leppmann, *Rilke*, 1984, p. 6.
7. Leppmann, *Rilke*, 1984, p. 201.
8. Quoted in Mandel, Siegfried, *Rainer Maria Rilke: The Poetic Instinct*, preface Henry T. Moore, Southern Illinois University Press, Carbondale, 1965, p. 4 (my itals).
9. Torgersen, Eric, *Dear Friend: Rainer Maria Rilke and Paula Modersohn-Becker*, Northwestern University Press, Evanston, IL, 1998, p. 13.
10. Rilke, Rainer Maria, *Rilke: Selected Letters*, ed. Harry T. Moore, Anchor, New York, 1960, p. 263.
11. Rilke, Rainer Maria, *Letters of Rainer Maria Rilke 1910–1926*, trans. Jane Bannard Greene & M. D. Herter Norton, W. W. Norton & Co., New York, 1969 (1947), p. 296.
12. Rilke, Rainer Maria, *Letters of Rainer Maria Rilke 1910–1926* (Greene & Herter Norton), 1969 (1947), pp. 350, 346.
13. Gass, William H., *Reading Rilke: Reflections on the Problems of Translation*, Basic Books, New York, 1999, p. 10.
14. His mother demanded the "exclusive privilege" of washing his gloves. In Hendry, *The Sacred Threshold*, 1983, p. 105.
15. Rilke, Rainer Maria, *Letters of Rainer Maria Rilke 1910–1926* (Greene & Herter Norton), 1969 (1947), pp. 237–9.
16. "Nothing caused him more distress than his awareness that he had taken on some of mother's worst qualities." In Kleinbard, David, *The Beginning of Terror: A Psychological Study of Rainer Maria Rilke's Life and Work*, foreword Jeffrey Berman, New York University Press, New York, 1993, p. 65.
17. Freedman, Ralph, *Life of a Poet: Rainer Maria Rilke*, Farrar, Straus and Giroux, New York, 1996, p. 10.
18. Rilke, *Letters of Rainer Maria Rilke 1910–1926* (Greene & Herter Norton), 1969 (1947), p. 90.
19. "Oh sage Dichter, was du tust?" (December 1921, Muzot), in Rilke, Rainer Maria, *Die Gedichte*, Insel Verlag, Frankfurt a. M., 2006, p. 681. (Trans. Mark S. Burrows, 2009.) In "Birds' voices are starting to praise," Rilke writes: "We're the ones in masks, oh God, and in costumes!" Rilke, Rainer Maria, *The Unknown Rilke*, trans. Franz Wright, Oberlin College Press, Oberlin, 1990, p. 171.
20. Leppmann, *Rilke*, 1984, p. 29.
21. Phillips, Brian, "The Angel and the Egoist," *The New Republic*, 8 May 2000.
22. *"Sie sagen mein und nennen das Besitz,"* in Mandel, *Rainer Maria Rilke*, 1965, p. 55.

ENDNOTES

23. Rilke, Rainer Maria, *Rilke's Late Poetry*, trans. Graham Good, Ronsdale Press, Vancouver, 2004, p. 135.
24. Rilke & Andreas-Salomé, *The Correspondence* (Snow & Winkler), 2006, p. 247.

WHAT ARE POETS FOR?

1. Bernstein, Michael André, *Five Portraits: Modernity and the Imagination in Twentieth-Century Writing,* Northwestern University Press, Evanston, IL, 2000, p. 29.
2. Bernstein, *Five Portraits*, 2000, pp. 29–30.
3. Ritzer, Walter, *Rainer Maria Rilke Bibliographie,* Wien, 1951, quoted in Peters, H. F., *Rainer Maria Rilke: Masks and the Man*, McGraw-Hill, New York, 1963, p. 205.
4. Matthew 18:3.
5. Peters, H. F., *Rainer Maria Rilke: Masks and the Man*, McGraw-Hill, New York, 1963, p. 9 (my itals).
6. Rilke, Rainer Maria, *Letters to a Young Poet*, trans. M. D. Herter Norton, W. W. Norton & Co., New York, 1993 (1934), pp. 29–30.
7. Marcel, Gabriel, *Homo Viator: Introduction to a Metaphysic of Hope*, trans. Emma Craufurd, Henry Regnery Company, Chicago, 1951, pp. 263–4.
8. *"Du Dunkelheit, aus der ich stamme"* (in *Das Buch vom mönchischen Leben/ Das Stunden-Buch*): Rilke, Rainer Maria, *Die Gedichte*, Insel Verlag, Frankfurt a. M., 2006, pp. 204–5. (Trans. Mark S. Burrows, 2009.) The last line is literally a credo: "I believe in nights." (*Ich glaube an Nächte.*)
9. Quoted in Peters, *Rainer Maria Rilke*, 1963, p. 9.
10. Rilke, Rainer Maria, *Uncollected Poems*, trans. Edward Snow, North Point Press, New York, 1996, p. 191. (Written in Muzot, 1924.)
11. Burrows, Mark S., "'To Taste with the Heart': Allegory, Poetics, and the Deep Reading of Scripture," *Interpretation,* Vol. 56, No. 2, April 2002, p. 171 (my itals).
12. Burrows, Mark S., private correspondence, 2008.
13. Heidegger, Martin, *Poetry, Language, Thought*, trans. & intro. Albert Hofstadter, Harper Perennial, New York, 2001 (1975), pp. 89, 90, 92.
14. Furtak, Rick Anthony, in Rilke, Rainer Maria, *Sonnets to Orpheus*, trans. & intro. Rick Anthony Furtak, University of Scranton Press, Scranton & London, 2007, p. 6.
15. Bachelard, Gaston, *The Poetics of Space: The Classic Look at How We Experience Intimate Places*, trans. Maria Jolas, Beacon, Boston, 1994 (1958), p. xx.
16. Heidegger, *Poetry, Language, Thought* (Hofstadter), 2001 (1975), pp. 93, 94–6.
17. It is sobering to note that Hans-Georg Gadamer was to say of Heidegger, whose student he had been, in relation to the latter's considerable and never entirely regretted enthusiasm for German National Socialism, that he was "the greatest of thinkers, but the smallest of men." And while Gadamer may, with his wit, have been point-scoring, his "point" about Heidegger remains relevant in this context, less as an invitation to self-righteous judgment than as further demonstration of the quandary readers may experience as they attempt to mediate the tension between a thinker and his or her thoughts.
18. Gadamer, Hans-Georg in Palmer, Richard E., ed., *Gadamer in Conversation: Reflections and Commentary,* Yale University Press, New Haven, 2001, p. 72.
19. Rilke, Rainer Maria, *Letters to Merline 1919–1922*, trans. Jesse Browner, Paragon House, New York, 1989 (1950), p. 29.
20. *"Werkleute sind wir"* (in *Das Buch vom mönchischen Leben/ Das Stunden-Buch*): Rilke, *Die Gedichte,* 2006, p. 212. (Trans. Mark S. Burrows, 2009.)

ENDNOTES

LOOKING WITH ALICE AND JAMES

1. Miller, Alice, *For Your Own Good: Hidden Cruelty in Child-Rearing and the Roots of Violence*, trans. Hildegarde & Hunter Hannum, Faber & Faber, London, 1983, pp. 4, 243.

2. Miller, Alice, *The Drama of the Gifted Child and the Search for the True Self*, trans. Ruth Ward, Faber & Faber, London, 1983 (1979), p. 81.

3. Miller, Alice, *The Body Never Lies: The Lingering Effects of Cruel Parenting*, trans. Andrew Jenkins, W. W. Norton & Co., New York, 2005, p. 113.

4. Miller, Alice, *The Untouched Key: Tracing Childhood Trauma in Creativity and Destructiveness*, trans. Hildegarde & Hunter Hannum, Virago, London, 1990, pp. 168–9.

5. Miller, *The Body Never Lies*, 2005, p. 206.

6. In Freedman, Ralph, *Life of a Poet: Rainer Maria Rilke*, Farrar, Straus and Giroux, New York, 1996, p. 11.

7. From the Fourth Elegy, in Rilke, Rainer Maria, *Duino Elegies: Bilingual Edition*, trans. Edward Snow, North Point Press/Farrar, Straus and Giroux, New York, 2000, p. 25.

8. Gass, William H., *Reading Rilke: Reflections on the Problems of Translation*, Basic Books, New York, 1999, p. 12. Gass follows this with one of the worst of the trivializing misfirings in this otherwise fascinating book: "Kid, Kitchen, Kirk, Koffee in which to dip a Kookie: they add up to Komfort."

9. Gass, *Reading Rilke*, 1999, p. 17.

10. Hass, Robert, in Rilke, Rainer Maria, *The Selected Poetry of Rainer Maria Rilke*, ed. & trans. Stephen Mitchell, intro. Robert Hass, Picador, London, 1987, p. xi.

11. Mandel, Siegfried, *Rainer Maria Rilke: The Poetic Instinct*, preface Henry T. Moore, Southern Illinois University Press, Carbondale, 1965, p. 23 (my itals).

12. Quoted in Hendry, J. F., *The Sacred Threshold: A Life of Rilke*, Carcanet, Manchester, 1983, p. 13.

13. Readers of the Rilke biographies are likely to be struck by the similarities between Rilke's affair with Magda von Hattingberg—"Benvenuta"—in 1914 and his longer affair with Elizabeth (Baladine) Klossowska—"Merline"—which began in 1919.

14. Some of this strange, off-putting essay appears in Rilke, Rainer Maria, *Where Silence Reigns: Selected Prose by Rainer Maria Rilke*, trans. G. Craig Houston, foreword Denise Levertov, New Directions, New York, 1978, pp. 43–50.

15. Peters, H. F., *Rainer Maria Rilke: Masks and the Man*, McGraw-Hill, New York, 1963, pp. 141–2.

16. Miller, *The Drama of the Gifted Child*, 1983 (1979), pp. 126, 127.

17. Rilke, Rainer Maria, *Diaries of a Young Poet*, trans. & intro. Edward Snow & Michael Winkler, W. W. Norton & Co., New York, 1998, pp. 221–2.

18. *"Der Dichter"* (in *Neue Gedichte*): Rilke, Rainer Maria, *Die Gedichte*, Insel Verlag, Frankfurt a. M., 2006, p. 451. (My translation.)

19. 24 January 1912, in Rilke, Rainer Maria, *Letters of Rainer Maria Rilke 1910–1926*, trans. Jane Bannard Greene & M. D. Herter Norton, W. W. Norton & Co., New York, 1969 (1947), p. 49.

20. Rilke, Rainer Maria, *Duino Elegies*, trans. J. B. Leishman & Stephen Spender, The Hogarth Press, London, 1948, p. 20.

21. Rilke, Rainer Maria & Andreas-Salomé, Lou, *Rainer Maria Rilke and Lou Andreas-Salomé: The Correspondence*, trans. & intro. Edward Snow & Michael Winkler, W. W. Norton & Co., New York, 2006, p. 166.

22. *"Ich bete wieder, du Erlauchter"* in Rilke, Rainer Maria, *Rilke's Book of Hours: Love Poems to God*, trans., preface & intro. Anita Barrows & Joanna Macy, Riverhead Books, New York, 1996, pp. 97–8.

ENDNOTES

23. From Third Elegy, Rilke, *Duino Elegies* (Snow), 2000, p. 21.
24. Hillman, James, *The Soul's Code: In Search of Character and Calling*, Random House, Sydney, 1996, pp. 63, 68, 78, 77 (my itals).
25. See Leppmann, Wolfgang, *Rilke: A Life*, trans. Russell M. Stockman, Fromm, New York, 1984, p. 13.
26. Salis, J. R. von, *Rainer Maria Rilke: The Years in Switzerland*, trans. N. K. Cruickshank, University of California Press, Berkeley, 1964 (1936), p. 131.
27. Gass, *Reading Rilke*, 1999, p. 31.
28. Hillman, *The Soul's Code*, 1996, pp. 28–9.
29. Salis, *Rainer Maria Rilke* (Cruickshank), 1964 (1936), p. 131.
30. In 1912 Rilke came close to seeking psychoanalysis, but it was Lou Andreas-Salomé who urged against it, a decision he came to value. See Rilke & Salomé, *The Correspondence* (Snow & Winkler), 2006, pp. xv–xvii, 175ff. See also Rilke's own remark: "Psychoanalysis is too fundamental a help for me, it helps once and for all, makes a clean sweep of things, and to find myself swept clean one day might be even more hopeless than this disarray," p. 177.
31. *"Ich liebe meines Wesens Dunkelstunden"* (in *von mönischen Leben/Das Stunden-Buch*): Rilke, *Die Gedichte*, 2006, p. 202. (Trans. Mark S. Burrows, 2009.)
32. Hillman, *The Soul's Code*, 1996, p. 111.
33. Letter to Ellen Key, 3 April 1903, in Rilke, Rainer Maria, *Rilke: Selected Letters*, ed. Harry T. Moore, Anchor, New York, 1960, pp. 43–4. This striking "animation" of things (and sense of comfort from things as "people" failed him) is taken forward in Section Two in relation to Rilke's "thing poems."
34. Hillman, *The Soul's Code*, 1996, p. 112.
35. Rilke, Rainer Maria, *The Poet's Guide: The Wisdom of Rilke*, ed. & trans. Ulrich Baer, Modern Library/Random House, New York, 2005, p. 48.
36. From "Straining so hard," in Rilke, *The Selected Poetry of Rainer Maria Rilke* (Mitchell), 1987, p. 127.
37. Bernstein, Michael André, *Five Portraits: Modernity and the Imagination in Twentieth-Century Writing*, Northwestern University Press, Evanston, IL, 2000, p. 30.
38. Wydenbruck, Nora, *Rilke: Man and Poet*, Appleton, New York, 1949, p. 347.
39. Salis, *Rainer Maria Rilke: The Years in Switzerland* (Cruickshank), 1964 (1936), p. 243.
40. Freedman, *Life of a Poet*, 1996, p. 544.
41. Wydenbruck, *Rilke*, 1949, p. 360.
42. Freedman, *Life of a Poet*, 1996, p. 544.
43. Rilke, *Rilke* (Moore), 1960, p. 43.
44. From "Turning," sent to Lou with a letter from Paris, 20 June 1914, in Rilke, *Letters of Rainer Maria Rilke 1910–1926* (Greene & Herter Norton), 1969 (1947), p. 117. The poem is given in full and discussed in Section Two.
45. Bachelard, Gaston, *The Poetics of Space: The Classic Look at How We Experience Intimate Places*, trans. Maria Jolas, Beacon, Boston, 1994 (1958), pp. xix–xx.

THE LANGUAGES OF LONGING

1. This statement, often attributed directly to Nietzsche, appears through the voice of the madman in *The Gay Science*, 1882. In his introduction to the Penguin Classic edition of *Beyond Good and Evil* (1886), Nietzschean scholar Michael Tanner writes: "The man is regarded as mad precisely because he makes such a fuss about God's death, which seems to be a matter of indifference to the people in the marketplace. Nietzsche is of

ENDNOTES

course the madman, and everything he produced after this proclamation is written in its shadow." Penguin, London, 2003 (1886), p. 26.

2. "God speaks," Rilke, Rainer Maria, *Rilke's Book of Hours: Love Poems to God*, trans., preface & intro. Anita Barrows & Joanna Macy, Riverhead Books, New York, 1996, p. 88.

3. Rilke, Rainer Maria, *The Poet's Guide to Life: The Wisdom of Rilke*, ed. & trans. Ulrich Baer, Modern Library/Random House, New York, 2005, p. 169.

4. Quoted in Otto, Rudolph (Rudolf), *Mysticism East and West*, trans. B. L. Bracey & R. C. Payne, Collier Books, New York, 1962 (1932), pp. 81, 87–8.

5. Hick, John, *An Interpretation of Religion: Human Responses to the Transcendent*, 2nd ed., Palgrave, Basingstoke, 2004, p. 151.

6. Quoted in Romanyshyn, Robert D., *Ways of the Heart: Essays Toward an Imaginal Psychology*, Trivium, Pittsburgh, 2002, p. 162.

7. Otto, *Mysticism East and West* (Bracey & Payne), 1962 (1932), p. 83.

8. From Rilke, Rainer Maria, "Archaic Torso of Apollo" (in *New Poems*): see p. 327, n. 28.

9. Rilke, *The Poet's Guide to Life* (Baer), 2005, p. 112.

10. From *"Ich bin, du Ängstlicher"* (in *Das Buch vom mönchischen Leben/Das Stunden-Buch*): Rilke, Rainer Maria, *Die Gedichte*, Insel Verlag, Frankfurt a. M., 2006, p. 208. (My translation.)

11. *"Du siehst, ich will viel"* (in *Das Buch vom mönchischen Leben/Das Stunden-Buch*): Rilke, *Die Gedichte*, 2006, p. 206. (Trans. Mark S. Burrows, 2009.)

12. Komar, Kathleen L., in Metzger, E. A. & Metzger, M. M., eds., *A Companion to the Works of Rainer Maria Rilke*, Camden House, Rochester, NY, 2001, p. 189.

13. From Wordsworth, William, "Ode: Intimations of Immortality from Recollections of Early Childhood," in Ricks, Christopher, ed., *The Oxford Book of English Verse*, Oxford University Press, Oxford, 1999, p. 351.

14. The meaning may express more yearning than "homesickness": *". . . du Großes Heimweh, das wir nicht bezwangen."* In Rilke, *Rilke's Book of Hours* (Barrows & Macy), 1996, p. 70.

15. Quoted in Ferrucci, Piero, *Inevitable Grace*, trans. David Kennard, Crucible, Wellingborough,1990, p. 99.

16. Rilke, *The Poet's Guide to Life* (Baer), 2005, p. 89.

17. Mojtabai, A. G., in Gass, William H. & Cuoco, Lorin, eds., *The Writer and Religion*, Southern Illinois University Press, Chicago, 2000, pp. 64–5.

18. Baer, in Rilke, *The Poet's Guide to Life* (Baer), 2005, p. xiii.

19. Rilke, *The Poet's Guide to Life* (Baer), 2005, pp. 172, 173.

20. Rumi, Moulana, *Masnavi III*, 4398–9 (various translations; my itals).

21. Barks, Coleman & Moyne, John, trans., *The Essential Rumi,* HarperSanFrancisco, San Francisco, 1995, p. 205.

22. Griffiths, Bede, *The Golden String*, Fount Paperbacks, London, 1979 (1954), p. 142 (my itals).

23. Part II, XXI, *Sonnets to Orpheus*, in Good, Graham, trans. ed. & commentary, *Rilke's Late Poetry*, Ronsdale Press, Vancouver, 2004, p. 105.

24. From Tenth Elegy, in Rilke, Rainer Maria, *The Selected Poetry of Rainer Maria Rilke*, ed. & trans. Stephen Mitchell, intro. Robert Hass, Picador, London, 1987, p. 211.

25. O'Donohue, John, *Divine Beauty: The Invisible Embrace*, Bantam, London, 2004, p. 90.

TERROR AND INSPIRATION

1. From "The Song of the Women to the Poet," in Rilke, Rainer Maria, *New Poems*, trans. & intro. Edward Snow, North Point Press, New York, 2001, p. 45.

ENDNOTES

2. In Rilke, Rainer Maria, *Selected Letters 1902–1926*, trans. R. F. C. Hull, intro. John Bayley, Quartet Encounters, London, 1988 (1946), p. 285.

3. Burrows, Mark S., "Prayers to a Dark God: Rainer Maria Rilke Among the Mystics," article forthcoming.

4. Burrows, Mark S., "Raiding the Inarticulate: Mysticism, Poetics, and the Unlanguageable," *Spiritus*, Vol. 4, No. 2, Fall 2004, p. 184.

5. Griffiths, Bede, *A Human Search: Bede Griffiths Reflects on His Life*, ed. John Swindells, foreword Wayne Teasdale, Triumph, Liguori, 1997, p. 100.

6. Rilke, Rainer Maria, "Du bist die Zukunft" (from *Das Stunden-Buch*) in Bly, Robert, *The Soul Is Here for Its Own Good*, Ecco, Hopewell, NJ, 1995, p. 105.

7. Rilke, Rainer Maria, *Diaries of a Young Poet*, trans. & intro. Edward Snow & Michael Winkler, W. W. Norton & Co., New York, 1998, pp. 219–20.

8. Rilke, *Diaries of a Young Poet* (Snow & Winkler), 1998, pp. 222–4.

9. Letter to Leopold von Schlözer, quoted in Pasternak, Boris, Tsvetayeva, Marina & Rilke, Rainer Maria, *Letters Summer 1926*, trans. Margaret Wettling & Walter Arndt, Oxford University Press, Oxford, 1988, p. 5.

10. Quoted in Wydenbruck, Nora, *Rilke: Man and Poet*, Appleton, New York, 1949, p. 60 (my itals).

11. 11 August 1924 to Nora Wydenbruck in Rilke, *Selected Letters 1902–1926* (Hull), 1988 (1946), pp. 386–7 (3rd para: my itals).

12. Khan, Hazrat Inayat, "Bowl of Saki," extracts from *Sufi Mysticism Vol X*, http://wahiduddin.net/mv2/X/X_4_8.htm

13. Letter to Nanny Wunderly-Volkart, undated, postmarked 29 July 1920, in Salis, J. R. von, *Rainer Maria Rilke: The Years in Switzerland*, trans. N. K. Cruickshank, University of California Press, Berkeley, 1964 (1936), p. 242. A slightly different version is given in Gass, *Reading Rilke: Reflections on the Problem of Translation*, Basic Books, New York, 1999, p. 183, and I used that in Section One.

14. From *"Und du erbst das Grün"* (in *Das Buch von der Pilgerschaft/ Das Stunden-Buch*): Rilke, Rainer Maria, *Die Gedichte*, Insel Verlag, Frankfurt a. M., 2006, p. 243. (My translation.)

15. Rilke, *Selected Letters 1902–1926* (Hull), 1988 (1946), p. 265.

16. Rilke, Rainer Maria, *Rilke: Selected Letters*, ed. Harry T. Moore, Anchor, New York, 1960, pp. 275–6.

17. From Rilke's final collection, *Vergers suivis de quatrain valaisans*, published in 1926. French text in Wydenbruck, *Rilke*, 1949, p. 344. (My translation.)

18. Rilke, *The Poet's Guide to Life: The Wisdom of Rilke*, ed. & trans. Ulrich Baer, Modern Library, Random House, New York, 2005, p. 175.

19. Bachelard, Gaston, *The Poetics of Space: The Classic Look at How We Experience Intimate Places*, trans. Maria Jolas, Beacon, Boston, 1994 (1958), p. 36 (my itals).

WAYS OF KNOWING

1. Shree, Purohit Swami & Yeats, W. B., *The Ten Principal Upanishads*, Faber & Faber, London, 1970 (1937), pp. 49–50.

2. Yeats, W. B., in Shree & Yeats, *The Ten Principal Upanishads*, 1970 (1937), p. 11.

3. Rilke, Rainer Maria, *Selected Poems of Rainer Maria Rilke*, trans., intro. & commentary Robert Bly, Harper & Row, New York, 1981, p. 49.

4. In Peters, H. F., *Rainer Maria Rilke: Masks and the Man*, McGraw-Hill, New York, 1963, p. 125.

5. "For Fräulein Maria von Hefner-Alteneck," December 1919, in Rilke, Rainer Maria, *Poems 1906–26*, trans. J. B. Leishman, The Hogarth Press, London, 1976 (1957), p. 243.

ENDNOTES

6. Zaehner, R. C., *At Sundry Times: An Essay in the Comparison of Religion*, Faber & Faber, London, 1958, p. 26.

7. Griffiths, Bede, *A Human Search: Bede Griffiths Reflects on His Life*, ed. John Swindells, foreword Wayne Teasdale, Triumph, Liguori, 1997, p. 101.

8. Griffiths, Bede, *The Other Half of My Soul: Bede Griffiths and the Hindu–Christian Dialogue*, ed. Beatrice Bruteau, The Theosophical Publishing House, Wheaton, IL, 1996, p. 93.

9. *Bhagavad Gita* 9:16.

10. Psalms 139:24.

11. Andreas-Salomé, Lou, *You Alone Are Real to Me: Remembering Rainer Maria Rilke*, trans. & intro. Angela von der Lippe, BOA Editions, Rochester, NY, 2003, p. 38.

12. Freedman, Ralph, *Life of a Poet: Rainer Maria Rilke*, Farrar, Straus, and Giroux, New York, 1996, p. 325.

13. *"Ich liebe dich, du sanftestes Gesetz"* (in *Das Buch vom mönchischen Leben/Das Stunden-Buch*): Rilke, *Die Gedichte,* 2006, p. 211. (Trans. Mark S. Burrows, 2009.)

14. Rilke, Rainer Maria, *Rilke: Selected Letters*, ed. Harry T. Moore, Anchor, New York, 1960, p. 108.

15. Rilke, Rainer Maria, *The Poet's Guide to Life: The Wisdom of Rilke*, ed. & trans. Ulrich Baer, Modern Library/Random House, New York, 2005, p. 170.

16. "Sonnett II, XXIX" (in *Die Sonette an Orpheus*): Rilke, Rainer Maria, *Die Gedichte*, Insel Verlag, Frankfurt a. M., 2006, p. 748. (Trans. Mark S. Burrows, 2009.) Judith Ryan notes that "From Goethe, Rilke also adopted several items of vocabulary . . . notably the *word Übermaß* (excess, in the sense of something splendidly overwhelming) . . ." Ryan, Judith, *Rilke, Modernism and Poetic Tradition*, Cambridge University Press, Cambridge, 1999, p. 135. This poem is particularly difficult to translate. Stephen Mitchell, for example, offers: "*In this immeasurable darkness, be the power/that rounds your senses in their magic ring."* *The Selected Poetry of Rainer Maria Rilke*, intro. Robert Hass, Picador, London, 1982, pp. 254–5. Edward Snow translates: "*In this night of fire and excess, stand/as magic power at your senses' crossroads,/be the meaning of their strange encounter."* Of those lines, Snow writes: ". . . what emerges is one of the most beautiful instances of absolute utterance in all of poetry," in Rilke, Rainer Maria, *Sonnets to Orpheus*, trans. Edward Snow, North Point Press, New York, 2004, p. xvi.

17. Kidder, Annemarie S., in Rilke, Rainer Maria, *The Book of Hours*, trans. Annemarie S. Kidder, Northwestern University Press, Evanston, IL, 2001, pp. xi, xii.

18. Rilke, *The Poet's Guide to Life*, 2005, p. 78.

19. Peters, *Rainer Maria Rilke*, 1960, p. 11.

20. Rilke, *The Poet's Guide to Life*, 2005, p. 127.

21. Rilke, Rainer Maria, *Letters of Rainer Maria Rilke 1910–1926*, trans. Jane Bannard Greene & M. D. Herter Norton, W. W. Norton & Co., New York, 1969 (1947), pp. 380–3.

22. Quoted in Mitchell, Stephen, ed., *The Enlightened Mind: An Anthology of Sacred Prose*, Harper Perennial, New York, 1991, p. 36.

23. The nineteenth-century Hindu saint Ramakrishna has had a profound effect on many Western seekers both directly and indirectly (for example, via writers like Christopher Isherwood or Joseph Campbell). It should also be noted in this context that in the Eastern traditions the hours before "break of day" are regarded as the most potent for meditation.

24. Rilke, *The Poet's Guide to Life*, 2005, pp. 78–9.

25. Rilke, Rainer Maria, *Diaries of a Young Poet*, trans. & intro. Edward Snow & Michael Winkler, W. W. Norton & Co., New York, 1998, p. 196.

26. Rilke, *Rilke* (Moore), 1960, p. 359 (my itals).

27. Dillard, Annie, *Living by Fiction*, Harper & Row, New York, 1988 (1982), pp. 98, 106–7.

ENDNOTES

28. Rilke, *Rilke* (Moore), 1960, p. 359 (my itals).
29. In Leppmann, Wolfgang, *Rilke: A Life*, trans. Russell M. Stockman, Fromm International, New York, 1984, p. 365.

SEEKING BEAUTY

1. O'Leary, Joseph S., "The Palm of Beauty: Yeats, Rilke, Joyce," *Journal of Irish Studies*, 21, 2006.
2. Phelan, Joseph, "Awe and Shock: Beauty, and the lack of it, in the life of art," in *The Weekly Standard*, July 2007. There are recent exceptions to this argument. Three examples quoted within this study are: philosopher John Armstrong's *The Secret Power of Beauty*, Penguin, London, 2005; the more overtly spiritual book from theological philosopher and poet John O'Donohue, *Divine Beauty: The Invisible Embrace,* Bantam, London, 2004; and Robert Baker's *The Extravagant: Crossings of Modern Poetry and Modern Philosophy*, University of Notre Dame Press, Notre Dame, 2005.
3. Macy, Joanna, in Rilke, Rainer Maria, *Rilke's Book of Hours: Love Poems to God*, trans., preface & intro. Anita Barrows & Joanna Macy, Riverhead Books, New York, 1996, p. 2.
4. Armstrong, *The Secret Power of Beauty*, 2005, pp. 72, 73.
5. Steiner, George, *Language and Silence: Essays on Language, Literature and the Inhuman*, Atheneum, New York, 1967, p. 45.
6. In Gadamer, Hans-Georg, *The Relevance of the Beautiful and Other Essays*, ed. & intro. Robert Bernasconi, trans. Nicholas Walker, Cambridge University Press, Cambridge, 1986, p. 15.
7. *"Wenn es nur einmal so ganz stille wäre"* (in *Das Buch vom mönchischen Leben / Das Stunden-Buch*): Rilke, Rainer Maria, *Die Gedichte,* Insel Verlag, Frankfurt a. M., 2006, p. 203. (Trans. Mark S. Burrows, 2009.)
8. Augustine, "Entering into Joy," quoted in Easwaran, Eknath, *God Makes the Rivers to Flow*, Nilgiri Press, Tomales, CA, 2003, p. 230.
9. O'Leary, "The Palm of Beauty," 2006.
10. Armstrong, John, *Love, Life, Goethe: How to be Happy in an Imperfect World,* Allen Lane/ Penguin, London, 2006, pp. 99–100.
11. "The term '*Dinggedicht'* [singular: "thing poem"] is not Rilke's; it was introduced by the critic K. Oppert in 1926." Waters, William, "Answerable Aesthetics: Reading 'You' in Rilke," *Comparative Literature*, Vol. 48, No. 2, Spring 1996, p. 128.
12. Quoted in Sword, Helen, *Engendering Inspiration: Visionary Strategies in Rilke, Lawrence and H. D.*, University of Michigan Press, Ann Arbor, 1995, p. 44.
13. Brodsky, Patricia Pollock, *Rainer Maria Rilke*, Twayne, Boston, 1988, p. 84.
14. Quoted in Rilke, Rainer Maria, *The Selected Poetry of Rainer Maria Rilke*, ed. & trans. Stephen Mitchell, intro. Robert Hass, Picador, London, 1987, p. 303.
15. Rilke, Rainer Maria, *Uncollected Poems*, trans. Edward Snow, North Point Press, New York, 1996, p. 101.
16. Rilke, Rainer Maria, *Letters on Cézanne*, ed. Clara Rilke, trans. Joel Agee, Vintage, New York, 1991, p. 33.
17. *"Am Rande Der Nacht"* (in *Das Buch der Bilder*): Rilke, *Die Gedichte*, 2006, p. 305. (My translation.)
18. Sword, *Engendering Inspiration,* 1995, pp. 45–6.
19. *"Das Rosen-Innere"* (in *Neue Gedichte*): Rilke, *Die Gedichte*, 2006, p. 526. (My translation.)
20. Rilke, Rainer Maria, *Auguste Rodin*, trans. Daniel Slager, intro. William Gass, Archipelago Books, New York, 2004 (1903), p. 68.
21. Lines from "Part I, IV," "Part I, XII," "Part II, XX" in Rilke, Rainer Maria, *In Praise of Mortality: Selections from Rainer Maria Rilke's Duino Elegies and Sonnets to Orpheus*, trans. Anita Barrows & Joanna Macy, Riverhead Books, New York, 2005, pp. 73, 85, 125.

ENDNOTES

22. Rilke, *Auguste Rodin* (Slager), 2004, p. 68.
23. Snow, Edward, in Rilke, Rainer Maria, *New Poems*, trans. & intro. Edward Snow, North Point Press, New York, 2001, p. 5.
24. Rilke, Rainer Maria, *Pictures of God: Rilke's Religious Poetry*, trans. Annemarie S. Kidder, First Page Publications, Livonia, MI, 2005, p. 140.
25. Barnacle, B. D., *Rilke: Space, Essence and Angels in the Poetry of Rainer Maria Rilke*, Crescent Moon, Kidderminster, 1993, p. 22.
26. Rilke, *Letters on Cézanne*, 1991, p. 9.
27. Stafford, William, *The Answers Are Inside the Mountain*, University of Michigan Press, MI, 2003, pp. 3, 39. Stafford is also the author of a book called *You Must Revise Your Life*, echoing Rilke: "You must change your life."
28. "*Archaïscher Torso Apollos*" ("Archaic Torso of Apollo" in *Neue Gedichte*): Rilke, *Die Gedichte*, 2006, p. 483. (My translation.) This is an exceptionally famous poem—not least for its final line calling so explicitly for transformation—yet none of the translations I had to hand seemed quite to capture it. My attempt is far from ideal, but the "vegetative imagery" that critics have found striking is lost in Bly and even Snow. Galway Kinnell used "eye-apples," but also "his gaze, screwed back to low," which rendered his translation impossible for me to use. Mitchell used "ripening fruit," even though Rilke was so specific with his choice of fruit: *Augenäpfel*.
29. Baker, *The Extravagant*, 2005, p. 6.
30. This recalls Joseph Campbell's warning: "Writer's block results from too much head. Cut off your head. Pegasus, poetry, was born of Medusa when her head was cut off." Campbell, Joseph, *Reflections on the Art of Living: A Joseph Campbell Companion*, ed. Diane K. Osbon, Harper Perennial, New York, 1991, p. 270.
31. Rilke, Rainer Maria, *Letters to Merline 1919–1922*, trans. Jesse Browner, Paragon House, New York, 1989 (1950), pp. 78–9.
32. LaoTzu, *Tao Teh Ching*, trans. John C. H. Wu, Shambhala, Boston, 1989, pp. 47, 89.
33. From Second Elegy (*Duino Elegies*), in Gass, William H., *Reading Rilke*, Basic Books, New York, 1999, p. 193.
34. "Mourning," 1914, in Rilke, Rainer Maria, *Selected Poems of Rainer Maria Rilke*, trans., intro. & commentary Robert Bly, Harper & Row, New York, 1981, p. 163.
35. Leppmann, Wolfgang, *Rilke: A Life*, trans. Russell M. Stockman, Fromm International, New York, 1984, p. 289. Rilke's First Elegy is also a tremendous example of the explicit conjunction of beauty and terror.
36. Hattingberg, Magda von, ed., *Rilke and Benvenuta: An Intimate Correspondence*, trans. Joel Agee, Fromm International, New York, 1987. Snow and Winkler note that Agee "uses a severely truncated edition" of the original published correspondence. In Rilke, Rainer Maria & Andreas-Salomé, Lou, *Rainer Maria Rilke and Lou Andreas-Salomé: The Correspondence*, trans. & intro. Edward Snow & Michael Winkler, W. W. Norton & Co., New York, 2006, p. 389.
37. Snow, Edward, in Rilke, *Duino Elegies* (Snow), 2000, p. xii.
38. Rilke, *Duino Elegies* (Snow), 2000, p. 43.
39. "William Gass's Rilke" in Coetzee, J. M., *Stranger Shores: Essays 1986–1999*, Vintage, London, 2002, p. 75.
40. "William Gass's Rilke" in Coetzee, *Stranger Shores*, 2002, p. 86.
41. "William Gass's Rilke" in Coetzee, *Stranger Shores*, 2002, p. 78.
42. Ryan, Judith, *Rilke, Modernism and Poetic Tradition*, Cambridge University Press, Cambridge, 1999, p. 111.
43. Yeats, W. B., in Shree, Purohit Swami & Yeats, W. B., *The Ten Principal Upanishads*, Faber & Faber, London, 1970 (1937), pp. 9–10 (my itals).
44. Rilke, *Duino Elegies* (Snow), 2000, p. 43.

ENDNOTES

MYSTICISM AND THE HOLY

1. Hendry, J. F., *The Sacred Threshold: A Life of Rilke*, Carcanet, Manchester, 1983, p. 173.

2. Rilke, Rainer Maria, *Letters of Rainer Maria Rilke 1910–1926* (Greene & Herter Norton), 1969 (1947), p. 355.

3. Ryan, Judith, *Rilke, Modernism and Poetic Tradition*, Cambridge University Press, Cambridge, 1999, p. 3.

4. Burrows, Mark S., "Prayers to a Dark God: Rainer Maria Rilke among the Mystics," article forthcoming.

5. Quoted in Hick, John, ed., *Classical and Contemporary Readings in the Philosophy of Religion*, Prentice Hall, Englewood Cliffs, NJ, 1990 (1964), pp. 265–6. The Scottish poet John Burnside comments: "[Wittgenstein] is not talking about metaphysics. He is saying you can't talk about some things using the tools of language. There are some things you can only be silent about . . . Poetry is a mode of discourse that can express that space . . ." Burnside, John, in "Spectrum," *Sydney Morning Herald*, 24 May 2008.

6. Underhill, Evelyn, *Concerning the Inner Life*, Oneworld, Oxford, 1999 (1926), p. 25.

7. Carlson, Thomas A., "Locating the Mystical Subject," in Kessler, M. & Sheppard, C., eds., *Mystics: Presence and Aporia*, University of Chicago Press, Chicago, 2003, p. 207.

8. From Ninth Elegy, in Rilke, Rainer Maria, *The Selected Poetry of Rainer Maria Rilke*, ed. & trans. Stephen Mitchell, intro. Robert Hass, Picador, London, 1987, p. 199.

9. Rolleston, James, *Rilke in Transition: An Exploration of His Earliest Poetry*, Yale University Press, New Haven, 1970, p. 5.

10. Rilke, Rainer Maria, *Rilke: Selected Letters*, ed. Harry T. Moore, Anchor, New York, 1960, p. 193.

11. Letter to Countess Margot Sizzo, 6 January 1923, in Rilke, *Letters of Rainer Maria Rilke 1910–1926* (Greene & Herter Norton), 1969 (1947), pp. 314–5.

12. Rilke, *Rilke* (Moore), 1960, p. 388. The translation in Rainer Maria Rilke, *Selected Letters 1902–1926*, trans. R. F. C. Hull, intro. John Bayley, Quartet Encounters, London, 1988 (1946), differs: "In that most vast, open world all beings are—one cannot say 'contemporaneous,' for it is precisely the passage of Time which determines that they all *are*. This transitoriness rushes everywhere into a profound Being." p. 393.

13. Gambini, Roberto, *Soul & Culture*, Texas A&M University Press, College Station, TX, 2003, p. 124.

14. Quoted in Otto, Rudolf, *The Idea of the Holy: An Inquiry into the Non-rational Factor in the Idea of the Divine and Its Relation to the Rational*, trans. John W. Harvey, Oxford University Press, Oxford, 1958 (1923), p. 95.

15. "A Walk" (Muzot, March 1924), in Bly, Robert, ed., *The Winged Energy of Delight: Poems from Europe, Asia and the Americas*, Harper Perennial, New York, 2005, p. 176.

16. Romanyshyn, Robert D., *Ways of the Heart: Essays Toward an Imaginal Psychology*, Trivium, Pittsburgh, 2002, p. 144.

17. Romanyshyn, *Ways of the Heart*, 2002, p. 144. The writer is quoting from the Ninth Elegy. In his notes, elsewhere, Romanyshyn quotes a letter from Keats, dated 21 April 1819: "Call the world if you please 'The Vale of Soul-Making,'" and then adds that "Then you will find out the use of the world." p. 181.

18. From "Uncollected Poems" (Muzot, 1924), in Rilke, Rainer Maria, *Selected Poems of Rainer Maria Rilke*, trans., intro. & commentary Robert Bly, Harper & Row, New York, 1981, p. 175.

19. From "Part I, III" (in *Die Sonette an Orpheus*): Rilke, Rainer Maria, *Die Gedichte*, Insel Verlag, Frankfurt a. M., 2006, pp. 723–4. (My translation.) The German here is typically complex: *Ein Gott vermags. Wie aber, sag mir, soll/ein Mann ihm folgen durch die schmale Leier?/Sein Sinn ist Zwiespalt. An der Kreuzung zweier/Herzwege steht kein Tempel für Apoll.*

ENDNOTES

"No temple to Apollo can stand where the two roads of the heart divide" is another possibility. Rilke, *Die Gedichte*, 2006, p. 723.

20. Letter to Countess Aline Dietrichstein, 1 November 1916, in Rilke, *Letters of Rainer Maria Rilke 1910–1926* (Greene & Herter Norton), 1969 (1947), p. 155.
21. Otto, *The Idea of the Holy*, 1958 (1923), pp. 94–5 (my itals).
22. Dillard, Annie, *Holy the Firm*, Harper Perennial, New York, 1977, p. 11.

THE SOUL'S SEARCH FOR GOD

1. Otto, Rudolf, *The Idea of the Holy: An Inquiry into the Non-rational Factor in the Idea of the Divine and Its Relation to the Rational*, trans. John W. Harvey, Oxford University Press, Oxford, 1958 (1923), p. 104.
2. "Und seine Sorgfalt ist uns wie ein Alb," in Rilke, Rainer Maria, *Rilke's Book of Hours: Love Poems to God*, trans., preface & intro. Anita Barrows & Joanna Macy, Riverhead Books, New York, 1996, p. 105.
3. From First Elegy in Rilke, Rainer Maria, *Duino Elegies: Bilingual Edition*, trans. Edward Snow, North Point Press/Farrar, Straus and Giroux, New York, 2000, p. 7.
4. Rilke, Rainer Maria, *Diaries of a Young Poet*, trans. & intro. Edward Snow & Michael Winkler, W. W. Norton & Co., New York, 1998, p. 221.
5. Rilke, Rainer Maria, *Letters of Rainer Maria Rilke 1910–1926* (Greene & Herter Norton), 1969 (1947), p. 325 (2nd para: my itals).
6. Phia Rilke outlived her only child and died in 1931.
7. Hendry, J. F., *The Sacred Threshold: A Life of Rilke*, Carcanet, Manchester, 1983, p. 9.
8. The reference to "American Christians" is particularly unkind. "Christians" and "Americans" as distinct groups were the target of Rilke's scorn. In combination, he saw them as literal-minded and limited. Rilke did not ever visit America and was also unenthusiastic about the English.
9. Rilke, Rainer Maria, *The Poet's Guide to Life: The Wisdom of Rilke*, ed. & trans. Ulrich Baer, Modern Library/Random House, New York, 2005, pp. 168–9.
10. From "*Mein Leben ging—Herr Jesus*" (in *Die Gedichte 1906–1910*): Rilke, Rainer Maria, *Die Gedichte*, Insel Verlag, Frankfurt a. M., 2006, p. 416. (My translation.)
11. From "*Vor der Passion*" (in *Das Marien-Leben*): Rilke, *Die Gedichte*, 2006, p. 559. (My translation.)
12. Rilke, Rainer Maria, *The Unknown Rilke*, trans. Franz Wright, Oberlin College Press, Oberlin, 1990, pp. 130–31.
13. Rilke, Rainer Maria & Andreas-Salomé, Lou, *Rainer Maria Rilke and Lou Andreas-Salomé: The Correspondence*, trans. & intro. Edward Snow & Michael Winkler, W. W. Norton & Co., New York, 2006, p. 106.
14. Gass, William H., *Reading Rilke: Reflections on the Problems of Translation*, Basic Books, New York, 1999, p. 9.
15. "Sonnet I, VII" (in *Sonette an Orpheus*): Rilke, *Die Gedichte*, 2006, p. 725. (My translation.)
16. Hamlin, Cyrus, in Rilke, Rainer Maria, *The Best of Rilke*, trans. Walter Arndt, Dartmouth University Press of New England, Hanover, 1983, p. xiii.
17. Rilke, *The Best of Rilke*, 1983, pp. 2–3.
18. Freedman, Ralph, in Metzger, E. A. & Metzger, M. M., eds., *A Companion to the Works of Rainer Maria Rilke*, Camden House, Rochester, NY, 2001, p. 90. Professor Freedman's essay is a jewel in this outstanding collection of scholarly essays on Rilke's work.
19. Otto, *The Idea of the Holy*, 1958 (1923), p. 8.
20. Otto, *The Idea of the Holy*, 1958 (1923), pp. 10–11 (my itals).
21. Khan, Hazrat Inayat, "Bowl of Saki," extracts from *Sufi Mysticism Vol. X*, http://wahiduddin.net/mv2/X/X_4_8.htm.

ENDNOTES

22. Bruner, Jerome, "James's *Varieties* and the 'New' Constructivism" in Proudfoot, Wayne, ed., *William James and a Science of Religions*, Columbia University Press, New York, 2004, p. 74.

23. *"Du siehst, ich will viel"* (in *Das Stunden-Buch*): Rilke, Rainer Maria, *Selected Poems of Rainer Maria Rilke,* trans., intro. & commentary Robert Bly, Harper & Row, New York, 1981, p. 27.

24. Campbell, Joseph, *The Inner Reaches of Outer Space: Metaphor as Myth and as Religion*, New World Library, Novato, CA, 2002 (1986), p. 39.

25. Olivero, Federico, *Rainer Maria Rilke: A Study in Poetry and Mysticism*, W. Heffer & Sons, Cambridge, 1931, p. 13.

"THE OPEN"

1. "Message to Poets," in Merton, Thomas, *Raids on the Unspeakable*, New Directions, New York, 1966, pp. 155–61.

2. Barnacle, B. D., *Rilke: Space, Essence and Angels in the Poetry of Rainer Maria Rilke*, Crescent Moon, Kidderminster, 1993, p. 3.

3. Thomas Merton is not a poet comparable to Rilke (few are). He was, however, a rare man who, like Rilke, wrote a vast amount and was utterly faithful to the complex vocation of making deep sense of life. For Merton, that took place within a framework of faith quite different from Rilke's experience. Merton's fiery, questioning intelligence makes him a tremendous companion for "yearning" readers.

4. Rilke, Rainer Maria, *The Selected Poetry of Rainer Maria Rilke*, ed. & trans. Stephen Mitchell, intro. Robert Hass, Picador, London, 1987, p. 193.

5. Mandel, Siegfried, *Rainer Maria Rilke: The Poetic Instinct*, preface Henry T. Moore, Southern Illinois University Press, Carbondale, 1965, pp. 147–8.

6. Mandel, *Rainer Maria Rilke*, 1965, p. 151.

7. Deutsch, Babette, in Rilke, Rainer Maria, *Poems from the Book of Hours*, trans. Babette Deutsch, New Directions, New York, 1975 (1941), p. 3.

8. Mandel, *Rainer Maria Rilke,* 1965, p. 147.

9. Quoted in Leppmann, Wolfgang, *Rilke: A Life*, trans. Russell M. Stockman, Fromm International, New York, 1984, p. 287.

10. From First Elegy, quoted in Wydenbruck, Nora, *Rilke: Man and Poet*, Appleton, New York, 1949, p. 158.

11. Quoted in Rilke, Rainer Maria, *Duino Elegies: Bilingual Edition*, trans. Edward Snow, North Point Press, New York, 2000, pp. vii–viii; Note also: "Rilke always carried [a] note-book in the breast-pocket of his black satin waistcoat, which buttoned right up to the neck . . . this was the only sartorial eccentricity in which he indulged" in Wydenbruck, *Rilke*, 1949, p. 174. The series would not be completed for another decade.

12. From First Elegy (in *Duineser Elegien*): Rilke, Rainer Maria, *Die Gedichte*, p. 689. (Trans. Mark S. Burrows, 2009.) Note also: "As mediator between God and man and a being equally at home in life and in death, the angel can only strike us as 'terrible' [or fearsome]." Quoted in Leppmann, *Rilke* (Stockman), 1984, p. 289. Rilke himself wrote, "The 'angel' of the Elegies has nothing to do with the angel of the Christian heaven . . .": in Wydenbruck, *Rilke*, 1949, p. 208.

13. Zaehner, R. C., *The City Within the Heart*, Unwin Paperbacks, London, 1980, pp. 100–1; Gospel of John, 17:21.

14. Heidegger, Martin, *Poetry, Language, Thought*, trans. & intro. Albert Hofstadter, Harper Perennial, New York, 2001 (1975), pp. 104, 105–6.

15. Letter to Witold von Hulewicz, 13 November 1925, Rilke, Rainer Maria, *Selected Letters*

ENDNOTES

1902–1926, trans. R. F. C. Hull, intro. John Bayley, Quartet Encounters, London, 1988 (1946), pp. 393, 395 (Rilke's caps).

16. Marcel, Gabriel, *Homo Viator: Introduction to a Metaphysic of Hope*, trans. Emma Craufurd, Henry Regnery Company, Chicago, 1951, pp. 252–3.

17. Burrows, Mark S., "Prayers to a Dark God: Rainer Maria Rilke Among the Mystics," article forthcoming.

18. Rilke sent the poem to Lou with the following note: ". . . here is a curious poem, written this morning, which I am sending you at once, since I instinctively called it 'Turning,' knowing that it represents that turning which surely must come if I am to live, and you will understand its meaning." Rilke, Rainer Maria & Andreas-Salomé, Lou, *Rainer Maria Rilke and Lou Andreas-Salomé: The Correspondence*, trans. & intro. Edward Snow & Michael Winkler, W. W. Norton & Co., New York, 2006, p. 242.

19. *"Wendung,"* June 1914, in Rilke & Salomé, *The Correspondence* (Snow & Winkler), 2006, pp. 243–4. Edward Snow offers a slightly different translation in his *Uncollected Poems* (pp. 91–3), but the version I have chosen is later and stronger.

20. Mandel, *Rainer Maria Rilke*, 1965, p. 109.

21. Hick, John, *The Fifth Dimension: An Exploration of the Spiritual Realm*, OneWorld/Oxford, Oxford, 1999, pp. 8–9.

22. Burrows, Mark S., "Raiding the Inarticulate: Mysticism, Poetics, and the Unlanguageable," *Spiritus*, Vol. 4, No. 2, Fall 2004, pp. 185, 184.

23. "In Denmark [Rilke] had noticed how even the most inexplicable phenomena are allowed their freedom and that the supernatural, and therefore the poetic also, enjoys an unusual hospitality." In Salis, J. R. von, *Rainer Maria Rilke: The Years in Switzerland*, trans. N. K. Cruickshank, University of California Press, Berkeley, 1964 (1936), p. 242.

24. From Seventh Elegy (in *Duineser Elegien*): Rilke, Rainer Maria, *Die Gedichte*, Insel Verlag, Frankfurt a. M., 2006, pp. 707–8. (Trans. Mark S. Burrows.)

25. Rilke, Rainer Maria, *Rilke: Selected Letters*, ed. Harry T. Moore, Anchor, New York, 1960, p. 94.

26. Merton, Thomas, *Conjectures of a Guilty Bystander*, intro. Thomas Moore, Doubleday, New York, 1989 (1968), pp. 156–7.

27. Wydenbruck, *Rilke*, 1949, pp. 210–11, 213.

28. From the monograph on Rodin, Part II, in Rilke, Rainer Maria, *Where Silence Reigns: Selected Prose by Rainer Maria Rilke*, trans. G. Craig Houston, foreword Denise Levertov, New Directions, New York, 1978, p. 133.

29. Rilke, Rainer Maria, *Diaries of a Young Poet*, trans. & intro. Edward Snow & Michael Winkler, W. W. Norton & Co., New York, 1998, p. 21.

30. "Between 20 September and 14 October [1899] he wrote the poems that were to become the first part of *Das Stunden-Buch* . . . In one night during this same period he wrote the first version of *Cornet* . . . Between 10 and 21 November came the stories *Vom lieben Gott und Anderes*, the first version of *Geschichten*. In January 1900 he produced the essay, 'Russische Kunst' (Russian Art)," in Brodsky, Patricia Pollock, *Rainer Maria Rilke*, Twayne, Boston, 1988, p. 57.

31. Rilke, Rainer Maria, *Stories of God*, trans. M. D. Herter Norton, W. W. Norton & Co., New York, 1963 (1932), p. 77 (my itals).

32. *"In tiefen Nächten grab ich dich"* (in *Von der Pilgerschaft/Das Stunden-Buch*): Rilke, *Die Gedichte*, 2006, p. 260. (Trans. Mark S. Burrows, 2009.)

33. Macy, Joanna, in Rilke, Rainer Maria, *Rilke's Book of Hours: Love Poems to God*, trans., preface & intro. Anita Barrows & Joanna Macy, Riverhead Books, New York, 1996, p. 3.

34. Salis, *Rainer Maria Rilke*, 1964 (1936), pp. 265–7 (my itals).

35. Rilke, *Diaries of a Young Poet* (Snow & Winkler), 1998, p. 85.

ENDNOTES

36. Rilke, Rainer Maria, *The Poet's Guide to Life: The Wisdom of Rilke*, ed. & trans. Ulrich Baer, Modern Library/Random House, New York, 2005, p. 152.
37. Gass, William H., *Reading Rilke: Reflections on the Problems of Translation*, Basic Books, New York, 1999, p. 160.
38. Salis, *Rainer Maria Rilke*, 1964 (1936), pp. 270–1.
39. *"Herbst"* (in *Das Buch der Bilder*): Rilke, *Die Gedichte*, 2006, p. 305. (My translation.)
40. Marcel, *Homo Viator*, 1951, p. 265.
41. Rilke, *Rilke* (Moore), 1960, p. 342.
42. Rilke, Rainer Maria, *The Unknown Rilke*, trans. Franz Wright, Oberlin College Press, Oberlin, 1990, pp. 77–80.
43. Salis, *Rainer Maria Rilke*, 1964 (1936), p. 285.
44. Freedman, Ralph, *Life of a Poet: Rainer Maria Rilke*, Farrar, Straus and Giroux, New York, 1996, p. 531.
45. Wydenbruck, *Rilke*, 1949, p. 363.
46. From First Elegy (in *Duineser Elegien*): Rilke, *Die Gedichte*, 2006, p. 691. (My translation.)

IRRATIONAL TRUTHS

1. Hattingberg, Magda von, ed., *Rilke and Benvenuta: An Intimate Correspondence*, trans. Joel Agee, Fromm International, New York, 1987, p. 85 (my itals).
2. *"Ich finde dich in allen diesen Dingen"* (in *Das Stunden-Buch*): Rilke, Rainer Maria, *Selected Poems of Rainer Maria Rilke*, trans., intro. & commentary Robert Bly, Harper & Row, New York, 1981, p. 32.
3. *"Ich finde dich"* (in *Das Buch vom mönchischen Leben/Das Stunden-Buch*): Rilke, Rainer Maria, *Die Gedichte*, Insel Verlag, Frankfurt a. M., 2006, p. 210.
4. Cross, Richard K., "Soul-Work: Reading as a Transformative Pursuit," *Modern Age*, Vol. 49, No. 2, Spring 2007.
5. Heidegger, Martin, *Poetry, Language, Thought*, trans. & intro. Albert Hofstadter, Harper Perennial, New York, 2001 (1975), pp. 94, 96.
6. Andreas-Salomé, Lou, *You Alone Are Real to Me: Remembering Rainer Maria Rilke*, trans. & intro. Angela von der Lippe, BOA Editions, Rochester, NY, 2003, p. 69.
7. Part II, X, in Rilke, Rainer Maria, *Sonnets to Orpheus*, trans. C. F. MacIntyre, University of California Press, Berkeley, 1960, p. 75.
8. Leishman, J. B., quoted in Peters, H. F., *Rainer Maria Rilke: Masks and the Man*, McGraw-Hill, New York, 1963, p. 121.
9. Peters, H. F., *Rainer Maria Rilke: Masks and the Man*, McGraw-Hill, New York, 1963, p. 121.
10. Leishman, J. B., in Rilke, Rainer Maria, *Duino Elegies*, trans. J. B. Leishman & Stephen Spender, The Hogarth Press, London, 1948, p. 20.
11. Raine, Kathleen, *The Inner Journey of the Poet*, George Allen & Unwin, London, 1982, p. 24.
12. Whyte, David, *The Heart Aroused: Poetry and the Preservation of Soul in Corporate America*, Currency/Doubleday, New York, 2002 (1994), pp. 239–40.
13. Raine, *The Inner Journey of the Poet*, 1982, pp. 23–4.
14. Raine, *The Inner Journey of the Poet*, 1982, p. 21.
15. Crasnow, Ellman, "Poems and Fictions: Stevens, Rilke, Valéry," in Bradbury, Malcolm & McFarlane, James, eds., *Modernism: A Guide to European Literature 1890–1930*, Penguin, London, 1991, p. 370.
16. From *"Daraus, daß Einer dich einmal gewollt hat"* (in *Das Buch vom mönchischen Leben/Das Stunden-Buch*): Rilke, *Die Gedichte*, 2006, p. 207. (My translation.)

ENDNOTES

17. Wydenbruck, Nora, *Rilke: Man and Poet*, Appleton, New York, 1949, p. 5.
18. "The Holy Longing," Goethe, Johann Wolfgang von, in Bly, Robert, ed., *The Soul Is Here for Its Own Joy*, The Ecco Press, Hopewell, NJ, 1995, p. 209.
19. Merton, Thomas, *Contemplation in a World of Action*, Doubleday, New York, 1973, pp. 164–5.
20. Rilke, Rainer Maria, *Letters to a Young Poet*, trans. & foreword Stephen Mitchell, Vintage, New York, 1986, pp. 7–8.
21. Final lines from Ninth Elegy (in *Duineser Elegien*): Rilke, *Die Gedichte*, 2006, pp. 712–3. (My translation.)

BIBLIOGRAPHY

Andreas-Salomé, Lou, *The Freud Journal*, trans. Stanley A. Leavy, intro. Mary-Kay Wilmers, Quartet Books, London, 1987.
——*Looking Back: Memoirs*, trans. Breon Mitchell, Marlowe & Co., New York, 1995.
——*You Alone Are Real to Me: Remembering Rainer Maria Rilke*, trans. & intro. Angela von der Lippe, BOA Editions, Rochester, NY, 2003.
Armstrong, John, *Love, Life, Goethe: How to Be Happy in an Imperfect World*, Allen Lane/ Penguin, London, 2006.
——*The Secret Power of Beauty*, Penguin, London, 2005.
Auden, W. S., "In Memory of W. B. Yeats," *Collected Poems*, ed. Edward Mendelson, Vintage, New York, 1991.
Bachelard, Gaston, *The Poetics of Space: The Classic Look at How We Experience Intimate Places*, trans. Maria Jolas, Beacon, Boston, 1994 (1958).
Baer, Ulrich, "The Perfection of Poetry: Rainer Maria Rilke and Paul Celan," *New German Critique*, No. 91, Winter 2004.
Baker, Robert, *The Extravagant: Crossings of Modern Poetry and Modern Philosophy*, University of Notre Dame Press, Notre Dame, 2005.
Barks, Coleman & Moyne, John, trans., *The Essential Rumi*, HarperSanFrancisco, San Francisco, 1995.
Barnacle, B. D., *Rilke: Space, Essence and Angels in the Poetry of Rainer Maria Rilke*, Crescent Moon, Kidderminster, 1993.
Bennett, Alan, "The Wrong Blond," in Spice, Nicholas, ed., *London Reviews*, Chatto & Windus, London, 1985.
Bernstein, Michael André, *Five Portraits: Modernity and the Imagination in Twentieth-Century Writing*, Northwestern University Press, Evanston, IL, 2000.
Bloom, Harold, *Omens of Millennium*, Fourth Estate, London, 1996.
Bly, Robert, *The Soul Is Here for Its Own Joy*, Ecco, Hopewell, NJ, 1995.

BIBLIOGRAPHY

Bly, Robert, ed., *The Winged Energy of Delight: Poems from Europe, Asia and the Americas*, Harper Perennial, New York, 2005.

Brodsky, Patricia Pollock, *Rainer Maria Rilke*, Twayne, Boston, 1988.

Bruner, Jerome, in Proudfoot, Wayne, ed., *William James and a Science of Religions*, Columbia University Press, New York, 2004.

Burrell, David B., "Religion and the University," *Crosscurrents*, Summer 2006.

Burrows, Mark S., "Prayers to a Dark God: Rainer Maria Rilke among the Mystics," article forthcoming.

——"Raiding the Inarticulate: Mysticism, Poetics, and the Unlanguageable," *Spiritus*, Vol. 4, No. 2, Fall 2004.

——"'To Taste with the Heart': Allegory, Poetics, and the Deep Reading of Scripture," *Interpretation*, Vol. 56, No. 2, April 2002.

Campbell, Joseph, *The Inner Reaches of Outer Space: Metaphor as Myth and as Religion*, New World Library, Novato, CA, 2002 (1986).

——*Reflections on the Art of Living: A Joseph Campbell Companion*, ed. Diane K. Osbon, HarperPerennial, New York, 1991.

Carlson, Thomas A., "Locating the Mystical Subject," in Kessler, M. & Sheppard, C., *Mystics: Presence and Aporia*, University of Chicago Press, Chicago, 2003.

Coetzee, J. M., *Stranger Shores: Essays 1986–1999*, Vintage, London, 2002.

Contogenis, Constantine, "Rilke in English" (a review of William H. Gass, *Reading Rilke*), *Essays in Criticism*, Oxford, Vol. 52, No. 2, April 2002.

Crasnow, Ellman, "Poems and Fictions: Stevens, Rilke, Valéry," in Bradbury, Malcolm & McFarlane, James, eds., *Modernism: A Guide to European Literature 1890–1930*, Penguin, London, 1991.

Cross, Richard K., "Soul-Work: Reading as a Transformative Pursuit," *Modern Age*, Vol. 49, No. 2, Spring 2007.

Dillard, Annie, *Holy the Firm*, HarperPerennial, New York, 1977.

——*Living by Fiction*, Harper & Row, New York, 1988 (1982).

Dirda, Michael, *Book by Book: Notes on Reading and Life*, Henry Holt, New York, 2005.

Dowrick, Stephanie, *Forgiveness and Other Acts of Love*, Allen & Unwin, Sydney, 2010 (1997).

——*Rainer Maria Rilke: Bearing Witness* (doctoral thesis, Writing & Society Research Group, University of Western Sydney, Sydney; http://library.uws.edu.au/adt.php), 2008.

Easwaran, Eknath, *God Makes the Rivers to Flow*, Nilgiri Press, Tomales, CA, 2003.

Eliot, T. S., *Selected Prose of T. S. Eliot*, ed. Frank Kermode, Harvest/Harcourt Brace, San Diego, 1975 (1935).

Ferrucci, Piero, *Inevitable Grace*, trans. David Kennard, Crucible, Wellingborough, England, 1990.

Freedman, Ralph, *Life of a Poet: Rainer Maria Rilke*, Farrar, Straus and Giroux, New York, 1996.

Gadamer, Hans-Georg, *The Relevance of the Beautiful and Other Essays*, ed. & intro. Robert Bernasconi, trans. Nicholas Walker, Cambridge University Press, Cambridge, 1986.

Gambini, Roberto, *Soul & Culture*, Texas A&M University Press, Texas, 2003.

Gass, William H., *Reading Rilke: Reflections on the Problems of Translation*, Basic Books, New York, 1999.

——*A Temple of Texts: Essays*, Knopf, New York, 2006.

Griffiths, Bede, *The Golden String*, Fount Paperbacks, London, 1979 (1954).

——*A Human Search: Bede Griffiths Reflects on His Life*, ed. John Swindells, foreword Wayne Teasdale, Triumph, Chicago, 1997.

——*The Other Half of My Soul: Bede Griffiths and the Hindu–Christian Dialogue*, ed. Beatrice Bruteau, The Theosophical Publishing House, Wheaton, IL, 1996.

BIBLIOGRAPHY

Hargreaves, Raymond, in *Notes and Queries*, Vol. 42, No. 1, March 1995.

Hartman, Geoffrey H., *The Unmediated Vision: An Interpretation of Wordsworth, Hopkins, Rilke and Valéry*, Yale University Press, New Haven, 1954.

Hattingberg, Magda von, ed., *Rilke and Benvenuta: An Intimate Correspondence*, trans. Joel Agee, Fromm International, New York, 1987.

Heidegger, Martin, *Poetry, Language, Thought*, trans. & intro. Albert Hofstadter, HarperPerennial, New York, 2001 (1975).

Hendry, J. F., *The Sacred Threshold: A Life of Rilke*, Carcanet, Manchester, 1983.

Hick, John, *An Interpretation of Religion: Human Responses to the Transcendent*, 2nd ed., Palgrave, Basingstoke, 2004.

——*The Fifth Dimension: An Exploration of the Spiritual Realm*, OneWorld/Oxford, Oxford, 1999.

Hick, John, ed., *Classical and Contemporary Readings in the Philosophy of Religion*, Prentice Hall, Englewood Cliffs, 1990 (1964).

Hillman, James, *The Soul's Code: In Search of Character and Calling*, Random House, Sydney, 1996.

Hirshfield, Jane, *Hiddenness, Uncertainty, Surprise: Three Generative Energies of Poetry*, University of Newcastle/Bloodaxe Books, Newcastle upon Tyne, 2008.

——*Nine Gates: Entering the Mind of Poetry*, Harper Perennial, New York, 1998.

James, William, *The Varieties of Religious Experience*, Collier, New York, 1902.

Khan, Hazrat Inayat, "Bowl of Saki," extracts from *Sufi Mysticism Vol X*, http://wahiduddin .net/mv2/X/X_4_8.htm.

Kirsch, Arthur C., *Auden and Christianity*, Yale University Press, New Haven, 2005.

Klee, Paul, *On Modern Art*, Faber & Faber, London, 1989 (1924).

Kleinbard, David, *The Beginning of Terror: A Psychological Study of Rainer Maria Rilke's Life and Work*, foreword Jeffrey Berman, New York University Press, New York, 1993.

Lao Tzu, *Tao Teh Ching*, trans. John C.H. Wu, Shambhala, Boston, 1989.

Leaves, Nigel, *The God Problem: Alternatives to Fundamentalism*, Polebridge Press, Santa Rosa, CA, 2006.

Leppmann, Wolfgang, *Rilke: A Life*, trans. Russell M. Stockman, Fromm International, New York, 1984.

Mandel, Siegfried, *Rainer Maria Rilke: The Poetic Instinct*, preface Henry T. Moore, Southern Illinois University Press, Carbondale, 1965.

Marcel, Gabriel, *Homo Viator: Introduction to a Metaphysic of Hope*, trans. Emma Craufurd, Henry Regnery Company, Chicago, 1951.

Mason, E. C., *Rilke, Europe, and the English-Speaking World*, Cambridge University Press, Cambridge, 1961.

McClatchy, J. D., "Rainer Maria Rilke," *Poetry*, Vol. 185, No. 1, October 2004.

McFague, Sallie, *Metaphorical Theology: Models of God in Religious Language*, Fortress Press, Philadelphia, 1982.

Mendelsohn, Daniel, "A Line-by-Line Safari," *New York Times Book Review*, New York, 30 January 2000.

Merton, Thomas, *Conjectures of a Guilty Bystander*, intro. Thomas Moore, Doubleday, New York, 1989 (1968).

——*Contemplation in a World of Action*, Doubleday, New York, 1973.

——*The Intimate Merton*, ed. Patrick Hart & Jonathan Montaldo, HarperSanFrancisco, San Francisco, 1999.

——*The Literary Essays of Thomas Merton*, ed. Patrick Hart, New Directions, New York, 1981.

——*Raids on the Unspeakable*, New Directions, New York, 1966.

BIBLIOGRAPHY

Metzger, E. A. & Metzger, M. M., eds., *A Companion to the Works of Rainer Maria Rilke*, Camden House, Rochester, NY, 2001.

Miller, Alice, *The Body Never Lies: The Lingering Effects of Cruel Parenting*, trans. Andrew Jenkins, W. W. Norton & Co., New York, 2005.

——*The Drama of the Gifted Child and the Search for the True Self*, trans. Ruth Ward, Faber & Faber, London, 1983 (1979).

——*For Your Own Good: Hidden Cruelty in Child-Rearing and the Roots of Violence*, trans. Hildegarde & Hunter Hannum, Faber & Faber, London, 1983.

——*The Untouched Key: Tracing Childhood Trauma in Creativity and Destructiveness*, trans. Hildegarde & Hunter Hannum, Virago, London, 1990.

Mitchell, Stephen, ed., *The Enlightened Mind: An Anthology of Sacred Prose*, Harper Perennial, New York, 1991.

Mojtabai, A. G., "A Writer and Religion" in Gass, William H. & Cuoco, Lorin, eds., *The Writer and Religion*, Southern Illinois University Press, Chicago, 2000.

Murdoch, Iris, *Metaphysics as a Guide to Morals*, Penguin, London, 1993.

Murray, Les, *Learning Human*, Duffy & Snellgrove, Sydney, 2003.

Nietzsche, Friedrich, *Beyond Good and Evil*, intro. Michael Tanner, Penguin, London, 2003 (1886).

O'Donohue, John, *Divine Beauty: The Invisible Embrace*, Bantam, London, 2004.

O'Leary, Joseph S., "The Palm of Beauty: Yeats, Rilke, Joyce," *Journal of Irish Studies*, 21, 2006.

Olivero, Federico, *Rainer Maria Rilke: A Study in Poetry and Mysticism*, W. Heffer & Sons, Cambridge, 1931.

Otto, Rudolf, *The Idea of the Holy: An Inquiry into the Non-rational Factor in the Idea of the Divine and Its Relation to the Rational*, trans. John W. Harvey, Oxford University Press, Oxford, 1958 (1923).

——*Mysticism East and West*, trans. B. L. Bracey & R. C. Payne, Collier Books, New York, 1962 (1932).

Paglia, Camille, *Break, Blow, Burn*, Vintage, New York, 2005.

Palmer, Richard E., ed., *Gadamer in Conversation: Reflections and Commentary*, Yale University Press, New Haven, 2001.

Pasternak, Boris, Tsvetayeva, Marina & Rilke, Rainer Maria, *Letters Summer 1926*, trans. Margaret Wettling & Walter Arndt, Oxford University Press, Oxford, 1988.

Perloff, Marjorie, "Reading Gass Reading Rilke," *Parnassus: Poetry in Review*, Vol. 25, No. 1–2, 2001.

Peters, H. F., *My Sister, My Spouse*, Gollancz, London, 1963.

——*Rainer Maria Rilke: Masks and the Man*, McGraw-Hill, New York, 1963.

Phelan, Joseph, "Awe and Shock: Beauty, and the lack of it, in the life of art" in *The Weekly Standard*, July 2007.

Phillips, Brian, "The Angel and the Egoist," *The New Republic*, 8 May 2000.

Prater, Donald, *A Ringing Glass: The Life of Rainer Maria Rilke*, Clarendon/Oxford University Press, Oxford, 1986.

Raine, Kathleen, *The Inner Journey of the Poet*, George Allen & Unwin, London, 1982.

Ricks, Christopher, ed., *The Oxford Book of English Verse*, Oxford University Press, Oxford, 1999.

Rilke, Rainer Maria, *Auguste Rodin*, trans. Daniel Slager, intro. William Gass, Archipelago Books, New York, 2004 (1903).

——*The Best of Rilke*, trans. Walter Arndt, Dartmouth/University Press of New England, Hanover, 1989.

——*The Book of Hours*, trans. Annemarie S. Kidder, Northwestern University Press, Evanston, IL, 2001.

BIBLIOGRAPHY

——*The Book of Images*, trans. Edward Snow, North Point Press, New York, 1991.

——*Diaries of a Young Poet*, trans. & intro. Edward Snow & Michael Winkler, W. W. Norton & Co., New York, 1998.

——*Die Gedichte*, Insel Verlag, Frankfurt a. M., 2006. (A single-volume edition of the collected works of 1955.)

——*Duino Elegies*, trans. J. B. Leishman & Stephen Spender, The Hogarth Press, London, 1948.

——*Duino Elegies: Bilingual Edition*, trans. Edward Snow, North Point Press/Farrar, Straus and Giroux, New York, 2000.

——*The Essential Rilke*, trans. Galway Kinnell & Hannah Liebmann, intro. Galway Kinnell, Ecco Press/HarperCollins, New York, 1999.

——*In Praise of Mortality: Selections from Rainer Maria Rilke's Duino Elegies and Sonnets to Orpheus*, trans. Anita Barrows & Joanna Macy, Riverhead Books, New York, 2005.

——*Letters of Rainer Maria Rilke 1910–1926*, trans. Jane Bannard Greene & M. D. Herter Norton, W. W. Norton & Co., New York, 1969 (1947).

——*Letters on Cézanne*, ed. Clara Rilke, trans. Joel Agee, Vintage, New York, 1991.

——*Letters to a Young Poet*, trans. M. D. Herter Norton, W. W. Norton & Co., New York, 1993 (1934).

——*Letters to a Young Poet*, trans. & foreword Stephen Mitchell, Vintage, New York, 1986.

——*Letters to Merline 1919–1922*, trans. Jesse Browner, Paragon House, New York, 1989 (1950).

——*New Poems*, trans. & intro. Edward Snow, North Point Press, New York, 2001.

——*The Notebooks of Malte Laurids Brigge*, trans. M. D. Herter Norton, W. W. Norton & Co., New York, 1964 (1949).

——*Pictures of God: Rilke's Religious Poetry*, trans. Annemarie S. Kidder, First Page Publications, Livonia, MI, 2005.

——*Poems 1906–26*, trans. J. B. Leishman, The Hogarth Press, London, 1976 (1957).

——*Poems from The Book of Hours*, trans. Babette Deutsch, New Directions, New York, 1975 (1941).

——*The Poet's Guide to Life: The Wisdom of Rilke*, ed. & trans. Ulrich Baer, Modern Library/Random House, New York, 2005.

——*Rilke's Book of Hours: Love Poems to God*, trans., preface & intro. Anita Barrows & Joanna Macy, Riverhead Books, New York, 1996.

——*Rilke: Selected Letters*, ed. Harry T. Moore, Anchor, New York, 1960.

——*Rilke: Selected Poems*, trans. C. F. MacIntyre, University of California Press, Berkeley, 1974 (1940).

——*Rilke's Late Poetry*, trans. Graham Good, Ronsdale Press, Vancouver, 2004.

——*Selected Letters 1902–1926*, trans. R. F. C. Hull, intro. John Bayley, Quartet Encounters, London, 1988 (1946).

——*Selected Poems of Rainer Maria Rilke*, trans., intro. & commentary Robert Bly, Harper & Row, New York, 1981.

——*The Selected Poetry of Rainer Maria Rilke*, ed. & trans. Stephen Mitchell, intro. Robert Hass, Picador, London, 1987.

——*Sonnets to Orpheus*, trans. & intro. Rick Anthony Furtak, University of Scranton Press, London, 2007.

——*Sonnets to Orpheus*, trans. C. F. MacIntyre, University of California Press, Berkeley, 1960.

——*Sonnets to Orpheus*, trans. Edward Snow, North Point Press, New York, 2004.

——*Stories of God*, trans. M. D. Herter Norton, W. W. Norton & Co., New York, 1963 (1932).

——*Uncollected Poems*, trans. Edward Snow, North Point Press, New York, 1996.

——*The Unknown Rilke*, trans. Franz Wright, Oberlin College Press, Oberlin, 1990.

BIBLIOGRAPHY

——*Where Silence Reigns: Selected Prose by Rainer Maria Rilke*, trans. G. Craig Houston, foreword Denise Levertov, New Directions, New York, 1978.

Rilke, Rainer Maria & Andreas-Salomé, Lou, *Rainer Maria Rilke and Lou Andreas-Salomé: The Correspondence*, trans. & intro. Edward Snow & Michael Winkler, W. W. Norton & Co., New York, 2006.

Rolleston, James, *Rilke in Transition: An Exploration of His Earliest Poetry*, Yale University Press, New Haven, 1970.

Romanyshyn, Robert D., *Ways of the Heart: Essays Toward an Imaginal Psychology*, Trivium, Pittsburgh, 2002.

Rumi, Moulana, *Masnavi* III, 4398–9 (various translations).

Ryan, Judith, *Rilke, Modernism and Poetic Tradition*, Cambridge University Press, Cambridge, 1999.

Salis, J. R. von, *Rainer Maria Rilke: The Years in Switzerland*, trans. N. K. Cruickshank, University of California Press, Berkeley, 1964 (1936).

Shree, Purohit Swami & Yeats, W. B., *The Ten Principal Upanishads*, Faber & Faber, London, 1970 (1937).

Stafford, William, *The Answers Are Inside the Mountain*, University of Michigan Press, Michigan, 2003.

Stearns, Mary Nurrie, "The Presence of Compassion: An Interview with John O'Donohue," personaltransformation.com.

Steiner, George, *Errata: An Examined Life*, Phoenix/Orion, London, 1997.

——*Language and Silence: Essays on Language, Literature and the Inhuman*, Atheneum, New York, 1967.

Sword, Helen, *Engendering Inspiration: Visionary Strategies in Rilke, Lawrence and H. D.*, University of Michigan Press, Ann Arbor, 1995.

Torgersen, Eric, *Dear Friend: Rainer Maria Rilke and Paula Modersohn-Becker*, Northwestern University Press, Evanston, IL, 1998.

Trapnell, Judson B., *Bede Griffiths: A Life in Dialogue*, State University of New York Press, New York, 2001.

Underhill, Evelyn, *Concerning the Inner Life*, Oneworld, Oxford, 1999 (1926).

——*Mysticism: A Study in the Nature and Development of Man's Spiritual Consciousness*, E. P. Dutton & Co., New York, 1910.

Waters, William, "Answerable Aesthetics: Reading 'You' in Rilke," *Comparative Literature*, Vol. 48, No. 2, Spring 1996.

Weil, Simone, *Waiting for God*, Harper & Row, New York, 1973.

Whyte, David, *The Heart Aroused: Poetry and the Preservation of Soul in Corporate America*, Currency/Doubleday, New York, 2002 (1994).

Wydenbruck, Nora, *Rilke: Man and Poet*, Appleton, New York, 1949.

Zaehner, R. C., *At Sundry Times: An Essay in the Comparison of Religion*, Faber & Faber, London, 1958.

——*The City Within the Heart*, Unwin Paperbacks, London, 1980.

INDEX

INDEX

INDEX

INDEX

INDEX

INDEX

INDEX

CREDITS

CREDITS

CREDITS

CREDITS

Page 149. "Ich bete wieder, du Erlauchter . . . / I am praying again . . ." from *Rilke's Book of Hours: Love Poems to God*, translated by Anita Barrows and Joanna Macy. Copyright © 1996 by Anita Barrows and Joanna Macy. Used by permission of Riverhead Books, an imprint of Penguin Group (USA) Inc.

Page 151. Excerpt from "Third Elegy" from *Duino Elegies* by Rainer Maria Rilke, translated by Edward Snow. Translation copyright © 2000 by Edward Snow. Reprinted by permission of North Point Press, a division of Farrar, Straus and Giroux, LLC.

Page 157. From "Straining so hard against the strength the strength of night" from *The Selected Poetry of Rainer Maria Rilke*, translated by Stephen Mitchell. Translation copyright © 1980, 1981, 1982 by Stephen Mitchell. Used by permission of Random House, Inc.

Page 160. From *Letters of Rainer Maria Rilke 1910–1926*, translated by Jane Bannard Greene and M. D. Herter Norton. Copyright © 1947, 1948 by W. W. Norton & Company, Inc., renewed © 1975 by M. D. Herter Norton. Used by permission of W. W. Norton & Company, Inc. This selection may not be reproduced, stored in a retrieval system, or transmitted in any form or by any means without the prior written permission of the publisher.

Page 161. "Dann bete du . . . / Now pray . . ." from *Rilke's Book of Hours: Love Poems to God*, translated by Anita Barrows and Joanna Macy. Copyright © 1996 by Anita Barrows and Joanna Macy. Used by permission of Riverhead Books, an imprint of Penguin Group (USA) Inc.

Page 163. "Gott spricht zu jedem . . . / God speaks to each of us . . ." from *Rilke's Book of Hours: Love Poems to God*, translated by Anita Barrows and Joanna Macy. Copyright © 1996 by Anita Barrows and Joanna Macy. Used by permission of Riverhead Books, an imprint of Penguin Group (USA) Inc.

Page 174. From *The Essential Rumi*, translated by Coleman Barks and John Moyne. Copyright © Coleman Barks. Reprinted by permission of Coleman Barks.

Page 175. From *Rilke's Late Poetry* by Rainer Maria Rilke, translated by and with an introduction and commentary by Graham Good. (Ronsdale Press, 2004.) Reprinted by permission.

Page 176. From "Tenth Elegy" from *The Selected Poetry of Rainer Maria Rilke*, translated by Stephen Mitchell. Translation copyright © 1980, 1981, 1982 by Stephen Mitchell. Used by permission of Random House, Inc.

Page 177. Excerpt from "The Song of the Women to the Poet" from *New Poems* [1907] by Rainer Maria Rilke, a bilingual edition translated by Edward Snow. Translation copyright © 1984 by Edward Snow. Reprinted by permission of North Point Press, a division of Farrar, Straus and Giroux, LLC.

Page 179. From *The Soul Is Here for Its Own Good*, edited and translated by Robert Bly. Copyright © 1995 by Robert Bly. Reprinted by permission of Georges Borchardt, Inc,. for Robert Bly.

Page 180. From *Diaries of a Young Poet* by Rainier Maria Rilke, translated by Edward Snow and Michael Winkler. Copyright © 1942 by Insel Verlag, 1997 by Edward Snow and Michael

CREDITS

Winkler. Used by permission of W. W. Norton & Company, Inc. This selection may not be reproduced, stored in a retrieval system, or transmitted in any form or by any means without the prior written permission of the publisher.

Page 180. From *Diaries of a Young Poet* by Rainier Maria Rilke, translated by Edward Snow and Michael Winkler. Copyright © 1942 by Insel Verlag, 1997 by Edward Snow and Michael Winkler. Used by permission of W. W. Norton & Company, Inc. This selection may not be reproduced, stored in a retrieval system, or transmitted in any form or by any means without the prior written permission of the publisher.

Page 190. From *The Selected Poems of Rainer Maria Rilke: A Translation from the German and Commentary* by Robert Bly. Copyright © 1981 by Robert Bly. Reprinted by permission of HarperCollins Publishers.

Page 191. From "For Fraulein Maria von Hefner-Alteneck" from *Poems 1906–26* by Rainer Maria Rilke, translated by J. B. Leishman. Copyright © 1957 by New Directions Publishing Corp. Reprinted by permission of New Directions Publishing Corp.

Page 192. "Gott spricht zu jedem . . . / God speaks to each of us . . ."from *Rilke's Book of Hours: Love Poems to God,* translated by Anita Barrows and Joanna Macy. Copyright © 1996 by Anita Barrows and Joanna Macy. Used by permission of Riverhead Books, an imprint of Penguin Group (USA) Inc.

Page 195. "Gott spricht zu jedem . . . / God speaks to each of us . . ." from *Rilke's Book of Hours: Love Poems to God,* translated by Anita Barrows and Joanna Macy. Copyright © 1996 by Anita Barrows and Joanna Macy. Used by permission of Riverhead Books, an imprint of Penguin Group (USA) Inc.

Page-204. From *Diaries of a Young Poet* by Rainier Maria Rilke, translated by Edward Snow and Michael Winkler. Copyright © 1942 by Insel Verlag, 1997 by Edward Snow and Michael Winkler. Used by permission of W. W. Norton & Company, Inc. This selection may not be reproduced, stored in a retrieval system, or transmitted in any form or by any means without the prior written permission of the publisher.

Page 214. Excerpt from *Uncollected Poems* by Rainer Maria Rilke, translated by Edward Snow. Translation copyright © 1996 by Edward Snow. Reprinted by permission of North Point Press, a division of Farrar, Straus and Giroux, LLC.

Page 219. Excerpts from "Sonnets to Orpheus," Part Two, Sonnet I in *In Praise of Mortality: Selections from Rainer Maria Rilke's Duino Elegies and Sonnets to Orpheus,* translated by Anita Barrows and Joanna Macy. Riverhead Books, 2005. Reprinted by permission of Janklow & Nesbit Associates.

Page 220. From *Pictures of Gold: Rilke's Religious Poetry* by Rainer Maria Rilke, translated by Annemarie S. Kidder. Livonia, Mich.: First Page Publications, 2005. Reprinted by permission of Annemarie Kidder.

Page 225. From *Reading Rilke* by William H. Gass. Copyright © 1999 by William H. Gass. Used by permission of Alfred A. Knopf, a division of Random House, Inc., and Janklow & Nesbit Associates.

CREDITS

CREDITS

system, or transmitted in any form or by any means without the prior written permission of the publisher.

Page 276. Preface by Anita Barrows from *Rilke's Book of Hours: Love Poems to God*, translated by Anita Barrows and Joanna Macy. Copyright © 1996 by Anita Barrows and Joanna Macy. Used by permission of Riverhead Books, an imprint of Penguin Group (USA) Inc.

Page 280. From *Diaries of a Young Poet* by Rainier Maria Rilke, translated by Edward Snow and Michael Winkler. Copyright © 1942 by InselVerlag, 1997 by Edward Snow and Michael Winkler. Used by permission of W. W. Norton & Company, Inc. This selection may not be reproduced, stored in a retrieval system, or transmitted in any form or by any means without the prior written permission of the publisher.

Pages 282–283. From *The Unknown Rilke: Expanded Edition* by Rainer Maria Rilke, translated by and with an introduction by Franz Wright. Copyright © 1990 by Oberlin College Press. Reprinted by permission of Oberlin College Press.

Page 287. From *The Selected Poems of Rainer Maria Rilke: A Translation from the German and Commentary* by Robert Bly. Copyright © 1981 by Robert Bly. Reprinted by permission of HarperCollins Publishers.

Page 289. From "Sonnet II, X" from *Sonnets to Orpheus* by Rainer Maria Rilke, translated by C. F. MacIntyre. Copyright © 1990 by University of California Press—Books. Reproduced with permission of University of California Press—Books in the format Textbook via Copyright Clearance Center.

Stephanie Dowrick, Ph.D., has the rare distinction of having written both fiction and nonfiction that have been critically acclaimed and commercially successful. Her best-selling books include *Intimacy and Solitude, Forgiveness & Other Acts of Love, Choosing Happiness,* and her most recent book, *Seeking the Sacred.* Formerly a publisher, and founder of the influential publishing house The Women's Press, London, she has lived in Sydney, Australia, with her family since 1983. Stephanie Dowrick teaches internationally on a variety of spiritual, psychological and literary issues. She is also an ordained interfaith minister and an adjunct fellow with the Writing & Society Research Group at the University of Western Sydney.